RIVERS OF
THE EASTERN SHORE

THE
RIVERS OF AMERICA

Edited by

HERVEY ALLEN and CARL CARMER

As Planned and Started by

CONSTANCE LINDSAY SKINNER

Associate Editor

JEAN CRAWFORD

Art Editor

BENJAMIN FEDER

RIVERS OF THE EASTERN SHORE

Seventeen Maryland Rivers

by

HULBERT FOOTNER

Illustrated by

AARON SOPHER

TIDEWATER PUBLISHERS

Centreville Maryland

Reprinted by arrangement with
Geoffrey Footner

ISBN 0-87033-092-6
Library of Congress Card Number: 89-139742

Manufactured in the United States of America
First Tidewater Publishers edition, 1964; fifth printing, 1996

Contents

1. BEGINNINGS 5
2. WILLIAM CLAIBORNE 24
3. COLONEL EDMUND SCARBURGH 40
4. THE PICAROONS 48
5. THE POCOMOKE RIVER 68
6. THE LITTLE AND THE BIG ANNEMESSEX . . 86
7. THE MANOKIN 104
8. THE WICOMICO 120
9. THE NANTICOKE RIVER 135
10. THE DORCHESTER MARSHES 152
11. THE LITTLE CHOPTANK 163
12. THE CHOPTANK RIVER, PART ONE . . . 170
13. THE CHOPTANK RIVER, PART TWO . . . 185
14. THE TOWN OF OXFORD 205
15. THE TRED AVON RIVER 218
16. ST. MICHAELS 236
17. THE MILES RIVER 255
18. THE LLOYDS OF WYE 269

19. THE WYE RIVER 294
20. THE CHESTER RIVER 309
21. CHESTERTOWN 326
22. THE SASSAFRAS AND BOHEMIA RIVERS . . 339
ACKNOWLEDGMENTS 360
SOURCES 362
INDEX 369

RIVERS OF
THE EASTERN SHORE

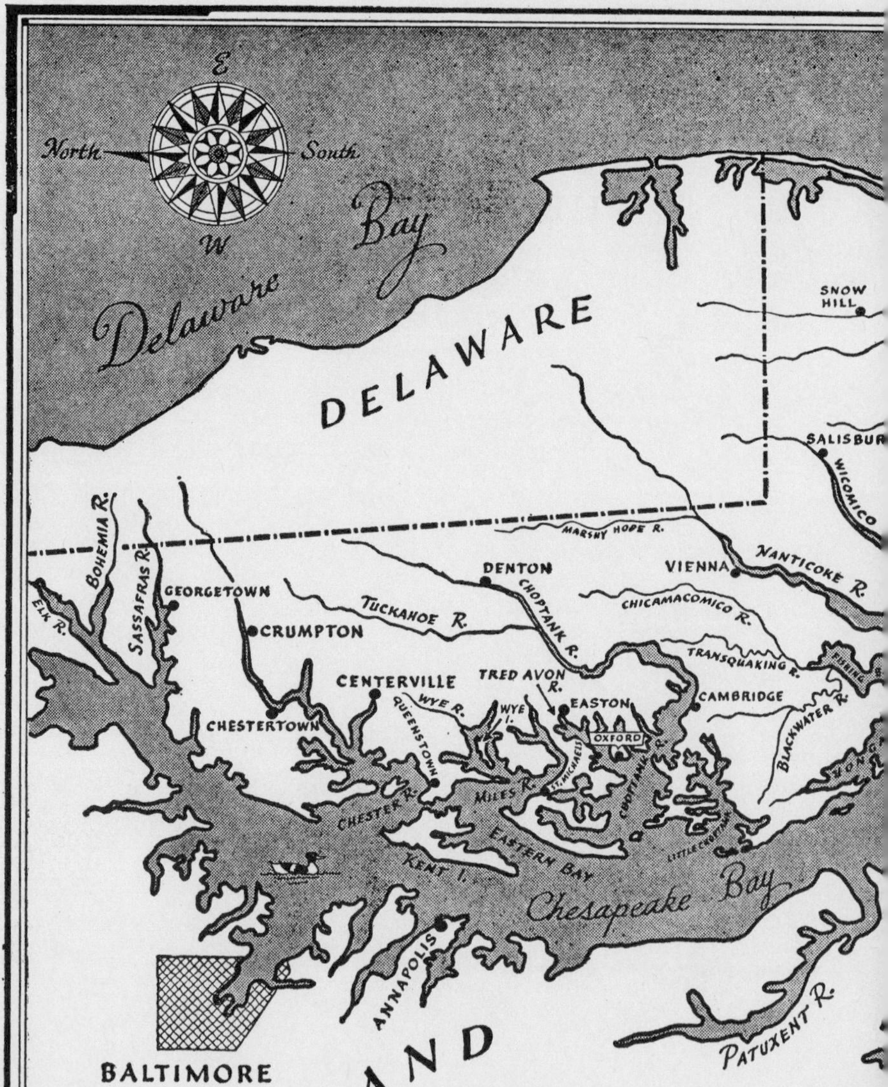
E
North
South
W
Delaware Bay
DELAWARE
SNOW HILL
WICOMICO
MARSHY HOPE R.
NANTICOKE R.
VIENNA
DENTON
CHOPTANK R.
CHICAMACOMICO R.
BOHEMIA R.
SASSAFRAS R.
ELK R.
GEORGETOWN
CRUMPTON
TUCKAHOE R.
TRANSQUAKING R.
TRED AVON R.
CENTERVILLE
WYE R.
WYE I.
EASTON
CAMBRIDGE
CHESTERTOWN
QUEENSTOWN
OXFORD
BLACKWATER R.
ST. MICHAELS
MILES R.
CHOPTANK R.
CHESTER R.
EASTERN BAY
KENT I.
Chesapeake Bay
ANNAPOLIS
PATUXENT R.
BALTIMORE
MARYLAND
WASHINGTON
MD.
VA.
MD.
VA

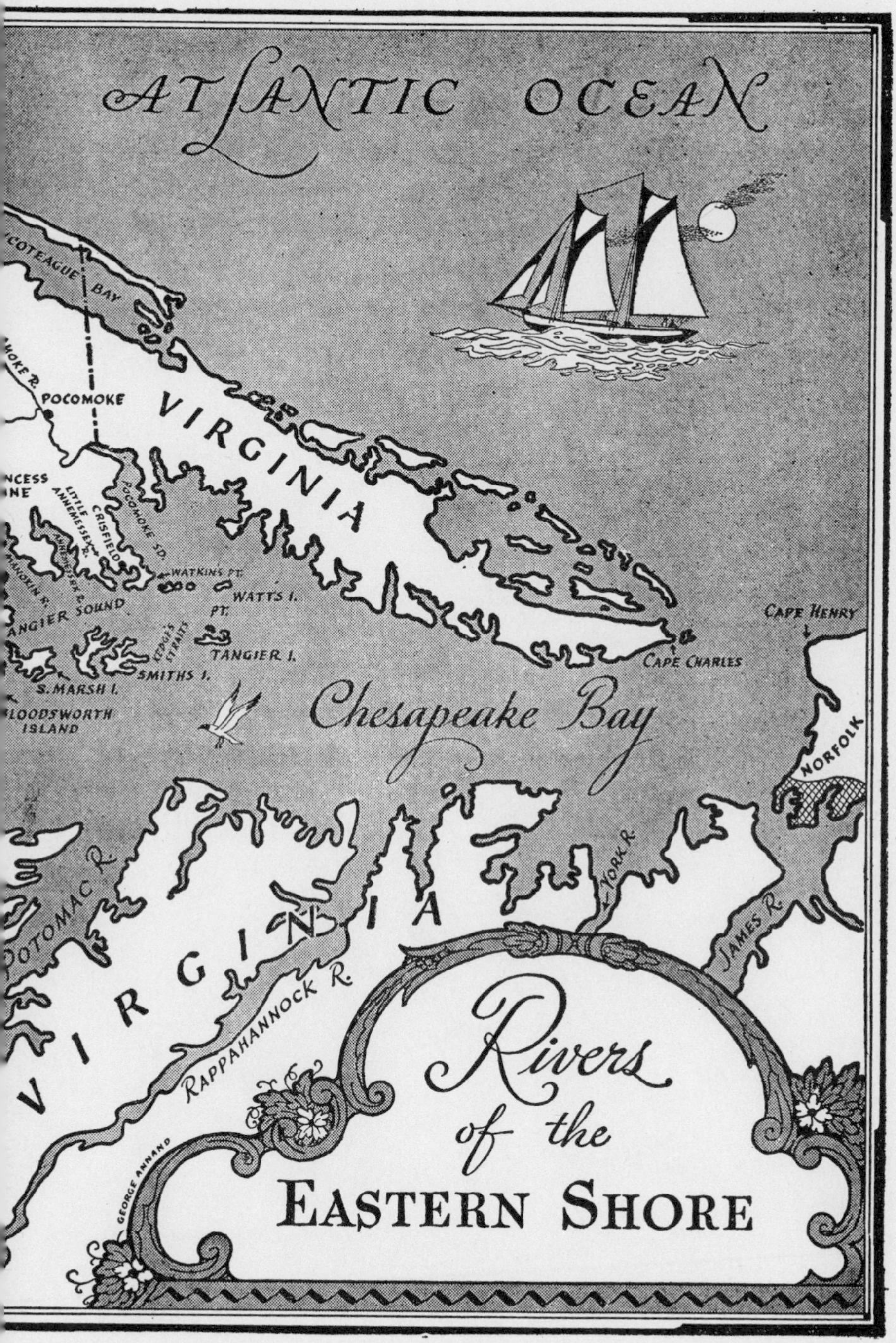
ATLANTIC OCEAN
VIRGINIA
POCOMOKE
LITTLE ANNEMESSEX R.
CRISFIELD
POCOMOKE SD.
WATKINS PT.
WATTS I.
TANGIER I.
SMITHS I.
S. MARSH I.
CAPE CHARLES
CAPE HENRY
Chesapeake Bay
NORFOLK
YORK R.
JAMES R.
RAPPAHANNOCK R.
VIRGINIA
GEORGE ANNAND
Rivers of the
EASTERN SHORE

CHAPTER I

Beginnings

THE "Eastern Shore," as every Marylander knows, comprises that peninsula lying between Chesapeake Bay and the Atlantic Ocean. More than three hundred years ago, the first white settlers in Virginia and Maryland established themselves on the western shore of the bay, and naturally they called the land on the other side the "Eastern Shore." To them no further designation was required, and it has been the Eastern Shore ever since.

In the language of the geologists, Chesapeake Bay is a "drowned" river, in other words, the Susquehanna, to which all the rivers which now empty into the bay on both sides were once tributary. In the course of ages, this part of the coastal plain sank beneath the sea, not once but four times, they say. The first time the land emerged, according to their theory, the Susquehanna River, coming down from the northwest, finding itself blocked by a great shoal or bank of detritus, was diverted to the south for a hundred and fifty miles before finding an outlet to the sea.

This bank was the first "Eastern Shore." It sank again, and the waves of the sea washed the base of the cliffs of the piedmont country, or foothills. Each time the shore sank it received deposits of detritus from the rivers, and it is in those various layers that the geologists read the story today. The ice-cap never extended quite as far south as this, but the rivers brought down great masses of ice laden with boulders and detritus. Such boulders are to be found buried on the Eastern Shore today. Here and there one lies on top of the ground, but the sight of a rock of any kind is rare in that country of silt and sand and clay.

The people of the Eastern Shore believe that their country is again sinking under the sea, and point to various evidences to prove it. The geologists say it *may* be so, but decline to commit themselves. Such a mighty change, they say, is not to be measured by a few generations of men. On the other hand, anybody can see the depredations of the winds and the tides in a land where there are no bulwarks of rock. The banks of the rivers and the bay shores are washing; the islands are going fast. Some islands have disappeared altogether within the space of recorded history.

Today the Eastern Shore comprises a peninsula shaped roughly like a bunch of grapes. It hangs down from a stem in the north, where only a few miles of land separate the waters of the Delaware from the Chesapeake, spreads out in a wide shoulder, and tapers off to a point (Cape Charles) at the south. It includes almost the whole of the little state of Delaware, with nine counties of Maryland, and two of Virginia. It is about 136 miles long and 55 miles wide at the shoulder.

In this small expanse there are no less than nineteen navigable rivers. As rivers go, they are small affairs; flowing through a "drowned" country, each widens into an immense tidal estuary. The Virginia end of the peninsula is a long strip of low land between bay and ocean, too narrow to need any rivers for drainage, while the Delaware part on the ocean, being slightly higher than the bay side, serves only for the sources of some of the longer streams, which thereupon flow through Maryland into the bay. For that reason, this book will deal almost exclusively with Maryland. On the bay side, winds and tides have shaped a shoreline fantastic in the number of its islands, rivers, bays, creeks, sounds and straits; in a sailboat one could spend the vacations of a lifetime in exploring its convolutions.

The Eastern Shore still bears the aspect of a great bank or shoal risen from the sea. Below Choptank it is as flat as a table, never more than fifteen feet above sea level, except for the low watershed near the ocean side, where it rises to a height of forty feet. As one travels north up the Shore, the land rises by infinitesimal degrees until we find the Sassafras flowing through a plain which averages eighty feet elevation. There is a gentle roll to this country.

The soil of the lower counties consists mostly of what the geologists call Norfolk sands, a coarse to medium brown sand averaging eight inches on a subsoil of friable orange-yellow sand several feet thick. Such a soil is best suited to quick-growing vegetables and melons. In the northern part, the soil is largely Sassafras loam, averaging ten inches on a heavy reddish-yellow loam subsoil three to six feet thick. This is a richer soil, and in the old days paid greater returns to its proprietors; but in these days of quick transportation when the early vegetables of Worcester and Somerset can be delivered fresh to half the continent, the accent is changing.

Through this rich, flat land flow the sluggish, tidal rivers never more than a few miles apart and winding interminably. The flatness of the land is its safeguard, since the topsoil washes but slowly into the streams. There is strange music in the sound of the Indian names: Pocomoke, Wicomico, Nanticoke, Choptank. Though they are so close together, they do not resemble each other; all are beautiful and each has a distinct character.

The Lords Baltimore were absolute proprietors of all this. They never granted land in fee simple, but always subject to a quitrent of two shillings per hundred acres. Thus they kept a string on it. This continued up to the time of the Revolution. The Baltimores would have been glad to establish an aristocracy in Maryland to hold things together, but the bill to accomplish this end was always defeated in the House of Delegates.

As to the people who occupy this favored land, their formal history is not particularly dramatic or exciting, but every necessary element was present to produce a rich and individual culture. The first settler took up land in 1619; many of his descendants are still occupying land in the neighborhood. Such were his accounts of the mildness and salubrity of the climate and the richness of the soil that many others followed quickly and the settlement of the country was completed very early; thus a culture has had ample time in which to ripen.

This first settler was an Englishman, and so were practically all the others who followed. Thus, as compared with other parts of our country, the Eastern Shore was homogeneous in its beginnings. It had an old culture as a foundation for that which was slowly erected upon it. Until the middle of the nineteenth century our whole country bore a more or less English stamp. Immigration then began to modify it; but the Eastern Shore, being completely settled long before, received no foreign immigration to speak of, and remained English in feeling. It is amusing to discover how often the present-day Eastern Shore will bring to mind the America of, say, 1860 as it has been described and pictured to us.

One still finds the English caste system shadowed forth on the Shore. White people are either gentlefolk or common. A gentle family will fight to maintain its prestige, come hell or high water. The possession of property has nothing to do with it. A gentleman may be reduced to hoeing his own corn, but he is still "quality." The word has passed out of use, but the feeling is almost as strong as ever. From time to time there have been efforts among the old families to establish primogeniture, but under our free institutions such efforts have always failed. Nevertheless, an English gentleman finds himself at home among the quality of the Eastern Shore. It is wonderful how many beliefs and feelings they still share with him, without ever finding it necessary to state them. Slavery was bad for such a people. Slavery was not a necessary institution under the mild climate of the Eastern Shore. It inculcated the vicious idea that manual labor was unworthy of a gentleman, and the white proprietors have been slow to get rid of that idea.

There is one profound difference which must not be overlooked. Since the first settler came, the idea of "freedom" has pervaded the Shore—that is what brought many of the first settlers over. There has never been any attempt to keep the common man down. As will be seen later, it was the greatest gentleman of the Shore that fought for free suffrage. Another gentleman pointed out that the common men had been treading hard on the heels of the gentlemen since the beginning. Some of the first families of the Shore trace their origin back to an indentured servant, and are proud of it—after he has receded far enough into the background.

Naturally, during the passage of three centuries the

original Englishness of the Eastern Shore has been modified in many directions. Owing to the salubrity of the climate and the richness of the soil, the Shoremen have never known the struggle for existence—or rather, they have only had to struggle hard enough to keep them from becoming enervated. The typical Eastern Shoreman, whether gentleman or fisherman, is a fine physical specimen, tall, lean and hardy.

It has always been easy come, easy go on the Shore, with all that that connotes both good and bad. Everybody may have enough without working himself to death. The waters are full of food; until recent years there was game for everybody also; the garden will produce two or three crops in a season. This has resulted in an easygoing character. After three centuries of easy living, the Eastern Shore has established a tradition of the good life which insists on superior eating and drinking, leisure, sport and sociability. They are the greatest visitors and gossips in the nation. Hardship may be good for the character; ease develops the personality. The Eastern Shore tradition enjoins a man (or a woman) always to speak his mind in company without fear or favor. This gives a pleasant, salty flavor to social intercourse.

Naturally there is a reverse side to this attractive picture. Openhandedness can be carried too far. It produced many a charming wastrel who left behind him a tradition and little else. The old families were forever ruining themselves through their lavish hospitality. They spent more than their incomes; they mortgaged their lands and the mortgages were foreclosed. That is why the common men were continually overtaking the gentlemen. As the story progresses, it will be seen that only a few of the first families have succeeded in maintaining their positions throughout. But all in all the rotation is a wholesome process.

The Eastern Shoreman has been strongly influenced by his proximity to the water. Every boy on the Shore has been brought up with boats. Even if his parents do not live on a river, the water is always near enough for him to go swimming, sailing, fishing, crabbing on holidays. Farmers become oystermen in the winter It has always been a seafaring people. The great planters frequently owned a ship or two. Some of the finest ships built by man hailed from the Eastern Shore. In the old days, it was their ships that prevented them from becoming *too* narrow and provincial. On the Eastern Shore they were always aware of the great world outside.

After the country became pretty well settled at the end of the seventeenth century, there was little interruption to the orderly process of developing a culture *sui generis.* For the Eastern Shore, being a peninsula, lies to one side of the main routes of travel. Until the railroad was built in modern times, nobody ever passed through the Eastern Shore; it was always the terminus of a journey. This makes a great difference in the development of a community. Few strangers came among them. They nourished and ripened and handed down their own notions undisturbed. Nowadays, these people are subject like the rest of us to the great leveling mediums of phonograph records, radio, motion pictures and comic strips. In the general uniformity, how refreshing it is to find a people who still obstinately cling to some notions of their own.

The first white man (that we know of) to set foot on the Eastern Shore was Giovanni da Verrazano in 1524. Verrazano was an Italian in the service of the king of France. Sailing north along the Atlantic coast in the ship *Dauphine* with a crew of fifty Frenchmen, he entered Chincoteague

Bay and landed in what is now Worcester County, Maryland. Because of the beauty of the trees thereabouts he called the land Arcadia.

As Verrazano stepped ashore, there appeared from among the trees a naked Indian youth of remarkable beauty, with olive-brown skin and his glossy black hair fastened back in a knot. He was very much frightened (as well he might be!) and stood hesitating, ready for flight. Then in friendly fashion he lifted a burning torch that he had, "as if to offer us fire."

Instead of responding to his overture of good will, one of the sailors crudely fired a shot in the air. The youth, overcome with fear, "prayed, worshipping like a monk, lifting his finger towards the sky and pointing to the ship and the sea, he appeared to bless us." Certainly the red man's manners were better than those of the white. When they made to approach him, the young Indian disappeared into the forest.

The landing party penetrated inland for eight miles and were then stopped by the swamps of the upper Pocomoke River. This fixes the spot of their exploration. The Indians fled from them in terror. They cornered an old woman and a young girl who vainly tried to conceal themselves in tall grass. Each woman was carrying three small children on her back. This is rather hard to picture, but so the account runs.

The sailors seized one of the little boys with the intention of carrying him away. It never occurred to them that these "salvages" might have feelings about children similar to their own. They attempted to take the girl too, who was "of much beauty and tall of stature," but her loud screams intimidated them and they let her go.

Verrazano had only this one walk ashore in Maryland, but what he recorded was absolutely new at that time. The people of this tribe may be identified as Assateagues. The women wore skirts made of the Spanish moss which apparently then hung from the cypresses along the Pocomoke. It grows nowhere in Maryland now. Besides game and fish, they lived on "pulse," or wild peas. They navigated the rivers in dugout canoes, formed by burning and scraping out the trunks of big trees. Their arrows were made of reeds headed with bone, since there was no stone in the country.

The Indian tribes inhabiting the lower Eastern Shore were a gentle, friendly people. The broad Chesapeake protected them from the forays of the fierce tribes to the north and west, and nature was lavish in supplying their wants. Their settlements were more or less permanent and they tilled the soil without interruption. They neither had to work very hard nor were they subject to the alarms of war. They never made trouble for white men, except on one or two occasions when they were provoked beyond bearing by encroachments on their lands.

For the greater part of a century after the visit of Verrazano they were left in peace. One can imagine the tradition that was handed down among them of strange, fantastically attired, white-skinned men from another world and their huge canoe. Certainly the story would have lost nothing in the telling. No doubt at times they looked nervously to sea in expectation of another visitation. At any rate, the next white man who came suffered as a result of his predecessors' rudeness.

This was Bartholomew Gilbert, son of the famous Sir Humphrey, who in midsummer of 1603 came cruising down the Atlantic coast from New England in a small bark of fifty tons, the *Elizabeth*. He was looking for the survivors of Sir Walter Raleigh's colony. Storms drove him into Chesapeake

Bay. Attracted by the inviting country and the mouth of what appeared to be a great river, he sailed north for a few leagues along the Eastern Shore. This seems to have been Bullock's Channel between Smith's Island and the mainland.

Captain Gilbert and three of his men went ashore to obtain fresh water. Leaving a boy to guard their boat, they struck inland. The Indians ambushed them. Falling on the little party without warning, they killed the captain and one of his men, and the others escaped to their ship with difficulty. They sailed home without any further attempts to find Raleigh's lost colony.

The next white visitor to the Eastern Shore was the redoubtable Captain John Smith, in June, 1608. Captain John was not so much an object of terror to the Indians because, in the first place, he was a man of good sense and good feeling and, secondly, he came in a little open barge with only a handful of men. The natives could comprehend such a boat.

Captain John Smith commands a highly entertaining and convincing style, and while it is hard to believe that so many adventures could be crowded within the span of one life, on the other hand, if you take what he wrote about the country we know as a measure, Virginia and Maryland, the reader cannot but be astonished at the keenness of his observation and the justness of his conclusions.

He made mistakes naturally—he was the first to see and report on these parts—but he neither falsifies nor exaggerates —much, and he is on the whole pretty modest, but not *too* modest, as to his own performances. Some of his accounts, though they bear internal evidence of having been written by him, were signed at his order by other men in his party: Walter Russell and Amos Todkill.

On June 2, 1608, Captain John Smith left the infant

settlement at Jamestown in an open barge "of three tunnes burthen" and a crew of fourteen including his good friend, Walter Russell, who was a doctor. Upon leaving Kecoughtan (Hampton, Virginia) at the mouth of the James, they crossed the bay to Cape Charles, the Virginia end of the Eastern Shore.

They were very ill-supplied, "having nothing but a little meale or oatmeale and water to feed us and scarce half sufficient of that. . . . provisions we got among the salvages and such rootes and fish as we caught by accident and God's direction. . . . And no mariners," Captain Smith goes on in his cheerful fashion, "nor any that had skill to trim the sayles or use the oares but two saylers and my selfe, the rest being Gentlemen, or them that were ignorant of such toyle and labour, but by the Captaine's diligence and example [he] taught them."

The first natives they encountered at Cape Charles were "two grimme, stout salvages, armed with poles headed with bone [javelins]." After considerable parley, they seemed to turn kind and directed the white men to their werowance (chief) at Accomac, who treated them well. This chief was Hicktopeake, brother of Debedeavon "the laughing king of Accomac," who was a good friend to white men as long as he lived. These Indians were technically subject to Powhatan (though they lived well out of his reach) and spoke his language; consequently, Smith had no difficulty in communicating with them.

The white men proceeded up the Eastern Shore and, being in want of fresh water, entered the first river which Smith calls the "Wighcocomoco," but it was the Pocomoke. This mistake of his made trouble for the province of Maryland in later years. However, Smith made a map which clearly indicated the truth of the matter to all but those who did not want to see.

The natives on this river, says Captain John, "at first with great furie seemed to assault us, yet at last made us welcome with songs, dances and much mirth." But the white men could only procure enough water to fill three barricoes and that was a sad puddle. They searched and dug in many places and at the end of two days "would have refused two barricoes of gold for one of the puddle water of Wighcocomoco." In the end they found on the dry land of the main a large pond of hot fresh water and filled their vessels from that.

The islands off Pocomoke they christened Smith's, in compliment to the captain, a name they still bear. Here they met with one of the terrific summer squalls that the watermen of the Chesapeake have reason to dread. "We discovered the winde and the waters so much increased with thunder, lightning and raine that our mast and saile blew overboard, and such mighty waves overracked us in that small barge that with great labour we kept her from sinking by freeing out the water."

They were forced to land and "for two dayes" continues Captain Smith, "we were forced to inhabite these uninhabitable Isles which for the extremitie of gusts, thunder, raine, stormes and ill weather, we called Limbo. [Then] repairing our saile with our shirts, we set saile for the maine and fell in with a pretty convenient river on the East called Kuskarawaok." (This was the Nanticoke.)

"By this river dwell the Soraphanigh, Nause, Arsek and Nantiquake." (Smith has been accused of making up the names of these tribes, except the last.) At sight of the white men these people "ran as amazed in troops from place to place, divers got in the tops of trees. Not sparing of their arrows, nor of the greatest passion they could express of their anger. Long they shot, we riding at anchor out of range, making all the signs of friendship we could.

"Next day they came [to the shore] unarmed, everyone

with a basket, and danced in a ring to draw us ashore. Seeing there was nothing in this but villainy, we discharged a volley of muskets charged with ball. They all tumbled to the ground, some creeping one way, some another into a thicket of reeds. There they lay in ambush.

"Towards evening we weighed and approaching the shore, discharged five or six shots among the reeds. We landed where they laid and found many baskets and much blood, but not a salvage. Seeing smoke across the river, we rowed over and found two or three little houses, in each a fire. We left pieces of copper, beads, bells and looking glasses and returned to the barge.

"Next morning four salvages came in from the Bay in a canoe, not knowing what had happened. We used them with such courtesie they bade us stay [while they went on to the village]. They came back with about twenty more and after a little conference, two or three thousand men, women and children came about us, everyone presenting us with something which even a little bead would so well repay, that they began to dispute who would fetch us water, stay with us for hostage, and give us the best content."

Finding the lower Eastern Shore, then as now, obstructed with shallow, broken, marshy islands, and fresh water being very difficult to find on the mainland (likewise marshy), they passed out "by the Straights of Limbo" (probably Cooper's Strait) and set sail for the western shore. At this point the bay was so wide they could scarcely distinguish the high cliffs on the other side.

They reported the western shore to be a pleasant, well-watered land of barren mountains and fertile valleys. Where they found mountains on the western shore I can't imagine, unless it was merely by comparison with the invariable flatness of the lower Eastern Shore. Without meeting any natives on this side, they sailed as far north as a river they called Bolus, which appears to have been the Patapsco.

After twelve days, Smith's men were tired out with rowing and disgusted with their food, which had been spoiled by water ("though their stomachs could still digest it," remarks the indomitable Captain John) and they began to tease the captain with continual complaints and beg him to turn back. He made them a memorable little speech which well illustrates the character of the man.

> What a shame it would be for you to force me to returne, scarce able to say where we have beene, nor yet heard of that we were sent to seeke. You cannot say but I have shared with you in the worst which is past. For what is to come of lodging, dyet or whatsoever, I am contented that you allot the worst part to myselfe. As for your feares that I will lose myselfe in these unknown large waters, or be swallowed up in some stormie gust, abandon these childish feares, for worse than is past is not likely to happen. There is as much danger to returne as to proceede. Regaine then your old spirits, for returne I will not, if God please, till I have seene the Massawomek [Iroquois Indians], found Patawomek [Potomac River] or the head of this water [Chesapeake Bay] you conceit to be endlesse.

This had the desired effect and the voyage continued.

But after several days of continuous bad weather, during which three or four of the men became really sick, their pitiful complaints persuaded Captain John to turn back.

They then discovered the mouth of the Potomac, which of course they had passed while sailing up the Eastern Shore. Their fears being lulled and their stomachs recovered, the men consented to explore it. They conducted themselves very warily among the natives of this side because they had reason to suspect that Powhatan, overlord of the tribes of Virginia, had been inciting them to betray the white man.

Smith's men dug unsuccessfully for gold, but acquired furs that were more valuable than gold in the long run. There was an abundance of fish. "For want of netts," says Captain John, "wee attempted to catch them with a frying pan, but found it a bad instrument to catch fish with."

Anchoring in the shallows, the captain then tried the expedient of spearing the fish with his sword and in that way took plenty. While thus engaged he met with an accident which almost put a period to his activities forever.

> But it chanced our Captain taking a fish from his sword (not knowing her condition) being much of the fashion of a Thornbacke [it was a stingray] but having a long tayle like a riding rodde, whereon the middest is a most poisoned sting of two or three inches long, bearded like a saw on each side, which she strucke into the wrist of his arme near an inch and a halfe; no bloud nor wound was seene, but a little blew spot, but the torment was instantly so extreme, that in foure hours had so swollen his hand, arme and shoulder, we all with much sorrow concluded his funerall, and prepared his grave in an island hard by, as himselfe directed, yet it pleased God by a precious oyle Dr. Russell at the first applyed to it with a probe, ere night his tormenting paine was so well asswaged that he eate of the fish to his supper.

Back at Kecoughtan, Smith's men regaled the familiar Indians there with tall stories of bloody battles and so forth, which was what they wanted to hear. "This rumor," says Smith, "went up the river [the James] faster than our barge." In a frolicsome spirit they stopped on the way up to trim their barge "with painted streamers and such devices as would make the Fort jealous of a Spanish Frigot."

Within a month the indefatigable Captain John set out again. On his second voyage, he proceeded up the western shore directly to the head of the bay, where they found that it "divided into four." These four divisions were probably the Susquehanna, North East, Elk and Sassafras rivers. Here they ran into a war party of the dreaded Massawomekes (Iroquois) in six or eight canoes. It was a ticklish situation because, Smith's men not yet having become seasoned, there were only five who were able to stand. Captain John covered the sick with a "tarpawling," mounted their hats on sticks, and arranged their guns to show over the side of the barge.

The Massawomekes gave them a wide berth, staring mightily meanwhile at the sailing of the barge. Sailing was an unknown art to these Indians. Smith's men took courage from the visible impression they were making, and finally dared to anchor close to the canoes. A long time passed before they were able to tempt the Massawomekes to visit them. Finally two came unarmed in a canoe. Each was presented with a little bell, and that brought all their fellows.

The white men could converse with them only by signs. The Indians loaded them with gifts: venison, bear meat, bows, arrows, shields, clubs and skins. These Indians had been fighting with the Tockwogh tribe on the Sassafras River, and showed their fresh wounds. An appointment was made for another meeting the following day, but the Massawomekes failed to keep it.

Smith's party then sailed across to the Tockwogh, or Sassafras, which is the next river south of the Elk on the Eastern Shore. Tockwogh is a variation of Tuckahoe, a water weed whose bulbous root supplied the natives with an article of food. As soon as they entered the river, the white men found themselves surrounded by a crowd of armed natives in boats. Luckily one of the Indians could speak the language of Powhatan, so it was possible to hold a friendly parley. Smith made believe that they had taken the gifts of the Massawomekes by force, and thus rose mightily in the estimation of the Tockwoghs.

The Sassafras is the loveliest river of the Eastern Shore, but Smith does not speak of that. He describes how the

Tockwoghs led them to their palisaded town "mantelled with the bark of trees," a few miles from the river's mouth, and threw a big party. Mats were spread for the white men to sit upon while the Indians danced and sang before them. Gifts of fruits, fish and furs were spread before them. The Tockwoghs were a gentle people.

Smith noted that they possessed hatchets, knives, pieces of brass, iron and so forth, and learned upon inquiry that they had procured these things in trade from their allies, the Susquehannocks, mortal enemies of the Massawomekes. Traded from tribe to tribe, such articles had come all the way from the Canadian Indians, who in turn had procured them from the French.

Following this pleasant visit, Smith retraced his course to the Susquehanna, with the object of making the acquaintance of the Indians who dwelt there. They ascended the big river, but were stopped by rocks before coming on any natives. Sending an interpreter and another man on upstream, they waited, and in due course about sixty of the Susquehannocks came down, bearing gifts.

Smith becomes lyrical in describing these Indians: "such great and well-proportioned men as are seldome seen, for they seemed like Giants to the English, yea, and to their neighbors, yet seemed of an honest and simple disposition. . . . the strangest people of all both in language & attire, for their language it well beseems their proportions, sounding from them as a voyce in a vault. . . . The calf of the greatest of the Werowances was three-quarters of a yard around, the rest of his limbs in proportion. The goodliest man that ever we beheld."

Smith is not very clear as to his next move, but it is indicated that he entered the Chester River, the next river on the

Eastern Shore, where he foregathered with a tribe he called the Ozinies. He then crossed back to the western shore, visiting the Patuxent, Potomac and Rappahannock rivers on that side, where his suspicions that Powhatan was trying to stir up trouble were confirmed. After one last furious storm on the bay that almost overwhelmed them, they arrived safe at Jamestown on September 7th.

At the conclusion of his second voyage Captain Smith writes:

> Thus have I walkt a wayless way with uncouth pace,
> Which yet no Christian man did ever trace.

CHAPTER 2

William Claiborne

THE story of the Eastern Shore naturally begins at Accomac on the Virginia end and works northward.

In 1613 Sir Samuel Argoll visited Accomac for the purpose of trading with the Indians for corn and fish to relieve the starving colonists at Jamestown. As a result of this visit, the colonists established a little saltworks on Smith's Island, and set up an outpost at Accomac under Lieutenant Craddock.

The first permanent settler on the Eastern Shore was Thomas Savage, who came from Jamestown in 1619. Savage had come to Virginia with Captain Smith in 1607 as a boy of thirteen. A bold young adventurer this! He was given to Powhatan as a hostage in exchange for an Indian boy and so learned the language. Debedeavon, the "laughing King," gave him a large tract of land which to this day is known as Savage's neck, and there he settled down with his wife, Hannah Tyng. They enjoyed peace and plenty during the years that Jamestown was sick, starving, and finally massacred (1622). Many of their descendants are still living in the neighborhood; thus the Savages may call themselves the first family of the United States.

Many settlers followed Savage, and it is hardly surprising that they were glad to exchange the sickly and dangerous surroundings of Jamestown for the breezy and salubrious Eastern Shore, with its almost subtropical climate, where a

farmer can raise three crops a year, and its wealth of fish and game, its peaceful, friendly Indians. By 1629 the inhabitants of Accomac were numerous enough to be entitled to a representative in the Virginia House of Burgesses. They chose Captain Edmund Scarburgh, father of the more famous Colonel Edmund, of whom we shall hear more. Three years later Scarburgh was appointed commissioner for Accomac, that is to say, the resident administrator.

Meanwhile in 1631, at the other end of the Eastern Shore, William Claiborne, secretary of state in Virginia and a member of the Governor's Council, had established a post for trading with the Indians. His headquarters were on Kent Island off the mouth of the Chester River, and he had an outpost on Palmer's Island in the Susquehanna. He enjoyed a license from King Charles I "to trade and make discoveries in any and all parts of North America, not already preempted by monopolies" and he owned a one-third share in the mercantile business of Cloberry and Company, London.

Claiborne was a man of great force of character. It was as the result of a chance conversation with Captain John Smith in London that he had been induced to emigrate. His rise in the colony was rapid. Since he was a thorn in the side of Lord Baltimore for more than twenty years, all the early writers on Maryland have abused him roundly. Now that the evidence is all in, even a Marylander may concede that Claiborne was at least as much sinned against as sinning. And it must be said in his favor that, when he was on top, he dealt mercifully with his enemies.

In July, 1631, Claiborne arrived from England in the ship *Africa* with a cargo of trade goods, twenty servants, "and a mayde to wash our linnen." He also had one Henry Pinke to read prayers but "he breake his legge and was unserviceable." At Kecoughtan he took aboard more volunteers to the number of one hundred men and proceeded to his post on the Eastern Shore. No man had ever been "implanted" there before him, he averred, and he contracted with the natives and bought the right to hold the island of the crown.

In the following year Captain Nicholas Martian represented the Kent Islanders in the Virginia Assembly.

On February 27, 1634, the *Ark*, a ship of three hundred tons attended by a small pinnace, the *Dove*, arrived at Kecoughtan bearing Governor Leonard Calvert and his company of nearly two hundred adventurers and servants to seat Lord Baltimore's province of Maryland. Calvert was his lordship's brother. Their reception was cool, for Virginia had a more or less shadowy claim to all the land covered by Baltimore's patent. The governor, Sir John Harvey, was friendly but, as he was hated in his own colony (and was soon after deposed), his friendship did not recommend the incoming Marylanders to the people of Virginia.

As for Claiborne, his settlement and post were right in the middle of Lord Baltimore's domain, and his feelings can be imagined. He appears to have been at Kecoughtan when the Baltimore ships called there, but he kept out of their way.

Lord Baltimore knew about Claiborne's settlement, and with his usual good sense and astuteness had given his brother explicit directions how to deal with him. This Cecil, the second Lord Baltimore, was the wisest of the founders of America and he should be better known among us. According to Lord Baltimore, Claiborne was to be given every encouragement to continue his trade, provided only that he acknowledged Baltimore's authority. Further, if Claiborne refused to respond to the first friendly overtures, he was to be let alone for a year before any action was taken against him.

Claiborne was a proud man and intensely loyal to the colony of Virginia. He had no intention of acknowledging Lord Baltimore as his landlord. Moreover, Baltimore's wise measures were immediately overset by malicious and interested gossip. There were other Indian traders in Virginia who had no desire to see the province of Maryland settled.

The incoming Marylanders were told that Claiborne was working among the Indians to inflame them against the new settlers; that he had told the natives Lord Baltimore's people were not English at all, but Spaniards who were bent on seizing their country and enslaving them. No proof of such treachery on Claiborne's part was ever forthcoming, but the rumor was enough to create bad blood between the two parties. Claiborne quite naturally claimed that the Marylanders had started the story themselves in order to excuse what he called their illegal acts. The first contests were for possession of Palmer's Island at the mouth of the Susquehanna. Later, Claiborne placed Captain Thomas Smith in command of his pinnace, the *Long Tayle,* and ordered him to proceed to the Patuxent River on the western shore to trade with the Indians there for corn and furs. This was a direct incitement to the Marylanders, because the Patuxent was only a dozen miles from St. Marys, the seat of the Maryland government. If Claiborne had been content to stay over on the Eastern Shore, further trouble might have been avoided—long enough at least to allow hot blood to cool.

The *Long Tayle,* incidentally, was the first vessel to be built on the Eastern Shore. Captain Claiborne had bought spikes, nails, iron and brass plates, a keel and rudder irons for her from Kecoughtan. From the same post came an anchor and cordage, as well as pitch, tar and brimstone to keep away the worms. She was supplied with a lamp, a quadrant, a compass and eighteen fathoms of sounding line. She could carry twenty men and was propelled by either sails or oars; she flew an "ancient" (ensign) and had several small boats for tenders. This vessel was the apple of Captain Claiborne's eye.

Let one of his men tell of the manner of their trading with the Indians:

> Our trade with the Indians for furs is alwaies with danger of our lives. We usuallie trade in a shallop or small pinnace, being sixe or seven Englishmen encompassed with two or three hundred Indians. And it is as much as we can doe to defend ourselves by standing upon our guard with our Armes ready & our gunnes present in our handes. Two or three men must looke to the trucke that the Indians doe not steale it, and a great deale of trucke is often stole by the Indians, though we looke ever so well to it. Alsoe a great parte of the trucke is given away to the Kings & great men of the Indians for presents, and commonlie one third parte is spent for [our] victualls and other occasions. . . .
>
> The Indians will be very long and tedious in viewing [the trucke] and doe tumble itt and tosse itt, & mingle itt a hundred times over, soe that it is impossible to keepe the severall parcelles asunder, and if any trader will not suffer the Indian soe to doe, they will be distasteful with the traders, & fall out with them & refuse to have any trade. Therefore it is not Convenient or possible to keepe an account in the Trade of every axe, knife or string of Beades, or for every yard of Cloth, especially because the Indians trade not by any certaine measure, or by the English weights or measures, & therefore every particular cannot be written downe distinctlie. All Traders find that it is impossible to keepe any more perfect account than att the end of the voiage to see what is sold & what is gained & what is left.

While the *Long Tayle* flying her "ancient" was thus engaged at Mattapony near the mouth of the Patuxent River, Captain Henry Fleet and Captain Humber appeared out of the woods with a company of men. They had come overland from St. Marys. The Kent Island men were greatly outnumbered and the Marylanders seized the *Long Tayle* without bloodshed. There was not room on the little vessel for both parties, so a number of Claiborne's men were unloaded and told to walk over to St. Marys. "Without any armes to defend themselves from the Indians," Captain Thomas Smith remarks indignantly. The *Long Tayle* with everybody else aboard dropped down the bay and ascended the Potomac to St. Marys.

There was a hearing before Governor Leonard Calvert. According to Captain Smith's story, the governor took a very arrogant and overbearing tone, but this hardly accords with other accounts of Leonard Calvert's character. Meanwhile, the *Long Tayle*'s cargo of truck was spread about and Captain Smith says rather surprisingly that he did some trading right under the noses of the St. Marys authorities. Smith concludes his story thus:

> Seeing noe hopes of having our vessell againe, I desired the Governor we might returne home . . . with some meanes. He graunted wee should goe, but said hee was sorrie hee had noe boate to send us home in, although having at that tyme three boates riding at his dore. I told him if there was noe other way I would make some meanes by the Indians, which hee graunted I should doe. The next day wee were sent in a cannow without either peece [arms] or victualls but one peece which I had myselfe, having twenty leagers to go [to Kent Island] without any means but such as wee should find from the Indians. With great danger it pleased God to send us safe home.

Naturally, Claiborne was infuriated by the news that his pinnace had been confiscated. This vessel had been sent to trade for corn, and the little settlement on Kent Island, for the lack of it, was suffering much hardship. Reprisals, as usual, followed reprisals. Claiborne sent Lieutenant Warren in a wherry (smaller than a pinnace) to St. Marys to demand the return of the *Long Tayle*. He didn't get it, but on his way home he seized a boat with trucking stuff belonging to Maryland and brought that back to Kent Island.

Later Claiborne received information that the Marylanders had dared to cross the bay in two pinnaces, the *St. Helen* and the *St. Margaret,* to trade with the Eastern Shore Indians, and that they were then cruising in Pocomoke Sound. This is the estuary of the river that Captain John Smith had mistakenly termed the Wighcocomoco twenty-five years before.

At Kent Island, Lieutenant Warren was now given the command of the shallop *Cockatrice* with a crew of thirteen men. His orders were to proceed to Pocomoke Sound and seize both pinnaces and their commander, Captain Thomas Cornwallis. The shallop was a smaller vessel than the pinnace, though the colonists did not use these terms with any exactness. At any rate, it is clear that the odds were greatly against young Warren.

It is easy to picture the scene of the action, for, after three hundred years, there is almost no change in it: the immense, sunny, blue estuary separated by low-lying islands from the still greater expanse of Chesapeake Bay; the far-spreading salt marshes on every side laced with silvery creeks and backed in the distance by the lines of dark pines. Such a scene somehow looks vaster and lonelier even than the sea.

In this great waste of water and marsh, the little vessels met. Lieutenant Warren and his men "charged with gunnes and pistolls, swords and other weapons upon the two pinnaces." Captain Cornwallis issued orders to his men to prepare to repel boarders. But the *Cockatrice* kept coming on. To avoid, if possible, a hand-to-hand fight, Cornwallis gave orders to fire, and the great stillness of the Pocomoke was for the first time in the world shattered by the sound of gunfire and the clash of steel.

The *Cockatrice*, though Warren and his men attacked bravely, was finally driven off. When it was over, Warren was dead and two of his crew. One of Cornwallis's men received a wound from which he presently died.

Claiborne's rage upon hearing of the result knew no bounds. In a memorial to his Majesty, King Charles I, he recited all his injuries at the hands of the Marylanders, and he later appealed to his Majesty's High Court of Admiralty in London. Charles turned the matter over to the lords commissioners for the plantations for adjudication.

Claiborne was never the man to be satisfied by appeals to the law. He fitted out two more armed expeditions, one under Philip Taylor, who was ordered to recover the pinnace and the men still detained at St. Marys, "or missing them, to make stay on such boates of theirs as you can light on." Taylor was cautioned to avoid violence and bloodshed so far as he could. The other expedition was under Captain Thomas Smith, who was ordered to capture Captain Cornwallis's pinnace, now cruising in the Wicomico.

Unfortunately, no record of what happened to these ventures has survived. It is likely that they enjoyed at least a measure of success, because during the two years that followed, Claiborne was suffered to trade with the Indians without interference from the Marylanders. During this time he appears to have confined himself to the Eastern Shore.

Meanwhile (in 1636) George Evelin had arrived at Kent Island as an emissary from Cloberry and Company, Claiborne's English principals. He brought a letter summoning Claiborne back to England for conference and directing him to leave Evelin in charge of the fort and settlement during his absence. Claiborne departed.

This Evelin was a treacherous creature. In Claiborne's presence he loudly supported his side of the quarrel and railed at Lord Baltimore, but within a few months of Claiborne's departure he paid a visit to Governor Leonard Calvert in St. Marys, where he was persuaded to accept a commission from the province of Maryland as governor of Kent Island.

Returning to the island, Evelin called a public meeting (by this time the community numbered a hundred and twenty men able to bear arms) and the astonished Kent Islanders heard him aver that, having examined Lord Baltimore's patent, he was convinced that Claiborne's commission had no effect or force in the Bay of Virginia but was for Nova Scotia and such places. "It would be better to live under the Government of Maryland than under the Government of Virginia," he urged, "for my Lord Baltemore hath ye patent & the Island is his."

The great seal of Maryland on Evelin's new commission failed to intimidate the Kent Islanders. When Evelin reported his failure to win them over to Governor Calvert, Calvert tried diplomacy, but the Islanders led by John Butler (who was Claiborne's brother-in-law) and the ever-faithful Captain Thomas Smith, proved obdurate. The old bogey was then resurrected, that Smith was inciting the Susquehannocks to attack the Marylanders.

With this for his excuse, Governor Calvert fitted out a force of twenty men which was to take Smith and Butler and subdue Kent Island. He was driven back to St. Marys by a week of bad weather. After waiting two months, he organized another expedition with thirty "choice musketeers" and set sail from St. Marys on February 25, 1638, the legislature being then in session. Leonard Calvert commanded in person, with Cornwallis as second in command. Evelin was in the party also.

In silence they made a surprise landing at the southern end of Kent Island before sunrise. Claiborne's house stood within a small palisaded enclosure; that was the "fort." The main gate, which faced the water, was locked, but somebody who knew the place (probably Evelin) found a way in at the back, opened the gate, and the whole party was inside before any alarm was given.

With the fort in his hands and all those who inhabited it taken prisoner, Calvert had no need to fear opposition from the scattered inhabitants outside. Butler lived on his plantation, the "Great Thicket," a few miles away and Smith near him, across a creek. Nobody had been able to escape from the fort to spread an alarm, and Calvert surprised and captured his chief enemies, one after another. They were sent down to St. Marys for trial. Deprived of their leaders, the Islanders quickly submitted to the Maryland government.

Captain Thomas Smith was brought to trial for piracy before the bar of the Maryland Assembly, which in this case constituted itself a court of last resort. The trial was a travesty on justice, because several men who served on the "grand inquest" which indicted Smith were men who had fought against him, and the same men served on the court which tried him. Smith was denied the advice of counsel but was permitted to speak in his own defense when the "evidence" was in. What he said was not recorded. He was found guilty and hanged. It is not a pretty episode in Maryland history.

Butler was merely censured by the Assembly and imprisoned for a while. Governor Calvert wrote to his brother,

Lord Baltimore: "I have taken him out of the Sheriff's custody into my owne howse, where I intend to have him remayne, until I have made further experience of his disposition, and if I can, win him to a good inclination to your Service."

The execution of loyal Captain Smith so enraged the Kent Islanders that they revolted against their new masters and Governor Calvert was obliged to set forth once more to bring them to order. This time he made a job of it, seizing their goods, burning some of their houses, and carrying many away as prisoners. Some of these were hanged without trial. The outpost at Palmer's Island was likewise reduced.

The Maryland Assembly, not satisfied with having confiscated all of Claiborne's property, then with doubtful legality proceeded to bring in a bill of attainder against William Claiborne "for the grievous crimes of pyracie and murther, and that he forfeite to the Lord Proprietarie all his lands and tenements, goods and chattels . . . In the province of Maryland."

George Evelin was made commander of Kent Island and presented with a manor.

In the same year (1638) the lords commissioners for the plantations, in England, decided unequivocally in favor of Lord Baltimore, and Claiborne's case seemed to be finally lost. He returned to Virginia quietly to await a better day, or, as they say on the Eastern Shore, "to lay low and chew poke root."

He had to wait fourteen years. In England during the interim, the king's cause had gone from bad to worse. Virginia under Sir William Berkeley was stanchly Royalist and Anglican, and Sir William began to make the Puritans there feel the weight of his displeasure. Lord Baltimore then (with an eye on the victorious Puritan Parliament in England) invited the Puritans to come settle in Maryland, promising them full religious freedom. Baltimore by this gesture hoped to secure toleration for his own Catholics, who were hated by both major parties in the English Civil War.

About a thousand of the Puritans accepted. In the meantime Leonard Calvert had died, and the prudent Baltimore had appointed William Stone, a Protestant, to be his governor of Maryland. In 1649, while the Virginia Puritans were on their way, the Maryland Assembly passed the famous Act of Toleration which guaranteed protection to all who believed in Jesus Christ. About the same time, the news arrived of the beheading of King Charles I.

The Puritans had hardly settled themselves in Maryland before they began to oppose Lord Baltimore's government, relying on the support of the Parliament of England. They objected to the oath of fidelity that Baltimore exacted in return for his grants of land.

In 1651 the English Parliament issued a commission to Captain Robert Denis and Mr. Thomas Stagge "to reduce all the plantations within the Bay of Chesapeake to their due obedience to the Parliament of the Commonwealth of England." In Virginia, Mr. Richard Bennett and Captain William Claiborne were to be associated with them in the execution of this commission.

On the way over, Denis and Stagge were lost at sea together with the original commission. It had been provided that in such a contingency Captain Edmund Curtis, who commanded the *Guinea*, frigate, was to serve in their place, and Curtis had been provided with a copy of the commission. In Virginia, Curtis was joined by Bennett and Claiborne, and that colony was brought to the heel of Parliament without any fighting. The commissioners then proceeded to Maryland with their somewhat dubiously worded commission. Claiborne's day had come at last.

It was Lord Baltimore's contention that the commission had no authority to disturb him in his patent. Maryland was at first specifically named in the warrant, he said, but upon his appointment of William Stone, a good Parliament man, as governor, the name of Maryland was stricken out.

Be that as it may, the *Guinea* appeared before St. Marys and summoned Governor Stone to surrender. He did. The frigate then sailed away, leaving Bennett and Claiborne to carry out the administrative details.

To Claiborne this was a sweet hour. To his everlasting honor, he exacted no revenge. None of his ancient enemies was punished; no man was imprisoned nor had his lands or goods confiscated. Governor Stone, upon refusing to issue writs excluding the name of Lord Baltimore, was deposed, and a commission of Puritans appointed to govern the province. The seat of government was removed from St. Marys to the house of one of the commissioners, Richard Preston of Patuxent. Bennett and Claiborne then returned to Virginia, where the one was now governor and the other his second in command. This was in 1652.

In Maryland the new government did not function satisfactorily and in three months Bennett and Claiborne returned. William Stone was now reinstated as governor, along with Thomas Hatton, secretary of the province. Stone very naturally felt justified in continuing to include the name of Lord Baltimore as proprietary, in all grants, writs, etc., issued by him. This angered the Puritans, and in 1654 Bennett and Claiborne summarily fired Governor Stone and increased the members of the Puritan commissioners from six to ten.

By this time a report of what had happened had reached Lord Baltimore in England. Oliver Cromwell was now lord protector of England; Parliament had been dissolved, and Baltimore took the position that its former acts had no force. Stone received letters from his lordship angrily rebuking him for having so tamely handed over the government to the Puritans. Stone then prepared to fight. Sending a couple of small expeditions against the provisional capital at Patuxent to recover the records and, it was said, to hang Mr. Preston, he got the records but Preston kept out of his hands.

Stone then gathered upward of a hundred men and, embarking them in small vessels, sailed to attack the principal Puritan settlement at Providence, on the Severn River, near the spot where Annapolis now stands. William Fuller, the commander of the Puritans, met him with a force of about the same size.

The battle which took place on what is now Horn's Point, while small in scale, was both bloody and decisive. The Puritans attacked with the cry: "In the name of God, fall on! God is our strength!" Lord Baltimore's men countered with: "Hey for St. Marys!" The Puritans asseverated that their cry was: "Hey for St. Marys and three wives!" but that is no doubt a canard. But they did cry: "Come on, ye rogues! ye roundheaded dogs!"

The Puritans had the advantage of an armed ship, the *Golden Lion*, in the river, whose fire caught the St. Marys men in the rear. Half of Stone's men were killed and wounded and the gorgeous proprietary standard of black and gold and red (still the flag of Maryland) went down. All the rest were captured by the Puritans except two or three who escaped by swimming. "The ground," says a Puritan account, "was strewed with Papist beads." William Stone was actually condemned to death by a drumhead court-martial, but was saved, it is said, by the intercession of the Puritan soldiers.

For three years thereafter the Puritan House of Burgesses and the Provincial Court continued to meet at the home of Mr. Preston (the house is still standing) without hindrance. All this while, the patient and astute Cecil Lord Baltimore was arguing his case before the authorities of England. Finally, in 1658 in London, an agreement was reached between Baltimore and Richard Bennett, restoring the government of Maryland into Lord Baltimore's hands. Baltimore must have smiled to himself when the Puritans exacted a promise that he should never repeal his own Act of Toleration.

After the Puritan commissioners were forced to restore the records (they said they had lost the Great Seal) to Josias Fendall, Lord Baltimore's new governor, William Claiborne returned to Virginia and never visited Kent Island again. But it was always in his heart. The county in which he lived in Virginia was christened New Kent. In 1677, when he was nearly ninety, he made a last pitiful petition to Charles II to have his island restored to him. It was not acted upon, and soon afterward he died.

CHAPTER 3

Colonel Edmund Scarburgh

Up to this time there had been little settlement on the Eastern Shore, except at Accomac down at the Virginia end. About 1660 the people of Accomac began to drift north into Maryland, some settling on the Pocomoke, the nearest river to their former homes, others going on to the Annemessex and Manokin rivers. Some of these new settlers were Quakers and other nonconformists who had been in conflict with the Virginia authorities, others were natural-born pioneers; all good people in a new land.

In 1661 Governor Calvert (this was Charles, eldest son of Cecil) found it necessary to appoint a commission for the Eastern Shore with authority to make grants of land south of the Choptank River. He named Colonel Edmund Scarburgh, of Accomac, Randall Revell, of Revell's Neck, and John Elzey, of Almodington on the Manokin.

Why Charles Calvert picked Scarburgh, nobody has ever been able to explain. While it is true that Scarburgh possessed lands on the Maryland side of the border, he was an ardent Virginian and a notorious Indian-baiter. An able, headstrong man, he also had a powerful interest at the English court, where his brother, Sir Charles Scarburgh, was physician in turn to Charles II, James II, and King William, and even the doughty Sir William Berkeley, governor of Virginia, was unable to keep him in order. Calvert may have had some idea of appeasing him.

Scarburgh was one of the first of that type of man who believes that the only good Indian is a dead Indian. It was said that smallpox and Colonel Scarburgh were the greatest

scourges of the gentle Assateagues. On one occasion, when he had been annoyed by some pilfering on his plantation, he summoned the neighboring Indians to his place on a Sunday morning, by promising them the Great Spirit would preach them a sermon if they gathered in a certain ditch. There was a cannon concealed in the ditch and when the Indians were assembled it was discharged. "The Great Spirit spoke so forcibly unto the natives that but few remained alive after his introductory remarks." The Indians called Scarburgh by the dread name of the "conjurer."

On another occasion, Scarburgh went after the Pocomokes, who lived beside the river of that name. After spreading the usual rumor that they were preparing to massacre the whites, he collected a troop of well-armed and experienced fighters and set out to find them. These unfortunate people possessed neither horses nor firearms. They were soon located. Many were killed in the first charge of the troopers, others slashed to death with sabers and long hunting knives, many taken prisoner. Two who, Scarburgh affected to believe, had been ringleaders were chained together neck and heels.

The Virginia authorities, aroused by this playful prank, summoned Scarburgh to appear before the Virginia Council at Jamestown and indicted him "for going in a hostile manner among the Indians and doing them outrages contrary to the known laws of Virginia." To placate the surviving Pocomokes, one hundred arm's lengths of roanoke was sent to their king and twenty arm's lengths given to each of the two who had been bound neck and heels.

Roanoke was a sort of wampum used by the Indians as currency. It was made of bits of white shell threaded on strings.

Scarburgh was not to be withstood. He was acquitted at his trial, and Governor Berkeley went so far as to beg him to accept for each of his two little daughters a ewe lamb.

The vindication of Scarburgh was a bad omen for the Eastern Shore Indians. It was not long before he was planning a campaign against the Assateagues, who lived over on the ocean side of the peninsula in both Virginia and Maryland. These were the Indians whom Verrazano had found more than a hundred years before, and this was the gentle tribe that had succored Colonel Norwood and his party within recent memory.

The ship *Virginia Merchant* was driven into Sinepuxent Bay (on the ocean side) in 1650. She was short of food and water and the crew was mutinous. Colonel Norwood, a passenger, volunteered to take a party ashore to search for fresh water, and they were landed on Fenwick's island. The mutinous crew took possession of the ship and sailed away, leaving them marooned. They found water, but were starving when the Assateague Indians came upon them.

The Indians welcomed the white men with joyful countenances, Colonel Norwood reported, and shook hands with all. They gave the white men corn and bread. Some of the whites had beads to give them in exchange, but the Indians fed those who had nothing just as generously. The white men were conducted to the Indian village, where a feast and entertainment were provided for them. The king made Colonel Norwood sit beside him "and was no less indulgent to feed and caress us than if we had been his children."

Guides were found for them and when they said goodbye: "He [the king] desired as a pledge of my affection that I would give him my camblet coat which he vowed to wear whilst he lived for my sake." Norwood said he was glad to comply, "because he was the first King I could call to my mind that ever shewed any inclination to wear my old clothes."

Norwood gave the king's daughter a piece of scarlet ribbon, scissors, "a French tweezer" and other such trifles that made her "skip for joy." She disappeared within a tepee and presently came out with ribbon, scissors, knives and bodkins hanging from her ears, neck and hair. She had painted her face yellow and green in honor of the white guests, and Colonel Norwood says: "I wished this young Princess would have contented herself with what nature had done for her, without this addition of paint, which I thought made her more fulsome than handsome."

This story was well-known to Scarburgh, yet he announced that he was going to attack the Assateagues because they "despise the English honnour and have so long triumphed in the ruines of Christian bloud." Both statements were made out of whole cloth.

Most of the Assateagues lived in Maryland, and Scarburgh asked the proprietary officials to send some men so that a joint attack might be made. Scarburgh planned to take three hundred footmen and sixty horse. Realizing that the Indians "were harder to find than to conquer," he intended to penetrate to the heart of their country "that they might neither plant corne, hunt, or fish and soe make them poore and famish them." A pleasant man, Scarburgh.

To their honor, the Maryland authorities refused to join in the attack. However, Scarburgh obtained troops from the western shore of Virginia and set out. How many of the simple Assateagues he massacred will never be known.

Such was the man chosen by Governor Calvert to be one of his commissioners on the Eastern Shore. Calvert was not long in discovering his mistake.

In the following year (1662) Randall Revell reported to St. Marys that there were fifty tithables (heads of families) seated at Annemessex and Manokin. The Nanticoke Indians who lived just to the north were made restive by this influx, and Revell asked that a treaty the commissioners had made with them should be ratified.

Under this treaty, the emperor of the Nanticokes was to receive six matchcoats from every white man who took up land in his territory. A matchcoat was a garment made of a rough blanket or frieze. The emperor was to get another coat for every runaway servant taken by him and returned. No murders to be committed by either side. The Indians promised not to trade with the Dutch so long as the English could supply their necessities. No Englishman was to pass through their territories without a pass from the governor or a magistrate.

The treaty was ratified. Scarburgh, Revell, and Elzey were reappointed commissioners; William Thorne was commissioned captain of a regiment of foot; Revell, Elzey, and Thorne were appointed magistrates qualified to hear any cause to the value of two thousand pounds of tobacco.

Next year the commissioners were named thus: John Elzey, Stephen Horsey, William Thorne, John Odber. Scarburgh and Revell were both dropped. By this time Scarburgh had shown his true colors, and Revell was suspected of being too friendly with him.

Later this year the dashing, haughty, domineering cavalier actually raided Maryland with forty horsemen for, as he explained, "pomp of safety and to repel that contempt which I was informed some Quakers & a foole in office had threatened to obtrude." He was now claiming that the country along the Annemessex and Manokin was rightfully within the borders of Virginia. This claim was founded on nothing more than the mistake Captain John Smith had made years before in calling the Pocomoke the Wighcocomoco (Wicomico). Everybody knew there was nothing in it.

So Scarburgh rode to exact the obedience of the settlers to Virginia. His report of his doings is a little masterpiece of invective. Of Stephen Horsey, the new commissioner who lived on Annemessex, he said: "An ignorant yet insolent officer and a factious and tumultuous person, constant in nothing, his children at great ages yet unchristened." Ambrose Dixon he characterized as a "prater of nonsense and much led by ye spirit of ignorance." George Johnson was "ye proteus of heresy . . . notorious for shifting, scismattical pranks . . . a known Drunkard & Reported by ye neighbors to be ye father of his negro Wenches' bastards." Dixon and Johnson were Quakers. Scarburgh marked the door of every planter who refused to submit to Virginia with "ye broad arrow" of confiscation.

When Governor Calvert heard of these goings-on, he sent word to the settlers that he would hang any man that submitted to "his Majestie's" governor of Virginia. Thus the Eastern Shore planters found themselves in a tight place. They had a third anxiety because the Nanticoke Indians (a more formidable tribe than the gentle Assateagues) were threatening to rise. When the settlers complained to St. Marys of this danger, the cool answer came back that they would have to "stand on their owne guards," and John Elzey said: "We lye between Sylla and Charibdis, not knowing how to gett out of this labarith."

Scarburgh appointed commissioners of his own, remitted some customs duties as a sop to the settlers, and returned home. The Nanticokes did not rise. Governor Calvert complained bitterly to Governor Berkeley of Virginia of Scarburgh's acts and was informed that the colonel had no authority to act on his own, or to use force.

The boundary quarrel dragged on for several years. Virginia had no case, and the original boundary which placed the Pocomoke, Annemessex, and Manokin rivers within Maryland was finally confirmed. Maryland continued vigorously to press charges against Scarburgh. But Scarburgh, surveyor general of Virginia, owner of vast lands and a fleet of ships, was one of the greatest gentlemen in the colony. He had survived so many accusations from his own people that he could afford to laugh at these foreign charges. All Maryland could secure from Virginia was an injunction forbidding the violent colonel to interfere with the boundary as established.

A Pocomoke chief is supposed to have said of Scarburgh's times—it sounds a little romantic for a redskin, but the facts are true enough:

> In the moon of the roasting ears [August] palefaces from the land of the Accomacs wanted war. The black wampum belt with the red hatchet painted on it was sent from chief to chief along the seaside and over beyond Pocomoke. The King of the bad whites was angry and came with horse and guns. After a while the cloud went down. The Quackels [Quakers] came into our land. The bad white chief and his friends had driven them out. They loved peace. But one time he put on his war paint and swam the rivers and followed them. He hated Quackels. . . . The Quackels were kind to Indians. Then the great father across the Bay said the bad white chief must stay beyond the marked trees.

CHAPTER 4

The Picaroons

LET us continue the story of the Pocomoke and adjacent waters. After the engagement of the *Cockatrice* with the *St. Margaret* and the *St. Helen*, the wide waters of Pocomoke Sound heard no warlike alarms for more than a hundred years. Governor Charles Calvert succeeded to his father's title as third Lord Baltimore in 1675, and in 1689 in the Protestant rebellion he was deprived of his governing powers. He died in 1715, shortly before they were restored. Charles was succeeded by the fourth lord, who enjoyed his honors for a few weeks only, and he by the fifth, another Charles. When the American Revolution broke out, the sixth and last lord was dead, and Maryland was paying rent to his illegitimate son, Henry Harford. But not for long!

During the years of the Revolution there was a numerous Tory element throughout the lower Eastern Shore which gave the patriots continual trouble. Forces of militia, one after another, were sent against them, either by land or by water. When such an expedition had a small success, it would disband and presently the job had to be done over. In the last and bloodiest fight at sea, the patriot force was badly beaten. Historians have slurred over this humiliating incident. Heretofore it has been accepted that the last blood shed in the Revolution was that of Captain Willmott at James Island, S. C., on November 14, 1782, but this battle of Kedge's Straits, it will be seen, with its many casualties occurred two weeks later.

The marshes and the islands of Pocomoke and Tangier sounds provided hundreds of hiding places to the Tory vessels —the patriots termed them refugee barges or picaroons. Occasionally the Tories secured a small schooner or two, but usually they operated in open boats of various sizes with a four-pounder gun and perhaps several swivels mounted fore and aft. They could be propelled by either oars or sail. After sallying out to plunder the patriot boats and plantations, they retired into some deep creek in the marshes where, when the mast was lowered, they could lie completely hidden, sure of protection and supply from their sympathizers on shore.

They had various leaders of whom the most notorious was one Joseph Whaland, who in time became a bogey with which to scare the patriot children up and down the Eastern Shore. He appears to have been wounded once and was twice taken prisoner, but he was a slick and plausible rascal who could talk himself out of jail. One of his victims has left this description of him:

> Whaland was a tall, slim, gallows-looking fellow in his shirtsleeves with a gold-embroidered waistcoat on, that he had robbed from some old trooper on the Eastern Shore.

During the early years of the Revolution there are few references in the records to the operations of the refugee boats; in 1780 they become frequent. During the summer of that year, Colonel Henry Hooper, a militia officer on the

Eastern Shore, reported to Annapolis that several small Tory boats were cruising in Hooper's Strait and that as a result of their activities the Nanticoke and Wicomico rivers were closed up.

The Council prepared to deal with the menace, but they moved very slowly (they had other troubles, too!) and it was December before the expedition was ready. It consisted of the *Porpuss (sic!)*, an armed sloop, the state boat *Dolphin*, and one or more barges under command of Major John Stewart. The enemy by this time was said to have five schooners and three or four barges and Major Stewart was urged to proceed with caution.

The only direct result of the expedition seems to have been the capture of the enemy's schooner *Active* by one of our barges under Captain Revelly, who gained great fame thereby.

But the expedition had the indirect result of driving Joseph Whaland under cover for a while. In December, 1780, he came to see Colonel George Dashiell, lieutenant and commissary for Somerset County. Whaland was not well-known as yet, but Colonel Dashiell had heard an ugly rumor concerning the activities of his boat. Whaland undertook to explain it away.

It was true, he said, that his boat had been concerned in one of the recent attacks on American vessels, but that was because it had been captured by the British. He, Whaland, had been put in irons and cast down below, and there he was forced to lie throughout the fight. On their return from up the bay, the British had returned his boat to him and dismissed him. He had immediately come up the Wicomico with his family, he said, so that they should no longer be exposed to the picaroons. In order to prove his loyalty he offered to serve against the Tories and to contribute to the expense of building a barge to be sent against them.

Dashiell was taken in, and wrote a letter to the governor, exculpating Whaland. It was no sooner sent than he received an "express" from the valuable Colonel Hooper asking him to arrest Joseph Whaland, "who has lately moved into your neighborhood." Hooper enclosed the affidavit of one Valentine Peyton who swore that he and his schooner had been captured by Joseph Whaland. Peyton described Whaland's boat with deadly particularity: "a small pilot boat with a white bottom and carries a Gib (!)."

Presumably Colonel Dashiell then arrested Whaland and sent him to Baltimore, though no record of it appears. But from a letter of Colonel George's kinsman, Colonel Joseph Dashiell, to the governor in the following year, we learn that: "Joseph Whaland, that old offender, is down in Somerset plundering again and we have reason to believe that the Gaoler in Baltimore is alone to blame, as Whaland's father told one of the Neighbors that he [the jailer] let him go at large. If I had direction to go into Somerset I think I could apprehend him. He has lately robbed a certain Thomas Reucher who, I think, would assist me to Trap him." Colonel Joseph Dashiell was the principal patriot officer in Worcester County.

However, Whaland was not apprehended at that time.

Meanwhile the men of Somerset County addressed a memorial to the Council at Annapolis, praying for protection, and offering the proposal of one Zedekiah Walley to build a barge. Order for the barge was immediately given, and by June she was reported to be almost ready. She appears to have been built at Pocomoke, and was christened *Protector*. They procured a twenty-four-pounder for her, a mighty gun for that service. Her full complement was a hundred men but she could operate with eighty.

At the same time the authorities at Annapolis were preparing another expedition comprising the state boat *Plater*, the armed boat *Decoy*, a state barge, and another boat, all under the command of Captain Alexander Trueman. This squadron set off in pursuit of an enemy barge with 120 men which had ascended as high as West River on the western shore, dangerously close to the capital, but nothing has been recorded of the outcome.

The picaroons were ever becoming bolder. Reports of fresh outrages came in almost daily, always from a different direction. Colonel Joseph Dashiell of Worcester wrote: "The enemy has four barges and 4 privateers in our Sound [Pocomoke]. I wish to God the armed boats and barges [the Annapolis outfit] would come down to act with Captain Walley who will be out in a few days I think."

Colonel George Dashiell reports from Somerset: "Captain Gale was taken out of his bed a few nights past by a person who called himself McMullen with 4 white men and 9 negroes in his command, and carried to Clay Island [at the mouth of the Nanticoke] where he was most inhumanly whipt with 36 lashes and afterwards hanged until they thought him dead. But some time after he was let down he recovered. McMullen endeavored, but could not prevail upon his crew to hang him a second time or drown him, but compelled him to take an oath not to bear arms against the King and dismissed him."

Another report from the same to the Eastern Shore Council: "Aaron Sterling, aged 66, a patriot of Annamessex, was plundered last fall by the British barges and four times this Spring, and all his provisions of every kind taken. His wharf and his houses have been burned and he has been obliged to move 17 miles from his plantation with his wife and children. That he was also wounded, beaten and bruised exceedingly. He is reduced to great difficulties, being obliged to depend much on the bounty and charity of others. His son Josiah Sterling being lately drafted, he can't get along without him in his present distresses, and prays your honours to discharge the said Josiah Sterling."

The Council answered that it had no power to discharge and suggests that Sterling apply to General Smallwood.

Colonel Henry Hooper reports to Matthew Tilghman (who was president of the Council for the Eastern Shore): "Two of the enemies barges came up to Vienna [on the Nanticoke River] where they plundered the inhabitants and took two or three loaded vessels. One proceeded up the river and took two more. The other retreated down river with her prizes. The militia recaptured three vessels and took three men. I posted militia on both sides the river cutting off the other barge. Her men ran her ashore and deserted her. She is now in our possession, but the men have got off. I despatched a party of light horse yesterday low down the river and on their reporting that the enemy's barge was not to be seen in the river, I discharged the militia.

"This morning at one o'clock I received an express that the barge had returned last night and made the inhabitants of Vienna prisoners. Orders now out for collecting a party to march to Vienna." Colonel Hooper concludes his report with an appeal for ammunition. He encloses the examination of the prisoners and asks for a light field gun. "Very usefull for cutting off the retreat of barges in the river."

Captain Walley, after all, was not ready to join the first successful cruise against the refugee boats. By this time the

Council had collected, armed, and manned three barges in the upper part of the Shore, and had put them under command of Captain Thomas Grason. The log that Grason kept of his first cruise has survived the vicissitudes of a hundred and sixty-odd years. From it we learn that Grason took several prizes and chased the picaroons down the bay.

On September 18th, the barge *Protector* being at last ready, Captain Zedekiah Walley was ordered to join Captain Grason's squadron to act as his second in command. They were to rendezvous at Jane's Island (at the mouth of Annemessex). It is likely that Walley had had at least a brief cruise on his own, because we find Joseph Dashiell joyfully reporting (no date) that Captain Walley's barge "had driven these gentry entirely from our Sound" (Pocomoke).

No second cruise was undertaken just then, for General Washington applied to Governor Thomas Sim Lee of Maryland for vessels to help transport his army to Virginia. Captain Walley was ordered to take his barge to Head of Elk for that purpose. In transmitting the order, Colonel Dashiell wrote exultingly: "The present happy concurrence of circumstances afford the most rational hopes that the whole of Cornwallis' army may fall into our hands." It did!

General Washington was desperately in need of supplies, too, and wrote movingly to Governor Lee on the subject: "An army cannot be kept together without supplies; if those fail us our operations must cease and all our highest Hopes will vanish into Disappointment and Disgrace."

Captain Grason was ordered to take all his barges to Baltimore to assist the army with food and transport.

During this same month, word came from North Carolina that Joseph Whaland and Michael Timmons had been captured. The Governor's Council immediately addressed the governor of North Carolina, speaking of the "horrid and wanton depredations" of these men, and offering to send and get them. No reply from North Carolina has been recorded. Some hitch must have arisen, for Whaland did not fall into the hands of the Maryland authorities, and in the following year he was as busy plundering as ever.

In October 1781 the British army had been finally defeated at Yorktown, but the war at sea went on. In March the principal farmers of the Eastern Shore agreed to fit out the barge *Experiment* with an attendant boat to cruise between Kent Point and Tilghman's Island. The enemy was reported to have increased his forces. At the same time the Assembly of Maryland undertook to equip and man four more barges, mounting two guns each and carrying 250 men. Maryland invited the co-operation of Virginia, but Virginia's reply (if any) has not been recorded. The depredations continued.

The main base of the picaroons was still thought to be on Tangier Island, and on April 13th Captain Grason was ordered to seek them out there and, if necessary, to depopulate the island and turn the men over to the lieutenants of their respective counties. By this time the Continental currency had become almost worthless, and the state authorities were experiencing heartbreaking difficulties in raising money. The records are sparse, but apparently three of the barges could not be manned for lack of money, and Captain Grason set off alone in the *Revenge* to carry out his orders.

Sometime in May the *Revenge* fell in with three of the enemy barges and bravely gave battle. The Americans were overwhelmed and Grason was killed. The date of this action has not been recorded. In fact, no mention of the battle is to be found anywhere except for a brief notice in the *Maryland Journal and Baltimore Advertiser* of May 14, 1782:

> A number of small Privateers, 5 of which are said to be armed Barges, manned principally by desperate Refugees, now infest our Bay and greatly annoy its Commerce. Three of the latter lately captured an armed Boat from Annapolis under Captain Grason's command, near the Tangier Islands, after a sharp Contest in which the brave Captain and several of his Men lost their Lives after performing Signal Acts of Valour.

The refugees were not always victorious. On July 5th the brig *Ranger*, Captain Thomas Simmons, outward bound from Alexandria, Virginia, was attacked by two barges off St. George's Island near the mouth of the Potomac. It was one o'clock in the morning and very dark; the picaroons were upon them before they could make a defense. There were about thirty men in each barge and Captain Simmons had but twenty-four. Unable to use the ship's guns, they repelled the boarders with pikes until all but three were broken. The sailors then "played them with cold shot," which did the greatest damage, and finally beat off the picaroons.

The action lasted for an hour and a half. The captain received a ball through his right leg, one of his men was killed and two wounded; a Negro from the barges was taken prisoner. The *Ranger* returned to Alexandria. Reports which came up the river later stated that one of the refugee captains (Barry) had been killed and the other (Joseph Whaland) wounded. One report said that 27 of their men had been killed, another 7. They buried their dead on St. George's Island and left two badly wounded men lying there. It was from these two that the information was had.

The indestructible Whaland could not have been badly wounded, for only three days later he was in action again. The *Journal and Advertiser* reports:

On the 8th instant [July] the schooner Greyhound, a beautiful boat laden with Salt, Peas, Pork, Bacon and some Dry Goods . . . was taken in Hooper's Straits by the Renegade-Pirate Joe Whaland. The prize was sent to New York but Mr. Furnival (who was unluckily on board) the Skipper and Hands were set on Shore at a place called Dan's [Dames] Quarter near Devil's [Deal's] Island after being detained 24 hours on board the Barge, during which time Mr. Furnival was plundered of his Money, Watch, Hat and indeed every Thing that the Thieves could lay their Hands on. Mr. Furnival saw several other Bay craft fall into the Fangs of the same Vultures before he was released. One Timmons (2 of whose brothers were executed some Time ago on the Eastern Shore) was Whaland's Lieutenant.

The militia in Worcester County was ordered out. These land soldiers were helpless against Whaland's vessels. The shortest distance between two points on the Eastern Shore is by water. Moreover, when the picaroons made a strike, they immediately went somewhere else. Piteous reports were now coming in from the rivers of Virginia's western shore: Rappahannock, Piankatank, Potomac.

Captain Zedekiah Walley was now in command of the remaining barges. In July he was ordered down the bay to report to the Chevalier de Villebrune, commander of the French fleet, and to co-operate with him; but in September the barges were still in Baltimore, unable to stir for want of pay for the men.

News of further depredations was received. Walley finally set out and returned with four American vessels recaptured from the picaroons. On the 24th he was ordered to sail again. On the 26th the order was repeated, and on the 28th he received peremptory orders to sail and "let Speddon's barge follow."

Many weeks must still have passed before he got away,

because on November 2nd the Council is writing him to suggest that Cherrystone is too far down the bay to appoint a rendezvous, and that he should choose a nearer place.

On November 15th he finally made contact with two enemy barges at Gwynn's Island and gave chase. Gwynn's Island is off the Western Shore of Virginia. Captain Solomon Frazier in the *Defense* captured one of the enemy's barges along with her commander and sixteen men. They chased the other barge around Cape Charles and clear out to sea.

Returning to the bay, they smoked out two more enemy barges under Smith's Island (off Annemessex on the Eastern Shore) and chased them around Cape Charles also, and behind the islands on the ocean side. These two escaped out through Wreck Island Inlet to the open sea and were lost in the dark. They took two lieutenants belonging to the barges routed out of Smith's Island, "one of whom is Peter Francks, a Portugee, who is notoriously known to be at and privie to almost every house burnt on the Eastern Shore."

Captain Walley, who from now on is termed commodore, received information that the enemy barges had made rendezvous in Chincoteague Bay (on the ocean side) and were awaiting him there, but he took it that his duty was to keep them outside the bay, and he returned inside to wait for them.

On November 27th the little flotilla was lying at the village of Onancock on the Eastern Shore of Virginia. With the wind at south, they saw seven sail standing up the bay. The commodore gave the signal to weigh anchor and pursue them. Night coming on, they were not able to make sure who they were, but supposed them to be British.

Early the next morning they discovered several vessels at anchor under lower Tangier Island which they took to be the same, but the wind was then blowing strong from the northwest and they were unable to sail into the teeth of it. The commodore consulted his officers, and since their little force was outnumbered by these suspicious strangers, it was agreed to dispatch an express back to Onancock asking for a barge that was lying there to join them, and also their prize that they had left there. They asked for volunteers to man both vessels.

At evening, as the messenger had not returned, the commodore gave orders to run into Onancock in order to speed matters. In the village they were told that the barge would be ready in the morning with sufficient men to man her, and also the prize taken from the picaroons. The latter vessel was called *Languedoc*.

Next morning the commodore desired Captain Frazier to man the *Defense* with forty picked men and proceed to Tangier Island to reconnoiter the enemy. Frazier arrived at Tangier without seeing any vessels. All the people on Tangier were British sympathizers. Flying British colors, Frazier landed at the house of one Crockett and asked where the American barges were. Crockett told him he knew nothing about them, but had seen five barges lying under Watts' Island the day before. Watts' Island lies east and a little south of Tangier, and these, of course, were the Americans.

Crockett, believing Captain Frazier to be British, further volunteered the information that six British barges had left his house early that morning for Fox Island (off Pocomoke Sound) and that they intended spending the night in Cager's (Kedge's) Straits (between Smith and South Marsh islands). Captain Frazier then returned to report to Commodore Walley.

Walley ordered the Onancock barge back because she

could not keep up with the others. A number of "gentlemen" volunteers from her transferred to the other barges. Next morning they set sail for Fox Island. This is really November 30th, though it would appear on the log as the 29th.

At Fox Island, Samuel Handy, second lieutenant in the commodore's barge, was sent ashore in the *Languedoc* to pick up what he could. He learned that the refugee barges had sailed north for Kedge's Straits the previous afternoon, and upon hearing his report, the American barges stood after them. They anchored at 4:00 A.M. with Kedge's Straits "bearing West and somewhat Northwardly."

At six o'clock in the morning, while Frazier was aboard the supply boat *Flying Fish,* drawing rations for his men, he saw six sail of the enemy entering the straits. The Americans immediately made sail and gave chase. Commodore Walley ordered Frazier in advance to bring the enemy into action. Upon Frazier's asking him in what position he would wish to engage them, he answered that he didn't think they would engage at all, but if they formed in line he would form in the same manner.

The enemy appeared to be under easy sail, standing away from them through the straits. In obedience to his orders, Frazier pushed a half mile ahead of the other American barges, who were following in this order: Captain Dashiell, Captain Speddon, the commodore, the *Languedoc,* and some distance astern, the *Flying Fish.* At eight o'clock the enemy took in sail, formed in line with five barges and started rowing toward Captain Frazier in the *Defense* with a light stroke. Their remaining barge rowed off to the right as if she did not mean to engage.

At a distance of two hundred yards the enemy hoisted his colors. He was still keeping in line and coming for Captain Frazier bow on. The latter took in sail and broke out his colors. At this point, he reports, Captain Dashiell rowed out of line and fell in behind Captain Speddon and the commodore, the *Languedoc* being still farther astern.

The enemy opened a heavy fire on the *Defense* from five barges. Captain Speddon and the commodore were coming up on her port quarter, and Captain Frazier backed slowly astern to form in line with them. He received two more volleys from the enemy which he returned with every gun he could bring to bear. The commodore and the gentlemen volunteers gave him three cheers as they came up, and both supporting barges opened fire on the enemy. The commodore was then holding the left of their line, Captain Speddon was in the center, Captain Frazier on the right.

For a while a brisk fire was maintained from both sides, and then occurred the accident that cost the Americans the battle. Fire broke out aboard the commodore's barge near the mizzenmast, and a number of volunteers leaped overboard from the stern sheets. Soon afterward a second fire broke out and many more men jumped overboard. Two of the enemy's barges rowed up to board the commodore and the other three kept up a constant fire on Captain Frazier. It was then seen that Captain Dashiell, the *Languedoc*, and the *Flying Fish* were retreating as fast as they could.

Captain Frazier rowed around without being able to discover any signals either for continuing the action or for retreating. Finally he made up his mind there was nothing for it but to get away if he could. Captain Speddon was now in retreat also; the commodore, having been boarded by the enemy, struck his colors. One enemy barge remained alongside him while the other five started after the retreating Americans.

Captain Dashiell bore away up the Tangier Sound with Captains Speddon and Frazier following; the *Languedoc* and the *Flying Fish* stood toward the mainland and by two o'clock had passed out of sight of the others. Captain Speddon's barge was a slow sailor and Frazier, seeing that he was likely to be overtaken, lowered his mainsail to wait for him and told him he would not forsake him. However, at 4:00 P.M. the enemy gave over the chase at the upper entrance to Hooper's Straits, and the two American barges sailed on up the bay and entered the Choptank River.

There they were detained by wind and weather until December 3rd. On that day they weighed anchor at Todd's Point ("Captain Dashiell having left us," Frazier said curtly) and that evening tied up at the Annapolis dock.

Governor Paca received other reports that must have made him a little heartsick. Captains Dashiell and Speddon tried to excuse themselves for running away. This Dashiell was also called George, but he was not the same as Colonel George, the lieutenant of Somerset. Captain Speddon said his six-pounder "bursted" the first time it was fired. He ordered his men to board the enemy, he said, but they would not row alongside the enemy barge.

Colonel George Dashiell, after hearing the stories of survivors, explained to the governor that the cause of the explosion on the commodore's barge was due to the gunner's breaking a cartridge. He had wet the spilled powder but not sufficiently. The men of the *Protector* fought with the greatest bravery. All of them were killed and thrown overboard except the bodies of Commodore Walley and Lieutenant Handy.

This report was an exaggeration, it appears from the report of Colonel Cropper. Cropper was the lieutenant of

Accomac County, Virginia, and a volunteer. He was wounded seven times. "I am so ill of my wounds I can scarcely write," he says. He is scathing on the subject of the barge captains. Frazier and Speddon fired a few shots, he says, but Dashiell ran away without discharging a gun. "There was never before on a like occasion so much cowardice exhibited." Cropper noted that it was the barge *Kidnapper* which boarded the *Protector*. The Americans killed or wounded more than twenty of her men before they were forced to strike. Commodore Walley was killed near the eighteen-pounder, a cool, intrepid, gallant officer. Lieutenant Joseph Handy fell near him, still nobly fighting though he had lost an arm.

On arriving in Annapolis, Frazier and Speddon asked for an inquiry, which was presently held. The proceedings have not survived, but the result is evident in the fact that Dashiell was discharged from the service while Speddon and Frazier were reinstated. Frazier now became commander of the barges.

The rest of the story makes painful reading. Somerset and Dorchester were left completely open to the depredations of the picaroons, and their complaints were pitiful. Governor Paca made an energetic attempt to refit the barges, only to find himself balked by the refusal of the crews (whose time was expiring) to re-enlist or to volunteer for service during the winter. He had to let them go, and he was under the humiliating necessity of writing the commander of the French fleet (after having applied to him for help) to say that he could not send out the barges.

Meanwhile, Whaland, who, it transpired later, was in sole command of the refugee boats, had the effrontery to build winter quarters for his men on Tangier. They were quiet for a few weeks, but in February they broke out again and Colonels George and Joseph Dashiell addressed another appeal to the governor. He answered, promising the *Pole Cat*, a brig of fourteen guns which had been offered him by the French admiral, also three sloops or schooners and three barges.

The unfortunate governor was hamstrung by the fact that the last year's bills for the barges had not been paid. He begged the intendant of the revenue for money, and addressed an eloquent appeal to the merchants of Baltimore for a loan of money and three armed ships, also extra men for the barges. "Every moment of delay is big with the ruin of some unfortunate family," he said to them.

The reply of the merchants apparently has not survived, but it is clear that they laid down conditions the governor could not meet. He wrote politely: "Neither our Power nor our Resources will enable us to obtain your assistance on the terms proposed."

He had already written to General Washington notifying him that Whaland had sacked the town of Benedict, thirty miles up the Patuxent, while on the Eastern Shore another party had come up as high as Kent Point, almost opposite Baltimore. Since King George III was said to have issued an order forbidding all offensive operations pending the peace, Governor Paca wanted Washington to make representations to the British authorities.

The *Pole Cat* was up for repairs and he did not get her, but in spite of all difficulties he outfitted and manned the schooner *Venus* and two barges, *Fearnought* and *Defense*. This expedition was to be commanded by Captain John Lynn of the army, and Lynn was to bring some soldiers aboard. Captain Frazier was told by the governor:

"As Captain Lynn knows very little of Naval affairs he

will consult and advise with you. Warned by experience, I hope you will be particularly careful of your ammunition."

And Captain Lynn was advised that he had better go on the *Venus* because of her better accommodation, but in action he should transfer to Captain Frazier's barge "as he is a Man of Sense and Bravery on whom, I think, you may rely for such advice as from your inexperience in Naval Matters it will be necessary for you to receive."

On March 22nd, Captain Lynn, writing from West River (on the Western Shore below Annapolis), said that all was ready and that he was impatiently awaiting the arrival of the schooner and barges. On the 29th, peace with England was proclaimed.

Scharf, in his *History of Maryland,* states that the expedition of Captain Lynn did attack the picaroon stronghold at Devil's or Deal's Island (which Scharf confuses with upper Tangier). According to Scharf, the expedition was successful. They captured a large quantity of plunder and, it is supposed, some of the enemy's barges. Scharf does not give his sources for this statement, and there is evidence, on the other hand, that after the peace was proclaimed Lynn's expedition was abandoned.

Until comparatively recent times there were many romantic stories current on the Eastern Shore about the Battle of Kedge's Straits. One Lawson, they said, found the body of a dead sailor floating in the bay and took his jacket. Later, being forced ashore by a storm, he turned his boat over and crept under it for shelter. Soon there was a terrible thumping on the bottom of the boat and he heard a hoarse voice shouting: "Give me my jacket! Give me my jacket!" Lawson flung it outside without daring to look, and the storm ceased.

Then there was the story of Hopkins, who found a body

floating in shallow water and, stripping it, left it. Thereafter the dead sailor haunted him. While he was fishing near a point of the marsh, he heard a loud "Hah! Hah!" and saw It come leaping at him from tuft to tuft like a jack rabbit. While he stood transfixed with terror, It leaped clean over

his head into the water. It made other appearances and Hopkins went to the parson for help, and was given a formula to lay the ghost. However, the next time It appeared, Hopkins forgot the words. The ghost eventually disappeared, for the brothers Richard and Solomon Evans found the body and buried it.

As to Joseph Whaland, there is nothing certain about

his end. Scharf says that he was killed by Captain Simmons, of the brig *Ranger*, but we know that is not so. There is also a report that his galley was captured near Ocracoke, North Carolina, but nothing about what happened to her commander. The fishermen of the Eastern Shore insist that he hid himself in the far-spreading marshes of Dorchester after the war. He went mad, and his screams and groans could be heard at immense distances. As an ending, it has poetic justice.

In 1783, the Assembly of Maryland passed an act adopting Thomas, son of Zedekiah Walley, and Maria, daughter of Thomas Grason, as wards of the state, appropriating money for their education (the governor was requested to take charge of it) and providing that £500 should be paid each of them upon coming of age.

CHAPTER 5

The Pocomoke River

WATKINS POINT was named in Lord Baltimore's patent as the southerly limit of his domain on the Eastern Shore. This point (now on an island) lies at the north side of the entrance to Pocomoke Sound. Colonel Scarburgh tried to move it to the mouth of the Wicomico some miles farther north, but Captain John Smith's map gave him the lie. The Fox Islands and Watts' Island vaguely indicate a division between Tangier and Pocomoke sounds. Far out in the Chesapeake lies Tangier, and to the north of it Smith's Island, a mere shadow on the water.

The northerly passage into Pocomoke Sound is called Cedar Straits. Inside, the sound stretches eastward for fourteen miles, and it is about as far to the invisible Virginia shore on the south. It is a dazzling sight on a fair summer day, for the salt marshes are as violently green as the water is blue. The marshes are backed by a distant dark line of woods. In summer the great expanse is likely to be as empty of shipping as it was that day more than three hundred years ago when the shallop *Cockatrice* sailed down on the pinnaces *St. Margaret* and *St. Helen;* but when fall comes, the oyster tongers singly and in small flotillas will be dotted here and there.

The first evidences of settlement are the oystermen's houses on Saxis Island, where the Virginia shore begins to close in. The river comes into a sound at a right angle, and in the pool thus formed lie the famous (or infamous) "Muds" of the Pocomoke. After trying for years to keep a channel open through this semiliquid stuff, the government has finally dug a canal through the low northerly bank which affords an unobstructed and shorter passage to the river within.

The river comes flowing in wide sweeps through the salt marshes. On a low shelf of dry land lies a picturesquely untidy hamlet known as Shelltown, which the vessel approaches first from one side and then from the other. An odd cypress tree or two appear, the sign manual of the Pocomoke. Cypresses will not grow in salt water, but the roots of these lonely trees have found fresh springs far below to keep them alive. As the course verges to the north, the state line strikes off to the right, and thereafter the Pocomoke is wholly contained within Maryland.

On the easterly bank, just over the line, stands Beverly of Worcester, the ancient home of the Dennis family. Long ago it was called Thrumcapped, a name so distinctive, it is a pity it was dropped. "Thrum" was the end of a weaver's thread. Perhaps the builder had in mind a line from John Sylvester:

> Thrummed halfe with ivie, half with crispèd moss.

The Dennises were established on this site by Donoch Dennis, an Irishman who arrived by way of Accomac. The present house is said to have been built at the beginning of the Revolution by his great-grandson, but it bears evidences of an earlier date. The lowness of the bank on which it stands brings the house into intimate relation with the narrow river. The dignified central block of weathered, painted brick, flanked by smaller wings, the ancient trees, and the family graveyard off to the left within its wall combine to make a picture of wonderful charm.

A pleasing feature is the delicate, wrought-iron work of the rails on the riverside steps, carrying a graceful arch overhead for holding a lantern to guide mariners up the crooked river at night. The arch is supported by a pair of odd wrought-iron creatures that are usually described as ducks, but it can be seen at a glance that they are intended to be coiled serpents. Ducks don't have forked tongues!

Within doors the house is no less beautiful, with its heart pine paneling lovingly carved by local workmen from English patterns. In its time it has given several valuable men to the state and to the nation. One of the mightiest of the Dennises, if not the most worthy, was John Upshur, whose life covered the first half of the nineteenth century. He owned a fleet of ships that carried Pocomoke cypress to the West Indies and brought back molasses. He had three wives and twenty-one children. He won his third wife in competition with his oldest son, and the stone for his second wife's grave arrived on the same ship with a carriage for number three!

Higher up the river, the first cypress forest appears beyond the marsh to the east, and upon the bluff facing it Francis Jenckins took up land in the late seventeenth century. Jenckins was an able, useful, and eventually a highly prosperous pioneer, but he is chiefly remembered as the husband of the lady whom he married in middle life. She was Mary, the daughter of Sir Robert King of Ireland, the first of his name to settle in Maryland. Sir Robert is usually referred to as a baronet, but actually nothing about his forebears has been established.

Mary was eighteen when she married Francis Jenckins. She quickly became the first great lady in this part of the world. She had a regal quality which so impressed her community that they called her "the king who became a queen." She was always addressed as "Madam" Jenckins, or Henry or Hampton, according to her husband of the moment. After their marriage, Jenckins rechristened his place on the Pocomoke "Mary's Lot."

Since her first husband was twenty-five years older than herself, it may be assumed that their marriage, while serene, was not exactly rapturous. Jenckins died in the course of time, leaving her rich, childless, and with a charming disposition and a still beautiful face. Unfortunately, no portrait of her has survived. A modern Presbyterian writer thus describes her as she appeared the first time Francis Makemie preached at Rehobeth, but I fear the portrait is a fanciful one:

> Madam Mary Jenckins, nineteen years old and in the prime of her beauty; elegantly dressed and very fascinating; a hat of green silk with a graceful pinner, a closely-fitting jacket also of green silk, a scarlet silk petticoat and scarlet silk shoes with very high heels. Lace floats about her like fleecy clouds over the moon.

Madam Jenckins married secondly, and for love, young John Henry, the pastor of nearby Rehobeth Church, and her life flowered. With his aid she founded one of the most distinguished families on the Eastern Shore. Francis Jenckins's memory was still green, too, for she had her first-born christened Robert Jenckins Henry. Both he and her other child, John Henry, achieved distinction in later years.

The Reverend John Henry died in 1717, and in the following year Madam Henry married another Presbyterian divine, the Reverend John Hampton, pastor of the church at Snow Hill on the upper Pocomoke. She had no more children. Hampton died in 1722, and for twenty-two years longer she lived on alone at Mary's Lot, which now came to be called Hampton, while her reputation for queenly elegance and authority spread far and wide.

Her house at Mary's Lot, or Hampton, has long since disappeared; even her grave was lost until a year or two ago, when one of her many-times-great-grandsons, who is an indefatigable antiquary, found it buried under a vegetable garden near the Pocomoke. He had the stone removed to the yard of Rehobeth Church. He told me that when the stone was lifted, he allowed every ounce of the earth beneath to sift through pious fingers, but without obtaining the least memento; no bit of jewelry, nothing of his queenly ancestress.

A mile or so above the site of Mary's Lot is the hamlet of Rehobeth, rich in historical associations. Here still stands Makemie's own church, so called because he built it on his own land in 1705. It is greatly revered by those of the Presbyterian persuasion, who look upon it as the oldest house of worship in the New World where their services have been continuously held. The plain little building has been restored and modernized, but it still keeps something of its old-time air.

In the churchyard lies the flat stone that marked Madam Mary Jenckins-Henry-Hampton's last resting place. The graceful old lettering runs:

Here lieth ye bodie of
Madam Mary Hampton
who died 1744
aged 70 years, lacking one day.

Nearby stand the ruins of another ancient church, Old Coventry, Episcopal. The first church was built here about 1697; there is a controversy about the date of the present ruined structure. In any case it is of the eighteenth century and, judging from the remains, was an imposing structure with a gallery and two tiers of windows. In front of the church stand three of the most magnificent sycamore trees I have ever seen, their trunks mantled with English ivy. The dank, overgrown churchyard is like something from the Old World; the whole composition, giant sycamores, ruined church, and the yard with its ancient broken cedars, is unforgettable.

In summer I made a brief exploration up and down the shores of the Pocomoke by car, having for my conductor a little gentleman who had spent the whole of his eighty-eight years beside the river. He was as active as a schoolboy, and he had all of a schoolboy's pleasure in this journey of ours. Everybody he met was his friend; every house, every crossroad, every patch of woods brought up some gentle reminiscence of the past. On that spot stood the school where he had taught when little more than a boy himself; in that house they were pressing grapes one day when he passed and they gave him a glass of fresh grape juice, the most delicious thing he had ever tasted.

In the churchyard of Old Coventry we came upon a broken slab which revealed a yawning grave beneath. On what was left of the stone was incised the grim text: "It is appointed unto man once to die." The name of the tenant was barely decipherable. After studying it, my companion said thoughtfully: "That must have been the fellow that used to court my auntie."

A short distance above Mary's Lot once stood the home of Colonel William Stevens, who brought the name Rehobeth here. That is what he called his plantation. "For now the Lord hath made room for us and we shall be fruitful in the land." Colonel Stevens was a truly broad-minded man; a faithful member of the Church of England himself, he could loyally support Lord Baltimore, the Catholic, through evil times and good; he was also an admirer of George Fox, the saintly Quaker, and entertained Fox when the latter journeyed through Maryland; finally, it was no other than Colonel Stevens who applied to the Presbytery of Laggan in Northern Ireland for a minister, as a result of which Francis Makemie was sent to Rehobeth.

Colonel Stevens, the antithesis of his contemporary, Colonel Edmund Scarburgh, had a way with the Indians and was continually chosen by the governor to make treaty or to settle trouble with the tribes, "because of his provident management and circumspection in affaires of this nature." So successful was he in placating the Nanticokes, Pocomokes, Assateagues, etc. that later he was fetched over to the western shore to save the province from the consequences of its own officers' treachery in massacring the Susquehannock envoys at Piscattaway.

Colonel Stevens died in 1687, rich and full of honors. He is said to have held twenty thousand acres of land. I found his grave out in the middle of a field. To keep the cattle off, there is a rough fence of four cement posts connected with logging chains. Not far away is a hole in the ground filled with briers and showing a bit of arched brickwork. This was the cellar of the colonel's house. The present owner said the ancient bricks were still so solidly mortared that they would break before separating.

The grave is covered with a mighty slab of bluestone, five feet by seven and four inches thick. That stone must have been brought from a great distance. The inscription reads:

> Here lyeth the Body of William Stevens, Esq.
> who departed this Life the 23 of December 1687
> aged 57 years. He was 20 years Judge of this County
> Court, one of His Lordship's Council, and one of ye
> Deputy Lieutenants of this Province of Maryland
> Vivii Post Funera Virtus

When we drove on, my elderly companion continued his gentle reminiscences: of how the swamps were scented with magnolia blossoms in spring; of the fun of gathering fox grapes in a canoe and the delicious wine and jelly made from them; of cooking before an open fire in the old days; the covered spider with embers raked underneath and on top, and how an unwary boy was like to get his feet scorched after the hearth had been swept.

He told of a bashful young clergyman who was persuaded to take part in a play the young people were getting up. He had to submit to being shot during the course of the action. The wag who was to shoot him slyly loaded the gun with a wad of cotton soaked in red ink. When it was fired, the clergyman clapped his hand to his breast and said in his gentle voice: "Gracious! I'm shot!" Then he looked at his hand and yelled: "My God! I AM shot!"

On the river, after passing around the big bend above Rehobeth, the salt marshes disappear for good and the

Pocomoke assumes its own unique character. These cypress trees grow nowhere else on the Eastern Shore; the narrow river, lined with dark trees standing in the water, has a tropical quality. It is said to be the deepest river in the world for its width. It has a certain sinister look, but not very sinister; it is too beautiful.

Yet it changes with the seasons. In spring the dark cypresses are mantled with a fairylike green. I went up in a boat in October and discovered that the trees were not all cypresses; the black river had burst into gorgeous color, the purple and crimson of the gums, orange and yellow ocher of the poplars, scarlet and vermilion of maple and dogwood, the whole picked out with rich green cedar. There are no cut-banks along the Pocomoke to scar its beauty; at high tide no earth at all is visible; the leafage springs directly from the water. When the tide is out, only a foot of sooty earth is revealed with grotesque cypress knees poking out of the water.

About ten miles from the mouth of the river as the crow flies stands Pocomoke City, the "metropolis" of Worcester County. The wild aspect of the river suddenly vanishes as a handsome bridge, a row of wharves and sheds come into view. Pocomoke City prides itself on its modernity. The central part of the town was destroyed by fire twenty years ago, and has been rebuilt in the latest style. The main street is more like that of a western town than of old Maryland. The main crossing of the river has been at this spot ever since the white man came. Colonel Stevens established the first ferry, and for a long time the place was called Stevens' ferry or Stevens' Landing; then Meeting-House Landing; Warehouse Landing, as the tobacco trade grew; afterward Newtown, and finally, since 1878, Pocomoke City. The public square has always been known as "the Hill" since it is all of ten feet higher than the river.

My traveling companion's grandfather has left an interesting picture of the town in the 1820's and 30's. In those days the mail stopped at Snow Hill once a week, and sometimes lay there a fortnight until the local postmaster got around to sending upriver for it. He would dispatch his three little boys in a canoe with two oars and a paddle. They went up on the flood tide and came back with the ebb. In Snow Hill they would be handed the Pocomoke letters in a little bundle tied with string. Often in the summer there were violent thunderstorms, and the boys' anxious mother would stand waiting at evening on the bank until she heard their welcome "Halloo!" and they came struggling up through the mud, the tuckahoe, and the briers.

Newtown was always a disorderly place: drinking, swearing, fighting, gambling, conjuration, witchcraft were prevalent. Even in families, it was the custom to serve toddy before breakfast to every member, while decanters, glasses, sugar and water were set out for all callers. On a counter of the store stood a pint and a pitcher, and every customer was invited to step up. Each would say as he took a drink: "Well, gentlemen, here's good and plenty!"

At the balls, four- and eight-handed reels were danced, and between times the hat was passed for the fiddlers. There was much capering and cutting of pigeonwings; the sets would break up and the couples dance all around the room. Every Saturday the country people would come in and dance the hoedown in the hotels. For the colored folks, booths were set up in the public square (the Hill) where cakes, candies, cider, beer, and oranges were sold. There would be boxing, wrestling, pitching quoits, and dancing to a fiddle (the banjo came in later) or perhaps only to patty-whack (juba) with many diverting antics. Here is one of the myriad versions of juba:

Juba do and Juba don't
Juba will and Juba won't;
Juba up and Juba down,
Juba all aroun' de town.

Sif' de meal and gimme de husk,
Bake de càke and gimme de crus',
Fry de pork and gimme de skin,
Ax me when I'se comin' agin.
Juba, Juba, Jubaree!

Yet with all the revelry, there was a strong religious element in Newtown. The two extremes are often found together. The hot-blooded little town from its first founding has been an ardent supporter of Methodism. It is recorded that as long ago as 1805 the famous traveling preacher, Lorenzo Dow, addressed two thousand persons in Newtown. They tell this story about Reverend Mr. Dow on another visit:

On his way to meeting he overtook a little colored boy named Gabriel, who happened to be carrying a tin horn. The conjunction of the horn and the name made Mr. Dow thoughtful, and after studying a little he pulled out a dollar and handed it to the boy. He promised him another dollar after meeting if he did exactly what he was told. "You are to climb up into the forks of the big elm tree in meetinghouse yard and sit there without making a sound while I am preaching, until I say: 'Blow, Gabriel!' Then you blow!"

The meeting took place in the yard, since the church was too small to hold the crowd. The Reverend Mr. Dow preached upon the subject of the resurrection and the Day of Judgment. He was like one inspired. Working up to a climax, he described the Angel Gabriel as standing with one foot on sea and one on land, his long silver trumpet in his hand. "Blow, Gabriel!" shouted Mr. Dow, and was instantly obeyed.

An indescribable scene followed; the congregation fell on the ground, crying for mercy or shouting salvation; the horses added to the uproar by squealing and stamping. Presently the boy was discovered in the tree and the shamed sinners looked at Mr. Dow threateningly. He was equal to the occasion.

"If a little boy can strike such terror into your hearts," he shouted, "what will you do when the great day really comes?"

In 1844, when the possibilities of the surrounding forests were realized, the cypress began to be cut and sawed and Newtown experienced a boom. Sawmills sprang up everywhere. There had always been shipbuilding along the river—two of Commodore Walley's barges were launched there; now they began to build decked schooners and even steamboats.

It was not until 1868 that steamboats began to ply regularly between Pocomoke wharves and the outside world. Before that, one traveled to Baltimore by schooner and it was customary to allow two weeks for the round trip. Among the early steamboats were the *Helen,* the *Maggie,* the *Sue,* the *Highland Light,* etc. Another old gentleman has described the last-named vessel to me:

"She was a side-wheeler with a heavy timber frame on the outside to prevent her from hogging [i.e., buckling in the middle]. The gents' cabin was down below deck, forward of the engine, with little portholes all around, which admitted

A. Sopher

scarcely any light and no air whatever. There was no partition dividing the cabin from the engine, but as a boy I liked that; I found the noise of the engine right conducive to sleep. There were three tiers of bunks all around, and I always tried to get a top one. No provision for washing aboard, and the toilets were just little boxes that stuck out over the water inside the paddle box.

"The ladies' cabin was similar. That was in the hold, aft of the engine room, and it also served as the dining room.

"I mind once when I was coming home from Baltimore, I climbed into a top bunk. I was wakened by the noise made by the passenger below me, flouncing around in his bunk. It was an old fellow with a magnificent set of whiskers. As I was lying there I saw a rat come out in the light of the swinging lamp, and the old fellow below me groaned pitifully. I didn't say nothing. After a while the rat came out again, and I heard another dreadful groan from below.

"I said: 'Why, there's a rat!' The old man sprang up, crying out 'Did you see it, boy? Did you see it?' 'Sure, I saw it,' I said, and he fell back in his bunk with a sigh of relief. 'I bought a gallon of whisky at Dan'l Samuels,' he said, 'and I thought I was seein' rats.'

"Dan'l Samuels kept a saloon on Light Street, Baltimore," my friend explained. "It was a favorite port of call for Eastern Shoremen. Many a fellow taking a trip up to town never got any further than Dan'l Samuels' bar, and was finally helped back aboard the steamboat, but he always claimed he had seen the whole town. The sign outside read: 'Daniel Samuels, Rectifier of Spirits, Two drinks for a nickel.' Dan'l rectified 'em all right."

Above the town the river immediately becomes even wilder and more deserted. Where the land back of the bank is cultivated, a thick screen of trees hides it. In the whole stretch between town and town, not more than three or four openings are to be seen. The old steamboat landings are rotting into the water and the roads leading to them have been taken by the jungle. No white steamboat ever cleaves the black water nowadays; only an occasional motor vessel carrying fertilizer up to Snow Hill or, more rarely, a big schooner almost filling the river as she is pushed slowly around the bends by a kicker.

The virgin timber was cleaned out long ago, but here and there along the way an occasional magnificent specimen has been left standing among the second growth. An aged cypress is the most individual and decorative of trees. Bird life is plentiful: reed birds and summer duck along the lower reaches; kingfishers, blue heron (which are white during their adolescence) and ospreys above, and even an occasional bald eagle, hanging about for a chance to steal the osprey's fish. It is a unique experience thus to be ascending an unbroken tropical-seeming river under a cool, northern sky.

Dividing Creek comes in sluggishly from the north, its black water winding through the tangle. In a lonely spot beyond stands a dignified eighteenth century dwelling known as the Barrel House—nobody could tell me why. It is supposed to have been a station on Patty Cannon's private underground railway—which led south! We shall hear more of Patty Cannon later.

A mile or two above, Nassawango Creek comes in from the north, a larger stream that rises up in Wicomico County. Much of the surrounding land is underlaid with bog ore, and above on Nassawango still stands an ancient iron furnace that was in busy operation up to 1847. In those days it was surrounded by a populous village with stores and a hotel. All that is gone except the ancient chimney; the green forest has covered it.

Above Nassawango, the Pocomoke is hemmed in on both sides by cypress swamps and the tortuous channel is broken by several swampy islands. It is the most characteristic and beautiful part of the stream. Then civilization obtrudes again in the town of Snow Hill, the county seat of Worcester. Snow Hill is at the head of navigation, though the river comes meandering down through the swamps all the way from the state of Delaware.

At Snow Hill the river is only six miles from Chincoteague Bay, on the Atlantic, and at various times the project of linking bay and ocean with a canal has been brought forward, but digging has never been started. The greatest elevation between the two waters is only 39 feet.

Snow Hill is a serene village with a slowly shrinking population. Nobody seems to worry about that. It is an ancient place, having been founded in 1686 by some settlers from Snow Hill, a suburb of London. No hill rises in the Maryland town, and but little snow falls there. There is a good deal of neighborly jealousy between Snow Hill and Pocomoke. In the former town they affect to look down on Pocomoke as being sunk in trade, while in Pocomoke they pretend to believe that the Snow Hillers are all lawyers and politicians. In Pocomoke they say that when a boy baby is born in Snow Hill, they turn his face toward Annapolis and tell him: "Son, there lies your meat and bread!"

Snow Hill may be called "slow" or "backward," but it provides a welcome refuge from a too-violent world! What a charming place to have been raised in! One might guess that such a place was noted for good food, and so it is. For terrapin stew, steamed oysters, and deviled crabs! A specialty of the place is Sunday pone or, more vulgarly, sweatpone, a damp but delicious delicacy. It is cooked all Saturday night in an iron pot. Our country will be the poorer when the last old-time village like this is spurred into modernity.

Under its serenity hot passions may slumber. Worcester County, owing to its remoteness from the rest of the state, especially in the old days of bad roads, has always been known for its strong county consciousness. They have their own peculiar ways down there; they wish to run their own affairs and deeply resent outside interference. In 1931 the world was violently made aware of the sleepy village of Snow Hill.

A Negro named Euel Lee murdered a whole family of white persons. It was a particularly brutal crime and feeling ran high, but an outbreak of lawlessness might have been averted had not a Baltimore lawyer turned up, charged by the International Labor Defense League to defend the murderer. This touched the citizens of Worcester in their tenderest place, and the mob broke out of control. Unable to get their hands on the Negro, they seized the "foreign" lawyer and his companions and beat them cruelly.

Lee was spirited away to the Baltimore County jail at Towson, Maryland. His case became a national *cause célèbre*. His first conviction was set aside by the Supreme Court of the United States on the ground that no Negro had served on the jury. At his second trial, Negroes were empaneled for the jury, but they were challenged by the prosecution and none served. However, in this case, the state successfully defended its challenges, and the Supreme Court declined to act. Lee was finally hanged at Towson in 1933.

CHAPTER 6

The Little and the Big Annemessex

THREE miles north of Watkins Point, the estuary of the Little Annemessex River makes in. Far out across Tangier Sound, the low-lying Smith's Island spreads like a stain across the horizon. The mouth of this river is a mile across and the estuary spreads out even wider within, but as a river it is very small potatoes; after a course of three or four miles it just ends.

The Little Annemessex is remarkable for only one thing, the town of Crisfield on its shore, which advertises itself as the "Seafood Capital of the World." No other town has ventured to dispute the title. There are really two Crisfields, "uptown," with its neat post offices and stores, its churches, and its rows of conventional white clapboarded dwellings, and "downtown," the port, which is unique.

The port started in 1868 when the Eastern Shore Railway established its terminal here by building a long trestle out through the marsh to the edge of deep water. From here the steamboat *Eastern Shore* carried its passengers and freight on to Norfolk. In due course, the railway line was extended down the middle of the peninsula to Cape Charles, and became the New York, Philadelphia and Norfolk—or the "Nyp an' N," as it is known locally. Crisfield was then left dangling at the end of an insignificant spur, but by that time the seafood business was established, and it has never ceased growing.

The port is built on made land, consisting of the shells of the millions of bushels of oysters that have been shucked here. First the railway trestle was filled in solid and odd little shacks and sheds began rising on piles down both sides, each connected with the track by a rickety footbridge. Gradually the buildings acquired a foundation of shells also, and now there is a broad street running from uptown to the port with the railway in the middle, all built on shell.

This street is lined with mismated little buildings, none of them old enough to have acquired any dignity, and no two alike. They may be built of brick, of wood, unpainted, or of stucco, peeling off. The whole has the rakish and slightly disreputable appearance generally associated with Sailor Town. Down at the end and off to one side, a considerable island has been created which is called Jersey. All over Jersey the packing houses are scattered in picturesque disorder.

Over the narrow waterway between island and shore is a drawbridge, a true drawbridge, the first I ever saw, because it draws back over rails on shore to allow a boat to pass through. The little harbor between island and railway terminal is called the Pot. There is only one train a day each way, a combination car, a freight car perhaps, and a couple of express cars for the seafood. This easy assignment has fallen to a mighty engine which used to pull the Congressional Limited. The train comes down in the afternoon and goes back next morning. All night the engine lies in the middle of the street, unhooked and breathing softly. What a temptation to a boy to take a joy-ride down the track! There is nothing else on the line.

In the packing houses the workers, male and female, white and colored, stand in long rows before zinc counters shucking oysters in winter and picking crabs in summer. They sway rhythmically while working, to get up speed, and often break into concerted song. Their expertness is astonishing. Good pickers have been known to pick a hundred pounds of crab meat a day. Anybody who has picked the meat out of one crab can appreciate this feat. The crabs are cooked by steam in immense wire baskets, which are then swung out into the air to cool. Soft crabs are shipped to market alive, packed in sea grass and ice.

Another feature of Jersey is the terrapin pound, a big plank enclosure running out into tidewater and shelving to a beach at the other end, where the terrapin may crawl out and lay their eggs. The eggs are an important constituent of terrapin à la Maryland—but not all are shipped to market. There are interstices in the plank walls to allow the baby terrapin to escape and make lives for themselves in the marshes.

Once upon a time, Maryland had to pass a law forbidding the planters to feed their slaves terrapin more than once a week; now the delectable creature fetches $100 a dozen. Like cattle, terrapin are denominated bulls, cows, and heifers. The cows grow the biggest! In the pound they are fed the rich yellow fat excavated from the hard crabs in the packing houses.

There is no recipe for terrapin Maryland; everything is left to the judgment of the individual cook. There is one hard and fast rule: no strong seasoning may be used to sophisticate the delicate natural flavor of the diamondback. When it is served, sherry is usually put on the table, but a real Maryland gourmet frowns even at the addition of sherry.

Tied up to the crab houses, or moored gunwale to gunwale in the Pot, lie scores of boats of every size and style. Not so long ago there were more sailing vessels registered from Crisfield than any other port in the country. Sail has gone out now, and there is a sad falling off in the picturesqueness of the scene, for a motor-driven shoe box on a scow has little beauty, but occasionally one of the old-time log canoes or bugeyes comes in to rejoice the eye.

Chesapeake Bay has produced a kind of boat all its own, the most elegant vessel ever devised by man. The log canoe is the descendant of the original Indian dugout, but with what a difference! The red man scraped out one big log and had only the crudest notions of shaping bow and stern; the white man used three or four logs—sometimes as many as seven. These he spiked together and hollowed and shaped with loving care, according to a plan made in advance. Little by little, the builder developed the clipper bow and the sharp stern until his slender craft slipped through the water in light airs making scarcely a ripple.

At first the canoe had lateen sails, but in the course of time the rakish gaff became the mast—with almost the same rake. The sails are triangular, having no gaff now, and the rake of the mast permits them to be hauled straight up from the center, making for greater speed and ease of handling. The old-time waterman on the Chesapeake loved his boat, and the result shows in the many little refinements and embellishments on the old-time canoes.

The bugeye is a larger vessel, broad-beamed, flat-bottomed, decked-over, for carrying cargo in and out of the shallow estuaries. It has the same elegantly raking masts and clipper bow. The pungy was still larger, sometimes carrying topmasts. All these were two-masters. The single sticker, called a bateau at Pocomoke or Crisfield, becomes a skipjack at Deal's Island and points north. I need not point out that the celebrated Baltimore clippers were built along these same graceful lines.

Crisfield produces many salty characters; consequently it's a great place for yarning—but what place on the Eastern Shore is not? There are grim anecdotes of the bad old days of oyster pirates when unwary sailors along the Baltimore waterfront used to be shanghaied aboard the oyster boats and carried down the bay. By transferring their catch to "run" vessels, the oyster boats could stay out the entire season, keeping their crews virtual prisoners. Starved, frozen, cruelly beaten by the mates, conditions aboard the vessels were often hideous. On the way home in the spring, the men, it is said, were often "paid off with the boom," i.e., knocked on the head and thrown overboard.

The last may be an imaginative touch, but there is no doubt that murder was a commonplace among this lawless element. An old-timer in Crisfield told of finding the nude body of a handsome young man frozen in the ice one morning after a sharp fall in temperature. He had attempted to swim ashore from a dredge boat and had become entangled in a fish net. It was odd to see how, after fifty years, this tough old customer was still impressed by the young man's beauty.

Pirates or not, the old-time oystermen were a turbulent lot. Men who owned private oyster beds alongshore were forced to club together and build a guardhouse on piles out in the middle of their beds. There they took turns at night watching, armed with a gun. For many years there was actual warfare between the Maryland oystermen and those of Virginia over the right to dredge certain choice beds. Under the

Jenkins Award of 1877, Maryland was forced to yield 23,000 acres of the best oyster bottoms to Virginia. The Smith's Islanders obstinately continued to dredge there in defiance of the Virginians and the patrol boats of both states.

In 1895 there was a pitched battle in Woman's Marsh between the rival oystermen, with many casualties. But both sides hated the patrol boats worse than they hated each other, and when a Virginia patrol appeared, they instantly suspended their battle, like husband and wife, and joined to drive it off. The Virginia patrol then sought out a Maryland patrol boat and the two came back and licked the combined oystermen. Trouble, however, continued until these particular oyster beds gave out about 1910. The oyster navies of both states were increased from time to time until at last they gained control. Nowadays the bay is as law-abiding as a duckpond.

Characteristic sayings of dead and gone characters are affectionately preserved in Crisfield. There was Uncle Haney, a Smith's Islander, a very religious man. Once, after a great storm tide had washed clean over the low-lying island, wrecking truck patches, oyster boats, crab houses, drowning a couple of the islanders, Uncle Haney was heard to remark: "I declare the Lord does as much harm as good!"

One Sunday over on the island, when they lacked a preacher, one of the congregation expressed a desire to preach. Being invited to take the platform, he gave out his text: "And Paul cast seven anchors from the stern of the ship." He then cleared his throat and asked for a glass of water, which was handed up. He gave out the text in a stronger voice: "And Paul cast seven anchors from the stern of the ship." He then looked around a little wildly, rubbed his hands up and down his pants, and said again: "And Paul cast seven anchors from the stern of the ship." "Brother," said Uncle Haney dryly, "reckon you've got her fast."

The first people who set up around the port after the railway was built had no wells, and they depended on the locomotive for a supply of fresh water. One day Uncle Haney came over from the island with a boatload of watermelons to sell. John W. Crisfield, the president of the railway, happened to be making a tour of inspection that day. He looked over the watermelons and asked how much. "Well, Mr. Crisfield," said Uncle Haney, "I askin' twenty cents, but your engine been so darn good to me with buckets of water, you can have your pick and your choice for nineteen cents."

By far the greatest number of the stories of Crisfield have to do with the Reverend Joshua Thomas, the parson of the islands, a truly remarkable man, who converted all the people hereabouts a hundred years and more ago. The odd part of it is, they have stayed converted. Thomas, an humble fisherman, was born on Potato Neck (between the Big Annemessex and the Manokin) in 1776. Feeling stirrings of grace one day when he was out fishing alone, he stood up in his boat and said: "Joshua Thomas, I baptize thee in the name of Father, Son and Holy Ghost, Amen." Later he heard of the practices of the Baptists, and fearing that he might have omitted something necessary, the next time he went out in his boat he jumped overboard for immersion.

Joshua Thomas was a very real and human person. Brother William Evans said that Brother Thomas as a lad surpassed all as a dancer for agility, gaiety and good humor. Several of his sermons have been preserved, and it is from them that we learn most about his life. He moved his hearers to shouts of laughter—and tears; he was much blamed by fellow preachers for drawing too intimately on his family experiences. Whatever they may have thought, his sermons even through the dry medium of print still have a wonderful eloquence.

His father died when he was a baby and his mother married for the second time a man called Pruitt. The family got along all right until the refugee boats came and burned their house; the stepfather took to drinking then, and treated them all with great cruelty. They were reduced to dreadful poverty. All they had to eat were oysters and crabs, and when the river froze they had nothing. "Our kind neighbors pitied my poor mother and her ragged little boys," says Joshua, "and brought her meal to keep us from starving."

Whenever the stepfather earned a dollar, he would cross Pocomoke Sound to Accomac to buy brandy. There is a short cut for small boats down to the sound through the marshes. After one of these trips, he failed to return and presently his boat was found empty and drifting. Joshua, now a big boy, went in search of his body and, finding it washed ashore, "buried it in a long grove on the beach of Accomac." The brandy bottle was in the dead man's pocket. Joshua presented it to the man on whose land he was, asking him to put it on the mantelpiece and tell the story to all who saw it. "In that way it may do some good."

Joshua describes his costume when he became a fisherman: "A little round hat, a light, striped jacket, pants rolled halfway to my knees, shoes generally carried under my arm. . . . When I caught a fish," he continues, "I always pulled off my hat, kneeled down in the canoe and thanked the Lord for it and asked Him to give me another. I often had all the fish I wanted when others had none. I was ashamed to pull off my hat and kneel in the presence of others, therefore I chose to go away from all the fishermen." It will be seen that Joshua even as a youth was very religious, though he did not feel that he had been "saved."

When he was twenty-three he prayed for a wife and was answered. He then built a little house on Tangier Island and was happy. "I watched the smoke curl up my clay chimney from the fire as I lay in my bed and it looked beautiful!"

I shall quote at length his own story of how he was converted, because it makes clear the processes of the movement which changed the whole character of the lower Eastern Shore. Joshua had heard there was to be a meeting in Williams' Woods near Roach Island in Annemessex, and he resolved to go. How could people pray without a book or

preach without a written sermon before them? he asked himself. On the way, he had to pass Uncle Levi's house. Uncle Levi said:

"If you go there they will have you down to worship them. They are nothing but a parcel of Irishmen run away from their own country to escape hanging. They know no other way to get a living but by going about and raising the devil by their preaching and carrying-on, and then make people worship them and give them money."

Joshua protested that they would not get *him* down to worship them.

Let him continue the story:

It was on Friday when I reached the camp. Worship was going on in a solemn and impressive manner. I listened and watched very closely, determined none of them should put a spell on me and make me fall down. [He then goes on to describe the various sermons and exhortations that followed.] I really desired that if there was such a thing as conversion to have my heart converted. I was opposed to their way, that is at the mourners' bench or altar in public. I wanted the blessing in secret.

During Saturday some were converted, including one of my neighbors. I began to feel very uneasy and much concerned. I went into the woods alone and prayed, but felt no better. So I returned again to the camp still praying secretly to be converted.

I felt so bad Saturday night I concluded I would go and kneel down with them at mourners' bench and try it once, determined that I would not fall down nor cry out as the others did. When praying persons came to talk to me, I rudely elbowed them. I tried to pray secretly until I became discouraged and concluded there was no reality in being converted and so I arose and went away.

On Sunday a great meeting, and many professed to be born from above. They shouted all over the ground and lay as dead on the earth; when they recovered they began to praise God wonderfully.

I went a great way in the woods again. After struggling a long time in prayer and receiving no answer, I concluded I would try what virtue there was in falling. So I looked me out a smooth place that was free from rocks and sticks, and kept my eye a little over one shoulder to see how to fall and not hurt myself. I came down full length on the earth. I lay about ten minutes praying to God to convert me there, and receiving no answer, arose completely discouraged and very impatient besides.

A Mr. Wiltbank preached in the evening which was to be the last sermon. I did not like his looks very well at first, a rather hard-looking face and given to speaking very loud and broad. He put it on the Methodists pretty hard. I was pleased with that.

As he became more and more animated I felt something rise up within me and say: "Behold the man, see how he is moved by the Holy Spirit!" I obtained faith. I gave up my whims and notions about getting converted in secret, and made up my mind to have it in the Methodist way if the Lord would forgive and convert me.

I felt something drawing me right to the feet of Jesus. Immediately on the invitation being given, I went to the altar and kneeled down and began to lift up my voice in earnest prayer that God would then convert my heart and set me at liberty.

Blessed be His Name! I did not have to wait long before I felt a gracious change run through my whole being! I did not say a word then to those about me but continued kneeling and wondering at the mercy and goodness of God.

My half brother came forward and kneeled close beside me bathed in tears. I reached out and took him by the hand to speak to him, but at that moment I was so filled with the Spirit of life and love I could not help shouting to the Glory of God with all my might!

That was the first time I ever cried out in praise or prayer in a congregation, but it was not the last. No, thank God! I have felt a heart to praise Him and have done it since that night more times than I can number.

They say when Joshua got home that night and met his wife, he began to leap and praise God and she was terrified lest he ruin their corn crop. But it was found that he had not trodden a single stalk, though he had been all over the patch.

Joshua then began to preach among the islanders and a religious awakening spread from Kedges Straits to Tangier Beach. He fasted because he said: "The Devil delights in full Christians." On Tangier, before Joshua preached, "the Devil and all his works had reigned with undisputed sway."

The greatest opportunity of Joshua's life arrived when the British fleet took Tangier Island during the War of 1812 and established their base upon it. Joshua converted the enemy! When they were about to set out to take Baltimore, the admiral commanded him to address the troops. Up to that moment they had been completely victorious, having beaten the Americans at the Battle of Bladensburg, and taken and burned Washington. Let Joshua tell what happened:

> I addressed 12,000 British on the eve of their expedition to Baltimore. I was afraid when I faced them that their officers with their keen glittering swords would cut me in pieces for speaking the truth. But after singing and praying, all fears left me. I told them what kind of a sinner I was and how He had saved me from sin. I described some of the seasons of refreshing we had enjoyed in that spot from the presence of the Lord, and I thanked them and the Admiral for their kindness [in sparing the camp-meeting ground] but I could not bid them God speed in what I understood they were about to do. I told them of the great wickedness of war and that God had said: "Thou shalt not kill!" If you do, I said, He will judge you at the last day or before, and he will cause you to perish by the sword!
>
> I told them that it was given me from the Almighty that they could not take Baltimore and would not succeed in their expedition.
>
> We saw them coming back some days later, and I went down to meet the first that landed. "Have you taken Baltimore?" I asked. "No," one answered, "but hundreds of our men have

fallen and our best General is killed. All the time we were fighting we thought of you and what you had told us. You seemed to be standing there before us, still warning us."

So perhaps Joshua Thomas *did* in his way help to save Baltimore!

So widespread and so lasting was the influence of this man, so many stories are still told about him, that you would think, to hear the old people of the lower Eastern Shore talking, he had left them only yesterday.

Four or five miles farther up Tangier Sound, the fine estuary of the Big Annemessex opens up, its marshy shores lined all around with coves and creeks. Few persons outside the Eastern Shore, I suppose, have ever heard of the Annemessex, but in another land where there was less competition among rivers it might well be celebrated for its beauty. The estuary narrows suddenly between Scott Point and Long Point; for a mile or two beyond, the river is still deeply lined with marsh. When dry land does appear, it is very low; the long pine-clad points slip imperceptibly underwater. This river presents an open, sunny scene; nothing could be less like the black Pocomoke.

The first settlers here were the Quakers and nonconformists driven from Accomac by the harsh laws of Virginia toward the end of the seventeenth century. The sturdy Stephen Horsey was the first settler and the leader of his community. Horsey was a notable man; he had once been thrown out of the Virginia Assembly for insisting on his rights. He was one of the six signers of the famous Northampton Protest, which raised the question of taxation without representation, a hundred and twenty-five years before the Declaration of Independence was drawn up. It was after he had been arrested six times for his refusal to pay tithes to the Church of England that he decided to emigrate to Maryland.

Horsey valiantly opposed Colonel Edmund Scarburgh, and it is to his honor that he earned Scarburgh's bitter enmity. It was Horsey whom Scarburgh termed "a factious and tumultuous person, a man repugnant to all government." The worst charge the colonel could bring against him was that he had failed to have his children bapitzed. In Maryland, Horsey was successively a commissioner, empowered to make grants of land, a magistrate, the first high sheriff, and a member of the little House of Burgesses. Unfortunately his life in Maryland was short; he died in 1671.

On the upper Annemessex, with a fine view across Gale's Creek and the river, stands a little old brick house of the seventeenth century that is now called Williams' Conquest, but it may have been built by Stephen Horsey; it is old enough and it stands on what was once his land. It is a story-and-a-half house of that earliest type which seems to grow out of the ground, big chimney, steep roof, and a row of what are known locally as "dormant" windows. That is good English, too; see Webster. The house stands forlornly in the midst of plowed fields, every vestige of a tree or a shrub having perished. Inside, there is some crude, early paneling and a little stairway that doubles on itself in the customary manner between chimney and wall. In places where the plaster has fallen, the old hand-riven laths are revealed, fastened with hand-wrought nails.

Across the fields from Williams' Conquest stands a later and much more imposing house known as Greenwood. This house is still surrounded and graced by its original trees, gigantic beeches, pecans and hemlocks. It is a wooden house of great size, the central block three stories high and the wings of two stories. It contains twenty-one rooms and a ballroom. There are no less than three fine stairways of paneled walnut, besides other good paneling. It is said to have been built by a member of the Williams family shortly before the Revolution.

Along the other side of the Big Annemessex stretches Potato Neck, famous for the richness of its land, and thickly settled by truck growers and other agriculturists.

Upon rounding Holland Point on the south shore, the river swerves abruptly to the east, and even south of east, as if making back to the Pocomoke. The wide stream narrows down and presently is crossed by a long wooden bridge, innocent of paint and silvery with age. Vincent Van Gogh would have loved to paint this scene, the silvery bridge, the winding stream, the mud (at low tide) of a special brown lusciousness, the green rushes, the gently rising fields. Off to the right there is an old farmhouse under trees to complete the composition.

Still higher up, where the Annemessex nowadays is no more than a ditch, stands Kingston Hall, one of the famous houses of the Eastern Shore. It now looks pretty forlorn, having been tenanted by Negroes for many years and raped of its magnificent box by a millionaire for his new house. However, it has lately come into the possession of people who are slowly bringing it back. Kingston Hall was built in the late eighteenth century by Thomas King, grandnephew of the magnificent Madam Jenckins-Henry-Hampton of Mary's Lot. We seem to have come a long journey from the Pocomoke, but as a matter of fact, Kingston Hall is only about six miles across the neck from the site of Mary's Lot.

All the Kings were great gentlemen and the old house

is enveloped in a tradition of high living. Thomas, the builder, had only one child, a daughter, who married Colonel Henry James Carroll of St. Marys County on the western shore, and the Carrolls proved worthy inheritors of the King tradition. In Somerset County they still tell of Colonel Carroll's grand coach and four with silver-mounted harness and outriders in the family livery, when he and Madam Carroll set off for a sojourn at the White Sulphur.

Another story tells of the great doings when young Thomas King Carroll, the colonel's son, brought his lovely girl bride, Juliana Stevenson, home to Kingston Hall. He was twenty years old, the colonel was dead, and the young man had come into his heritage. A hundred and fifty handsome male slaves in the green and gold livery of the house were lined up to receive the young couple. It was traditional with the Carrolls to breed and feed their slaves as carefully as their blooded cattle. Consequently, there was scarcely a man among them who was under six feet tall.

Thomas King Carroll turned out to be a superior man. His grandfather, old Thomas King, had made a point of training the boy himself. It was his habit to set young Tom across the fireplace from himself, and talk to him as to a contemporary, about politics and government, the chief interests of a gentleman in those days. As a result, it is hardly surprising to learn that young Thomas took his seat in the Maryland legislature on his twenty-first birthday. He continued to serve there uninterruptedly until that day in 1829 when he was elected governor of Maryland.

After serving his term, Governor Carroll, still a young man, became somewhat embittered because his state did not choose to send him to the United States Senate. Most of the balance of his life was spent at Kingston Hall. The Carroll fortune was ebbing now; the truth was, they were slave poor, yet in accordance with the humane tradition of the family, Governor Carroll would not sell off his Negroes. He is described as "a great somebody, ceremonious, punctilious, high-minded, &c."

His first child was a girl, Anna Ella Carroll, who was to become famous in her day as the "unacknowledged member of Lincoln's cabinet." Anna Ella was "plain but high-mannered." She is said to have been a great belle in her youth, but that may be doubted when we read of the sort of education she received. Her father, remembering the profit he had received from his grandfather, took to setting the child across the fireplace at Kingston Hall when she was little more than an infant, and reading Shakespeare and Scott to her. Politics, government and the law were still his interests, and as Anna Ella grew older, they progressed to Alison, the Scottish historian, to Kant, Coke and Blackstone.

Anna Ella developed a mind like a man's. She never married. In later years (her father being dead), she became an abolitionist and almost ruined herself by freeing her own slaves. She is credited with having saved Maryland to the Union. It was a pamphlet she wrote in answer to a speech of Senator Breckinridge of Kentucky that turned the scale. She is said to have distributed fifty thousand copies of this pamphlet at her own expense. President Lincoln, noting the favorable effect that the pamphlet was having on Union enlistments, wrote, encouraging her to keep on writing.

Later the president sent her to St. Louis to write of the proposed Union expedition down the Mississippi. She reported that the river was too heavily fortified for the expedition to have any chance of success, and recommended that the best line of attack would be by the unfortified Tennessee Valley.

Her strategy was accepted by the president and his Cabinet. Even after the campaign had been crowned by success, it is said that the generals were never told that the plan had been conceived by a female. When the capture of Vicksburg seemed to be impossible, Miss Carroll drew plans for attacking it from the land side, and in 1863 Vicksburg fell to a land attack. Congress never rewarded her, and after the war she was forgotten. She lived on in Washington until 1894, poor and paralyzed, supported by the wages of a sister who was a government clerk. It is a sorry conclusion to the story of Kingston Hall. If Lincoln had lived, it would have been different, no doubt.

CHAPTER 7

The Manokin

UPON coming out of the Big Annemessex and heading north along the Eastern Shore, one passes low-lying Hazard Point, and immediately begins to verge imperceptibly into the next river, the Manokin. The mouth is four miles across; South Marsh Island lies far to the west; on both sides the river is widened indefinitely by the green salt marshes, with here and there a narrow island of fast land, as the natives call it, bearing the white-painted houses of watermen.

Far across the river, beyond another stretch of marsh, lies a larger area of fast land with a numerous settlement of the white houses. This is Deal's Island, another village that claims Joshua Thomas as its own. Long ago, when it was a haunt of the picaroons, it was called Devil's Island, but after having been converted by Brother Thomas, the inhabitants changed its name. For the same reason Damned Quarter, a near-by settlement, became Dames Quarter. After conversion, the fiddles played hymns instead of dance tunes, but as the associations of fiddles were still considered dangerous, one by one they were burned or smashed on the picket fences.

Joshua moved here from Tangier Island in 1820 and built a little church. Deal's was a better center than Tangier for his preaching tours. A log canoe, the *Methodist,* was built for him, and it became famous among the islands, and as high up the rivers as it could go. Joshua was now known as the "shouting preacher." He looked on shouting as a means of grace; "I shout myself happy," he said. No man could do up a wedding better than Brother Thomas, it was said. He did a little trading too, and always threw in a good prayer to boot.

The *Methodist* was made from one of the largest trees ever felled on the Shore. It stood near Curtis' Chapel. Hance Cresswell bought it for ten dollars, and cut it down. Its fall shook the earth for a mile around. It was then hauled to King's Creek and towed down that creek, down the Manokin, and around Jericho Marsh to the Annemessex, where it was finished and launched. It was twenty feet long and had a beam of five feet. After thirty years of hard service, it was as good as new. An old engraving represents it as having the usual raking masts and triangular sails of a Chesapeake canoe.

The camp-meeting ground at Deal's Island became the most famous on the Shore. Five rows of permanent "tents," built of clapboards and shingled, were built in circles around the central space. To the south they were reserved for the Potato Neck people; to the north there were large tents for the pilgrims from Virginia, with an immense boarding establishment beyond, while away to the east the colored people encamped and held their lively exercises. The preacher's stand was on the highest point of the ground, and there were many "fire stands" all around.

These fire stands are still used at camp meetings. Little platforms are erected on a stand of tall posts, and thickly heaped with mud or sand. On such beds fires are kept burning to give light to the proceedings at night.

One night in 1838, while the meetings were in progress, a

terrific squall struck the camp and a hideous panic resulted. Trees fell, fire was whirled among the screaming people, boats were dashed ashore. The wind was followed by a deluge of rain. In the morning a scene of utter ruin met the eye; the people were ready to flee home, never to return. Joshua summoned them to the ground with trumpets and made the speech of his life, ending with:

Here I'll raise my Ebenezer
Hither by Thy help I've come;
And I hope by Thy good pleasure
Safely to arrive at home.

The debris was cleared away and the meetings went on.

In 1850, his people built Joshua a new and finer church on Deal's Island, which still stands, but the old trees around it have been destroyed in innumerable gales. The meeting ground was subsequently moved to a new site near the church, and when the horns were sounded for the first services Joshua preached his last sermon. He was seventy-seven and crippled with arthritis. They brought him to the ground in a wheelbarrow, and he addressed them from that. He ended his sermon by saying:

"My friends, will you meet me hard by the Throne? All who feel like trying for Heaven and Glory now rise up!"

The whole congregation sprang to its feet.

A few days later he was dead. They buried him according to his wish, close to the door of the new church "where he could hear the preached gospel Sunday after Sunday, and the shouts of the happy Christians." On his gravestone appears:

Come all my friends as you pass by,
Behold the place where I do lie,

Once as you are, so was I,
Remember, you are born to die.

Deal's Island cannot have changed much in appearance since Joshua Thomas's day. It fronts on wide Tangier Sound, with Bloodsworth Island lying athwart the horizon, and the back of it slides into the limitless salt marshes. It is covered by a biggish village, but the houses are sparsely and irregularly scattered. In a hundred years houses have burned down, of course, and new ones been built, but the clapboarded houses, old and new, follow the same severely plain style; they might all have been designed and built by the same carpenter.

It is a neat village, for the islanders, like all watermen, are just as particular about keeping their houses and fences fresh painted as their boats. In the spring nearly every yard will contain a boat blocked up to be painted. The oyster tongs with their fantastically long handles are leaning against the house wall, and the steel "drudges" piled up in a corner, waiting for next season. Tidy as it is, the general effect of the village is bleak, for nearly all the trees have been destroyed in the gales that sweep the island. Though the land is as flat as a table, the state road winds back and forth in a fantastic manner. Naturally, the politicians who were responsible for the state road tried to build it to the doors of as many voters as possible.

The main village merges into another down at the end of the island, called Wenona. There is a crab house on the point. The deep water makes around to the back of the island here, and comes up close to the shore, forming a natural harbor. Here the oyster boats are moored side by side in a long line. They are all skipjacks nowadays, that is to say, single-

HOME
SWEET
HOME

stickers with an engine. A marshy island protects the harbor from the south; the strip of deep water that runs between is called the Lower Thorofare.

One thing on Deal's Island that I feel sure has not changed at all is Webster's store—except that it contains more package goods today, with brighter labels. Before entering, I wondered why all the shutters were closed and barred on a weekday; inside I decided that it was to keep the stock from bursting out through the windows. The store was crammed with everything under the sun that customers buy; yet there were half a score of people wedged in also, sitting on bags, on boxes, and perched on the counters. Counters, showcases and shelves had certainly not been renewed since Joshua Thomas's day. The shelves were bending like bows under weight of the goods they carried. One of the customers, glancing around, asked the storekeeper when he was going to fix his shelves.

"Oh, when they finally break," he said.

It was a friendly crowd and the strangers were immediately made to feel at home. The young storekeeper's lady friend was sitting by the counter discussing a quart bottle of beer. We would have liked some beer, but the storekeeper regretfully explained that he was not permitted to sell beer; he could only offer it to his friends.

Another young woman came in with a little dog. The dog was sick and she was worried about him. Much advice was offered to her. An old colored woman in a snowy apron said solicitously:

" 'Deed, miss, you ought to take him to a vegetarian."

I asked this young woman, who was pretty and vivacious, to explain the significance of the odd little cement vaults I had seen planted all over the churchyards. The rounded top of each vault projected out of the earth. They all seemed to be new.

"They have come in since the big storm of August, 1933," she said. "In that storm the water washed clean over the island, and many of the old-style wooden coffins were washed out of their graves. There was a young colored woman whose mother had been buried the day before. She lived across the street from the colored church. The water was standing a foot deep on the lower floor of her house, and she and her children had taken refuge upstairs. At intervals she heard a strange knocking at her door, and finally she went down and splashed through the water to see who it was. When she opened the front door, her mother's coffin floated into the house. She said:

" 'My Lord of Mercy! Yo' can't even keep yo' daid in they graves nowadays!' "

The oddest thing in Webster's store was a canvas cot stretched on the floor in front of a side counter. A very much soiled pillow and a heap of bedding lay upon it. When I asked who slept there, I was told that the late proprietor, who had died some months before, had become very feeble toward the end of his life and, unable to walk back and forth, had taken to sleeping in the store. They just hadn't got around to removing his bed.

The Manokin River is of the same character as the Big Annemessex, but it is a bigger stream. As with the Annemessex, it was first settled by a little company of immigrants from Accomac, but this lot were Church of England men. Chief among them was Randall Revell, whose name has been perpetuated in Revell's Neck, lying between the river and Back Creek on the south side. Revell, it will be remembered, was chosen by Governor Calvert as one of the first commissioners for issuing land grants, but after a year in office he was dropped because he was too friendly with Colonel Edmund Scarburgh. The settlement at Manokin submitted to Scarburgh.

On a knoll in Revell's Neck, facing the river, stands the house Clifton, which is said to have been built by the second Randall Revell—the architectural detail suggests a later date. It enjoys a superb view out across a point of land decorated with straggling pines, to the open sound. Long a distressing ruin, Clifton has been purchased and restored in fine style—too fine, one might suggest, for the patina of age has been destroyed.

In 1688 Lord Baltimore ordered a town laid out on the Revell property, which was designed to be the county seat of Somerset and called Somerton. Little is known about this town; perhaps the river overwhelmed it. At any rate, at low tide some stones are uncovered off the point of Clifton that are supposed to be the foundation stones of the first courthouse. Across the river, some other stones near the shore are called the ruins of the original Somerset parish church, now submerged with all its graves.

Across the river rises Almodington, a dignified eighteenth century house supposed to have been built by Arnold Elzey, the son of John, who was one of Revell's fellow commissioners. John Elzey was faithful to Lord Baltimore. It was he who asked for protection against the Nanticoke Indians. "We are not in a Capacity to defend ourselves from the Pagans," he wrote, "who do grow very insolent & tell us we are Lyars." The construction of Almodington extended over a term of years. The very beautiful parlor paneling was purchased by the Metropolitan Museum of New York, where it is on display in the American Wing.

Across Goose Creek from Almodington once stood the house of William Bosman (or Bozman), another early commissioner, who gave his place the odd name of "More and Case It." A little farther down river is Elmwood, built by Arnold Elzey Jones at the beginning of the nineteenth century. His son, of the same name, was born here. He dropped the Jones, and as Arnold Elzey served in the Seminole and Mexican wars and became a major general in the Confederate Army. Another neighbor on this side was William Thorne of Thornton, the commander of the militia in John Elzey's day.

At the head of Goose Creek is the hamlet of Habnab, stretching along a former portage to Monie Creek. It took its name from an early land grant. In 1921 the inhabitants petitioned the post office for a more dignified name, and were awarded Venton. Venton it is still, officially, but few remember it. Habnab it always will be in the vernacular.

The next tributary of any size that joins the Manokin is King's Creek on the south, and a mile beyond, Jones' Creek on the same side. The land between is called Stewart Neck. On this pleasant little plateau once stood the principal village of the Manokin Indians. The Manokins, the Annemessex, and the Assateagues were all of the same gentle race; of a different blood were the hardy Nanticokes a little farther north.

King's Creek was so named for the important King family, of whom we have already heard something. Sir Robert, the first of his name in Maryland (the father of Madam Mary), came over from Calvert County in 1682, took up a grant along this creek, and called it Kingsland. Sir Robert was an opponent of the Lords Baltimore (from whom he held his lands), and he played a leading part in the Protestant Rebellion of 1689, as a result of which Lord Baltimore lost his palatinate.

Sir Robert's son, Robert King II, greatly increased the family holdings. Robert III died before his father. Thomas, a son of Robert III, was established, as we have seen, over at Kingston Hall. Kingsland, the original seat of the family, is now called Beverly—Beverly of Somerset, to distinguish it from the house of the same name in Worcester.

The present Beverly was built by Nehemiah King II during the closing years of the eighteenth century. It would be a great house anywhere in the world, and compares favorably with any of the famous houses of its period in Annapolis. The timbers for it were cut in the woods of the estate, and the English-mold bricks were baked on the spot. Dignity is the keynote of Georgian architecture, and this tall, square house with its big inside chimneys exemplifies it. Inside the rooms are lofty; the central hall both upstairs and down, of the noblest proportions. All the carving, such as moldings, rails, mantelpieces, is in the style of the Brothers Adam and exhibits an exquisite delicacy.

In 1937 the house, having just been completely restored, was gutted by fire. A former Negro servant confessed that he had sprayed it with kerosene in revenge because another Negro had been engaged in place of himself. The owner, still having the original plans, then set to work a second time to rebuild it. The restorations have been completed. The present house is perfect, and perfectly beautiful—yet it lacks something; it has never been lived in.

Many stories cling around the handsome building. The kitchen wing is obviously of a much older construction, a quaint story-and-a-half house with dormer windows. This is said to be the original King homestead. They say that Madam Nehemiah King, appalled by her husband's extravagance, was violently opposed to the building of the new house. As a last argument, she vowed that if it was built she would never set foot in it. It was built and she kept her vow. When she died, her husband had her carried into the new house and laid out in his princely parlor. "Now, Madam King," he said, "you are in!"

Beverly figured in one of the many schemes to rescue Napoleon from the island of St. Helena. Jerome Bonaparte, Napoleon's youngest brother, married Betsy Patterson of Baltimore in 1803. This did not suit the dynastic plans of the head of the family, and at Napoleon's order the marriage was annulled two years later. Jerome was consoled with the crown of Westphalia and a German princess. Notwithstanding the annulment, Jerome retained many friends in America, including the King family of Beverly, and when Napoleon was immured on his lonely island, the Kings were called upon to help rescue him.

Mayor Girod of New Orleans was the ringleader in the plot. Funds were raised to build a fast sloop; plans of St. Helena and its fortifications were studied and details of the attempt carefully rehearsed. The intention was to hide Napoleon in a secret room at remote Beverly until the hunt for him should subside, and he could be safely taken to New Orleans. Shortly before the sloop was to sail, news came of Napoleon's death.

The head of navigation on an Eastern Shore river was always the preordained site of a town. Here travelers transferred from canoe to horse and goods were loaded from the boats to oxcarts. Land in such a spot was always the first to be taken up. First the settler's house, then an ordinary, then a store, and at last the village.

The town at "Head of Manokin" is Princess Anne, the county seat of Somerset. Big schooners used to come up to the town bridge, but now the river bed is so silted up, a rowboat would have difficulty in making it. Somerset was erected as a county as long ago as 1666 and named, in the words of Lord Baltimore, "for our dear sister, Lady Mary Somersett." The town did not come into being until 1731. Good Queen Anne did so much for early Maryland, most of the townspeople believe that the county seat was named for her. In that belief a native son, who went out into the world and prospered, bought a contemporary portrait of Queen Anne by Sir Godfrey Kneller to present to his birthplace. It hangs in the courthouse. As a matter of fact, Queen Anne was gathered to her fathers some years before the town was thought of. Their particular Princess Anne was an undistinguished daughter of George II. Be that as it may, the town is the richer by the possession of a superb portrait.

Princess Anne, like Snow Hill, is looked upon as unprogressive by better-boosted towns. Its "unprogressiveness" constitutes its charm. Unlike Snow Hill, it is on the main line of the Nyp an' N, and is thus in quick and frequent communication with the great world. All the more honor to Princess Anne that it refuses to be flattened out by the steam roller of progress. Princess Anne is still itself.

The Somerset ideal of behavior is not necessarily that of Worcester, though the counties lie side by side. All the counties share in the Eastern Shore spirit, but each has decided notions of its own. Princess Anne with one exception (of which more later) is the most characteristic of Eastern Shore villages. And incidentally it is the most beautiful. This is due chiefly to the magnificence of the sycamore trees which form a lofty green vault through Washington and King William streets.

Charm is full of contradictions. Provincialism, for instance, is a term of reproach, yet Princess Anne's passionate interest in local matters constitutes no small part of its character. The people of larger places are apt not to have a passionate interest in anything. Factional fights are frequent, furious and bitter; they add to the spice of life. Gossip is the mainstay of the village; neighbors pretend to believe the worst about each other, yet fly to the assistance of the victim when real misfortune strikes.

But let it not be supposed that there is anything crude about the social life of Princess Anne. The great-grandfathers and great-grandmothers of these people knew what was what. Every good house will have hanging somewhere on the walls an illuminated coat of arms—perhaps several. It is one of the weaknesses of the Eastern Shore. All such families know each other, of course—know each other! they know all about each other to the remotest degree of consanguinity, including "kissing cousins." They therefore form one great family, the members of which have no illusions about the other members. Their family gossip is highly diverting; often spiced with inimitable mimicry.

Their code is never formulated; "quality" is a word that is not heard nowadays except once in a while from the very old-fashioned; but it is still in the air. An outsider finds the social distinctions that are drawn, inexplicable because he doesn't know what has gone before. Like the Bourbons, Eastern Shore people forget nothing. In the case of newcomers to the village, if they seem "nice," they will be received in the friendliest and most hospitable manner—but they will never *quite* be taken into the family unless some blood connection, however tenuous, can be established.

Many relics of the past survive in Princess Anne; and not only in the starred points of interest such as Beckford, the Teackle Mansion, the Washington Hotel, and the two ancient churches. Down every side street you will see little old houses of no importance whatever except that they add their bit to the mellow aspect of the place. In particular I have in mind three ancient, unpainted wooden tenements leaning crazily together, beautiful in decay.

Beckford ranks with Beverly of Somerset as one of the truly great houses south of the Nanticoke River. It dates from the best period of Colonial architecture, the outbreak of the Revolutionary War, and was built on what had been a part of the widespread holdings of Colonel William Stevens. Wide windows to admit the sun and great chimneys to furnish cheer express the utmost in human comfort. Everything about Beckford is on a sumptuous scale, the great brass locks on heavy paneled doors, the 12-foot ceilings upheld by handsome cornices, the carved mantels. Outside, the trees are adequate for such a house, in particular a monarch of a pecan tree famous in its own right.

The Teackle Mansion in the middle of the town is of later date and less fine in detail, but it has something that renders it unforgettable. With its three big sections and connecting galleries, a "five-part" house, it has a frontage on the street of two hundred feet. Long ago the bricks were painted, and they have weathered to a delicious shade of burnt ocher. The chief grace of the house is a row of tall elms along the front. When the level rays of the setting sun strike over the roof from behind into the foliage, the whole structure is bathed in a green-gold nimbus like a beautiful apparition.

The Teackle Mansion was built in 1801 by Littleton Dennis Teackle, Princess Anne's great man of that day. He was the proprietor of a successful iron furnace near-by, and became the town's first banker. Later he failed for $260,000, a sum so vast as to excite the wonder and respect of all.

The Washington Hotel, an indiscriminate wooden building at the entrance to the town from the north, was dispensing hospitality throughout the Revolution, and it is still a good point of call. The fireplaces are eked out by radiators nowadays, and candles have given place to electric bulbs; there is a telephone booth and several bathrooms, but much of the past still survives. For example, an odd double stairway with a partition down through the middle; one side was for the ladies, the other for the gentlemen. It is explained that in Revolutionary days the ladies were obliged to raise their voluminous skirts in tripping up and down stairs, and the partition was to keep the gentlemen from seeing more than was seemly.

The hotel, as well as the Teackle Mansion and other places around Princess Anne, furnish the scenes of an old-fashioned novel, still read in Maryland but perhaps forgotten elsewhere, *The Entailed Hat*. It is by George Alfred Townsend, who signed himself "Gath," a notable literary light during the Civil War and after. It is a good novel couched in the elaborate phraseology that was fashionable sixty years ago, but freshly observed.

A feature of the Washington Hotel that has endured through the generations is the "gentlemen's lounge," a small room to the left of the lobby. In the reckless games of poker that were played here a hundred and fifty years ago, gentlemen might wager their slaves and even their lands; their great-grandsons are satisfied with bridge at a penny a point.

But, as I am sure it was then, it still is the best gossip exchange in Princess Anne. The gentlemen, however they may deny it, are just as inveterate gossipers as the ladies, and their talk is freer. Life in Princess Anne is conducted at a leisurely pace, and all day and during the evening the older men keep dropping in and out of the lounge, sure of finding congenial company.

One of the things that helps to keep social life in Princess Anne amusing and stimulating is the tradition that a man (or a woman) should speak his mind boldly. Once, when I was writing a series of articles on Eastern Shore towns for a newspaper, I was introduced to a Princess Anne spinster of the old school. She said in an uncompromising voice:

"I have read what you wrote about Pocomoke and about Easton. Some things I liked, and some I did not like."

"Well," said I, anxious to be polite, "tell me the sort of thing you object to, and I'll try to avoid it in future."

She fixed me with a stern gray eye. "No, I shall not tell you. But I shall be waiting to see what you write about Princess Anne!"

CHAPTER 8

The Wicomico

THE next river is the Wicomico. At the head of navigation stands Salisbury, the first city of the Eastern Shore and the seat of Wicomico County. Wicomico was carved out of bits of Somerset and Worcester as recently as 1867; consequently, as a county it has hardly had time to develop a character of its own; to a great extent, Salisbury is Wicomico, and Wicomico is Salisbury.

In any congeries of country towns, all about the same size and equidistant from each other, one is bound at last to draw ahead of the others; whereupon the rest become tributary to it and Number One goes ahead by leaps and bounds. Such is the story of Salisbury. It had a fourfold advantage: it is in the center of the peninsula; it is at the head of a navigable river and at the crossing of principal highways; and it is on the right of way of the only up-and-coming railway. Consequently, four counties of Maryland, one of Delaware, and two of Virginia have their faces turned toward Salisbury. Thither the farmers proceed to sell their crops and the farmers' womenfolk to buy their dresses. During the decade 1920-1930, the population increased forty-six per cent.

Salisbury was laid out at the same time as Princess Anne, but fire has swept it on several occasions, and little that is old remains. Nevertheless, something of the grace of the old Eastern Shore still clings around the place, and the faces on the street are Eastern Shore faces. It is amusing to note that a special type of successful young businessman has been evolved; he dresses in the manner of his prototype in Philadelphia or Baltimore; he has the assurance furnished by a line of great-grandfathers; he is fond of good living; he is doing well in the world; yet there is that in his open glance and smile which suggests he is something more than a Babbitt.

In other respects, Salisbury is much like any prosperous small city in one of the older states. Generally speaking, the narrow winding main street, crowded with traffic, has the aspect of 1886, which was the date of the last big fire. But it also has a banking house that would not disgrace Fifth Avenue. Once the town was a kind of sink; not so long ago a councilman said: "The Wicomico has always smelled bad and it always will." All that is changed.

The growth of the place has been steady without any retrogressions; one important improvement after another has been proposed and pushed through to completion without undue fanfare. This is very unusual on the slowgoing Shore, where nothing new can be proposed without arousing violent opposition. Salisbury has, or is about to have, everything that pertains to a real city—including a model broadcasting station.

On a summer evening, to get a view of the Wicomico, I went aboard one of the little Diesel-engined freight boats that ply every night to Baltimore, the last surviving line from the Shore. She lay in a still black pool below Main

Street; the cries of the Negro stevedores on the wharf and the clatter of their hand trucks to and fro over the gang-plank brought back a homesickness for old steamboat days. It was something to be going aboard a boat once more. Across the pool lay the rotting wharf where the steamboats used to end their journeys. The most popular boat on this line was the *Joppa*. The river is so narrow here that the tanker *Willie*, sent up to the shipyard for repairs in 1941, had to be backed downstream for eighteen miles before she could turn around.

The little vessel I was on did not much resemble the elegant *Joppa* with her tall smokestack, her powerful walking beam and her big paddle boxes, but the feel of her underfoot, and the smell of her, combining scents of engine room, galley and cattle below, was much the same—the steamboat smell like nothing else on earth. An unkind person might have termed the present vessel a tub, but she could stow a lot of freight in her beamy hull and deckhouse. On the upper deck was a capacious wheelhouse, just as I remembered it from long ago, then cabins for the captain, mate and purser, the engine-room skylight, and abaft the skylight, the officers' mess and the galley.

A light rain was falling when we cast off, and I shared the wheelhouse with captain and mate. It transpired that the captain had served as mate on the *Joppa*, when she used to run up to Salisbury. He told me sadly that she was now stripped down to a Diesel-engined barge called the *City of Salisbury*, and was engaged in hauling lumber and telephone poles up from the South. For thirty-seven years the captain had been following Chesapeake waters, though he was still a trim, youthful-looking man.

There was a pleasant intimacy about the little vessel in

the quiet evening. A deck hand came out on the "forad" deck below to address the captain. He wanted to know if she was trimmed right. Squinting ahead, the captain said she had a list to "stabboard," though I couldn't see it. However, after issuing certain instructions about shifting the freight, he was

satisfied we were floating on an even keel, and we proceeded slowly. Captain said we had to go at half speed the first few miles in order to round the sharp bends.

We left the grimy waterfront of the city behind, and the passenger's heart lifted up. The rain stopped and one could see better. The banks of the narrow Wicomico, after all the flatness to the south, seemed very bold, all of forty feet in places. The air was fresh and cool after rain; the trees in the sunless light showed an intense, pure green. The tide was low, and shelves of sleek brown mud slid under the water on either side. Above the high-water line, masses of tuckahoe sprang from the mud, that fleshy bulbous weed that must have its roots in the water and its leaves in the sun. Of all the greens alongshore, the green of tuckahoe was most vivid.

The charred ribs of a vessel lay cradled in the mud to port. That was the schooner *Blackbird,* which burned to the water's edge at Salisbury and was hauled down here to get her out of the way. A great blue heron rose from the tuckahoe and lazily flapped away. In the pilothouse we were still exchanging reminiscences of old steamboat days. Some of the old vessels had been wrecked; others sent north, where they are still carrying passengers; one was serving the government as a mine-layer. Every time a steamboat changes hands, she gets a new name, thus making it difficult to follow her career.

"My father was a steamboat man before me," said the captain; "Civil War days. You ought to heard the stories he could tell. At the beginning of the Civil War, most of the steamboats on the bay were seized and operated by the Union Army. They had to put iron plates around the wheelhouses to protect the pilots against Confederate snipers on shore. Most of the people on the Eastern Shore were southern sympathizers.

"The steamboats were great places for southern spies, too. One of the smartest spies was Colonel Zarvona Thomas, of the Confederate Army. He used to dress up in women's clothes and the Union agents knew him as the veiled French lady. He kept out of their hands for a long time. Once, with the help of a couple of men, he overpowered the crew of a

Union steamboat and carried her down to Norfolk. He was planning to repeat the trick on board the steamboat *Mary Washington,* but the Union agents were on to him this time.

"When he saw he was watched and followed, he went down to the ladies' cabin and threw himself on the mercy of the female passengers. He was a good-looking fellow and he knew he would find sympathizers. And what did they do? Pulled out the drawers of a bureau and broke out the bottoms. Then he climbed in and they closed the fronts of the drawers on him. He would have made it, too, but the drawers fit so tight he near suffocated inside. The Union agents searched the ladies' cabin and were just leaving when the colonel gave himself away by his heavy breathing."

On rounding a point, the first tributary opened up on the left. This was Tonytank Creek, which gave us a pretty vista inland between its high banks. Half a dozen skipjacks lay in the mouth of the creek, at low tide only their raking masts showing above the tuckahoe. The bold point at the lower side of the creek is called Shad Point, in remembrance of the vast quantities of that fish netted here in former years.

Across the river from the mouth of Tonytank, but invisible from the wheelhouse, stands an appealing little house called Pemberton Hall. It was in a sad state of dilapidation when I visited it. Not a comfortable house to live in at any time, but a delight to the eye with its single tiny dormer in the gambrel roof on the river side, and a porch roof coming down low and out on the little kitchen wing, like a shade over its eyes. Indoors the paneling is remarkably fine for a house of this size and age.

During the Civil War, Pemberton Hall became a rendezvous for Confederate sympathizers, while Salisbury, a couple of miles away, was full of Union soldiers. Captain Allison

Parsons, who lived here then, gave the snap away because he insisted on firing a small cannon whenever news of a southern victory was received. After having been warned a couple of times, he was raided by the Union troops. He told them to their faces that the secessionists' arsenal of small arms was buried on the place, but they were unable to find it. Captain Parsons, his brother, and a faithful slave carried the secret to their graves. There has been much digging since, but in vain.

A couple of miles below Pemberton Hall, on the same side of the river, stands another ancient little house called New Nithsdale, and it too has its story. In 1730, Captain Levin Gale, whose house this was, put in to the Bermudas with his ship for food and water. He found the Negroes in revolt, and some white people engaged him to carry them away from the islands. That night, their baggage came aboard accompanied by a boy of four and a girl of six. The children knew their names only as John and Frances, but the name North appeared on a trunk and in some books. The parents failed to come on board, and Captain Gale was finally forced by a threatened attack from the Negroes to sail without them. He brought the children home to his new house. At the first opportunity, he returned to Bermuda but could find no trace of anybody belonging to the children. So John and Frances North grew up in their foster father's house. John was lost at sea as a young man, and Frances married Captain William Murray, a Scottish seaman, who named this house after his native Nithsdale. From them descended William Murray Stone, who became the third Episcopal bishop of Maryland in 1830.

A little way below New Nithsdale, Rockawalkin Creek comes stealing into the Wicomico on that side, its water almost hidden by the thick tuckahoe. Nobody knows the origin of this uncouth name. The Wicomico itself is denominated on some of the old maps as Rockawalkin River. Some say there was once a settler living on its banks called Rock, who refused to ride a horse, and it became the custom of his neighbors to say: "Here comes Rock a-walkin'." But that sounds like something invented after the fact.

In the quiet wheelhouse, the captain and the mate gossiped idly while they pulled the spokes of the big wheel over and back. No "mechanical mike" or steam steering gear on this little vessel! She did not answer instantly, and it was nice to see how accurately they gauged the point at which they must start putting the wheel over. Upon rounding the point, they let go the wheel and it spun back to center. Over their heads were two little signs reading: "right rudder," "left rudder," with arrows pointing. Surely this was unnecessary!

One Shorty came up from below to relieve the captain, who thereupon sat down beside me to continue his gossip of old steamboat days. Shorty, it appeared, was the butt of all the hands' jokes, some of them far from delicate. But he was used to it; he didn't appear to mind.

The mate was concerned about a report from the deckhands that there were "chinches" in their quarters below aft.

"I knew it!" said captain. "That's what comes of carrying a load of secondhand furniture to Baltimore fortnight ago. They stowed it near the engine and the heat brought those babies right out!"

A long discussion followed on the habits of chinches, the sailors' bane. "The *Pocahontas,*" remarked the captain, "had enough of them critters to eat her up!"

"I'll fix 'em before they get *that* bad," said the mate.

"One of the best captains on the bay was Charles W. Wright," said the captain. "He was another great storyteller. Many's the time in the pilothouse I heard him tell how the *Express* run into a twister while rounding Point Lookout, and had her upper works lifted clean off the hull and dumped into the bay. And how, when electric lights was introduced on the steamboats in the late eighties, an old fisherman from Poverty Point, who was a passenger, said to him: 'I took one of them 'lectric lamps home with me, cap'n, but I couldn't make her burn. What kind oil you use, cap'n?'

"Cap'n Wright commanded many vessels, the *Ruggles*, the *Minnie Wheeler*, the *Chesapeake*. All these was long before my time. In 1887 they gave him the new steamboat *Choptank*. She was a beauty in her day. Here's another of his stories: He left Baltimore on the last Saturday in August and turned in right away, because he expected bad weather. It was very rough when they got out in the bay. The men on duty heard cries of distress, so they called the cap'n and he ordered a boat launched. This was off Seven-foot Knoll. Cap'n went in the boat and steered her. They heard a faint voice crying: 'For God's sake save the kid!' Well, to make a long story short, they saved a boy of ten year and four men from off an overturned boat.

"Well, in 1921, that was thirty-four years after, Cap'n Wright and his daughter, they was taking a trip on a Merchants and Miners Line ship to Florida as passengers, and naturally they was invited to sit at the cap'n's table. The cap'n of that ship was William P. Pratt. Well, a lady at the table asks Cap'n P. to tell some of his experiences, and cap'n looks out the window and sees they was passing the light on Seven-foot Knoll, so that puts him in mind to tell of a yachting trip when he was a little boy, and how they capsized on that very spot and was rescued by the steamboat *Choptank*. 'That was in August, 1887,' Cap'n Wright puts in quietly. Big surprise around the table."

We passed a little flat-bottomed scow drawn up to the bank on our left. This was the Upper Ferry; the ferryman sat on the rail smoking his after-supper pipe while he waited for a fare. The narrow craft didn't look big enough to accommodate a motorcar, but they told me she could carry two, one in front of the other. This is one of the rope ferries of this part of the world. A steel cable made fast at each bank lies athwart the bed of the river. It passes over the rail of the ferry on rollers, and the ferryman pulls his boat by it. For this purpose he is provided with a stout bar, deeply notched near one end. He hooks the notch on the cable and, leaning back on the bar, walks backward the length of his boat, then goes forward and starts again. Extra bars are carried for the passengers if they wish to help. This ferry is free to residents of Wicomico County; "foreigners" must pay half a dollar.

The sun broke through for a moment and the whole earth was suspended in a luscious apricot medium. The river was wider now, the bends less acute, and the engine-room telegraph tinkled the signal for full speed. As we approached the mouth, the water became saltier and tuckahoe gave place to sea grass. The banks were lower, and from the upper deck, when the trees permitted, we looked over a wide stretch of flat country on either side.

We passed the rotting remains of old steamboat wharves: Quantico, then Truitt's. Near the former and beside a little creek rose a gigantic lumber mill and creosoting plant, an incongruous note in the wide empty wilderness. The banks of the lower Wicomico go down so steeply that, as the mate said, "You can't run aground unless you hit the bank head on. To build a wharf, all you've got to do is drive a line of piles parallel with the bank and put planks across."

The apricot light slowly deepened to a rose color like that on the sunny side of an apricot, and the whole scene was glorified beyond description. Then abruptly the color was gone and the wide marshes, the distant woods, the river were all washed with a cool aquamarine. A gentle chorus of peeping was heard.

"Frogs hollerin' tonight," remarked the mate.

On the right-hand side in the falling dusk, little Green Hill Church presently came in view, standing dangerously close to the bank's edge. Some of the graves have already fallen into the river; further depredations have been checked, it is hoped, by piling stone along the foot of the bank. Green Hill Church of Stepney Parish was built in 1732 and is the only old church on the Eastern Shore, so far as I know, that has been preserved just as it was built. On a previous visit I was charmed by the high box pews, the pulpit and the clerk's desk. The church possesses a fine old silver service, including a flagon twenty inches high. It is only brought out on St. Bartholomew's Day, the feast of this church's patron saint.

In the churchyard the stone over the grave of Captain James Parker's wife bears this quaint epitaph:

> This world, a city full of crooked Streets,
> Death is a Marketplace where all men meets.
> If Life was Merchandize that man could buy,
> The Rich would live ever—poor men dye.

Farther downstream, the Wicomico's principal tributary, Wicomico Creek, came in from the left. In the old records, it is referred to as the Little Wicomico. Several interesting old houses are built along its banks, though we could not see them now.

In the deepening darkness we slipped stealthily past the village of Whitehaven on the right-hand bank. In the past, I have had occasion to use the "lower ferry," which crosses here. It has a larger scow and does a brisk trade, so much so that the ferryman has been able to introduce a small motorboat to help him over, and so save his back. The village was once a busy place, an important point of call for the steamboats, with a good-sized shipyard and an important fishing industry. An old-timer told me with gusto of those days, when there were three saloons doing an enormous business because they sold rum cheaper than any other place on the Shore.

But the steamboats were withdrawn, shipbuilding was abandoned, the fishing fell off, the grogshops closed, and Whitehaven fell upon evil days. Since the beginning of the war, there has been some revival; the shipyard is being operated again by a big concern in the menhaden industry which builds its steamers here and repairs them. Whitehaven was like a deserted village until somebody on a tugboat at the wharf flashed a searchlight on us to discover who we were.

Below Whitehaven the Wicomico spreads out wide. On the right the salt marshes reach to the horizon, but off on the left a narrow strip of fast land borders the river with the fishing village of Mount Vernon straggling along it for a couple of miles. Its lights sparkled in the dusk. At the end of the road over there stood a little dance pavilion with a whole necklet of lights. When we rounded the point on which it stood, Wingate Point on the chart, we were out in broad water. Away to the south shone Great Shoals Lighthouse.

It was completely dark now. Although we were in effect out at sea, the water was very shallow and we had to stick to the narrow dredged channel. The men began to use the little searchlight mounted on the roof of the wheelhouse. It was operated by a wheel under the ceiling. While the captain steered, the mate turned the light this way and that until it picked up the buoy. Going out, black buoys had to be left to starboard, red to port. The buoys naturally were masculine. "There he is!" the men would cry simultaneously, and switch off the light until it was time to look for another. The south wind came mild and strong through the wheelhouse windows, and in the perfect darkness all the little waves were capped with a pale phosphorescence. That is one of the beauties of Chesapeake waters in the summer.

We were still in the Wicomico River, here a mile wide. When we left Nanticoke Point to starboard, we headed west across the broad mouth of the Nanticoke River for Sharkfin Light, a mere pin point ahead. Sharkfin is out in the middle of Tangier Sound. Tangier at its head ends in Fishing Bay, which is about three miles across. As we drew abreast of Sharkfin Light, standing in the water on long iron legs like a spider, the flashing light of Hooper's Strait appeared ahead and a little to starboard. We passed through the strait, though one would never have known it in that black waste, having Bishop's Head to starboard and Bloodsworth Island to port. Even yet we were not out in the bay; we had still to cross the four-mile mouth of the Honga (local pronunciation Hunger) River and round Lower Hooper's Island. The Honga is not a true river, but just another inlet running far up behind the three Hooper's Islands, Lower, Middle and Upper.

In these big waters there are plenty of shoals, and we still had to pick up an occasional buoy to keep on our course. To a landlubber it seemed a little miraculous how unerringly we hit them. The captain's watch was hanging in front of his eyes, and he knew the precise time it took to proceed from buoy to buoy. At intervals he said, "He ought to be somewhere around here." The mate would then switch on the light, swing it back and forth over the dusky surface of the water, and there, presently, he was! Passing one of the buoys, the captain remarked, "This here's a new one. They put him out without telling us, and first thing we knew we almost run him down."

A wheelhouse at night on the water has a special atmosphere not like anything on land. No lights can be permitted, of course; it is dark, quiet, companionable. Nobody feels obliged to talk. If a remark occurs to a man he utters it; unless an answer is required, there is silence again. But if somebody feels reminiscent, that's all right too. The mate had a special way of relating an anecdote, which he had developed to while away the long hours on watch at night. He would give out the first sentence, wait about half a minute, then continue with the next. It was just his way. When you got used to it, it was pleasantly soothing, but it was a little difficult to know when he had got to the end of his story.

It was long past midnight when we got out in the bay and the searchlight was turned off for the last time. Lights sparkled all around us near and far, fixed and flashing. To the landlubber, these lights spelled confusion, but the two men beside me knew the book of the bay by heart. The distant bright light abeam was Cedar Point Lighthouse on the western shore; the dim fixed light a little to the north was Drum Point at the entrance to my own river, the Patuxent; the flashing light still farther north was Cove Point. We shaped a course that would bring us within a mile of Cove Point on our way north.

The captain announced that he was turning in, and offered to show me my quarters. I was surprised at their luxuriousness; not knowing that there was even a spare berth aboard, I had been prepared to sit up all night. A large square cabin with windows on three sides and a comfortable bed in the corner with snowy linen—the *Queen Mary* could hardly have done me better. This was the purser's room, who was spending the night ashore.

In the morning the cook awakened me for breakfast and I came out on deck in the beaming early sunshine to find that we were in the Patapsco with Fort Carroll abeam, and Sparrows' Point enveloped in a smoky haze off the starboard bow. Breakfast was worthy of the best tradition of steamboat days. At seven o'clock we made our pier in the basin. Another little vessel of the same line was lying athwart the end of the pier, obstructing our entrance to the slip.

"It would serve that fellow right if I sliced off his bow," grumbled the captain.

But he did not. Casually making out not to be proud of his skill, he maneuvered his vessel around the bow of the other and brought her up to the side of the pier as delicately as if he were packing eggs.

CHAPTER 9

The Nanticoke River

As already mentioned, the Wicomico and Nanticoke rivers empty side by side into Tangier Sound. In point of volume and length the Nanticoke is much the greater stream; throughout its lower course it is over a mile wide, a very Mississippi of rivers. It rises far up in Delaware, and it is navigable for steamboats—if there were any steamboats—as far as the town of Seaford in that state. Yet the lore of the Nanticoke is scantier than that of any other river on the Eastern Shore. In the early days few men of the sort who leave legends appear to have settled on its banks.

Along the lower reaches of the Nanticoke the salt marshes of Dorchester, home of the muskrat and the blackhead duck, stretch endlessly away to the west; on the other side there is fast land settled by oystermen and fishermen. Their three sprawling villages which merge into each other are called Nanticoke, Bivalve and Tyaskin. Bivalve (aptly named!) is an important shipping point for oysters. Tyaskin fronts on a muddy creek, the Wetipquin. When steamboats came up the Nanticoke they were advertised to call at Tyaskin, "tide permitting." But it was a matter of pride with the captain to make it at any stage. As his propeller churned

up the mud astern in endless backing and filling, the assembled crowd on shore alternately jeered and applauded. But Cap'n Billy always made it in the end.

At Long Point, about fifteen miles above its mouth, the Nanticoke suddenly narrows to about half a mile, but still for many a long mile above that it continues to swing widely back and forth through the salt marshes. On the east there is nothing but marsh; on the west side fast land comes down to the river at the outside of each swing. Even on the fast land few houses are to be seen. It always was a lonely land and is so still.

Near Lewis Landing on the west bank rises Weston, the home of John Henry, a member of the Continental Congress, later governor of Maryland, and finally the first United States senator elected in Maryland. He was the grandson of that Reverend John Henry who married the regal Mary Jenckins of Mary's Lot on Pocomoke. During the 1780's the picaroons, on their way to burn Vienna, plundered Weston and set fire to it. Later, it was completely destroyed by fire.

The most notable feature of the present big house is the entrance door with graceful fanlight and sidelights.

It may be that the reason the early settlers gave the Nanticoke River the go-by was because of their wholesome respect for the Nanticoke Indians. The speech and customs of these Indians differed from those of the neighbor tribes, and the Nanticokes were the most warlike and numerous. Ethnologists call them a branch of the Delaware tribe, which belonged to the Algonquin race, originating on the shores of Hudson Bay. The Nanticokes liked fishing and trapping better than hunting, and that is undoubtedly why they settled beside the river which gave them their name. After all these years, it is still a trapper's paradise.

They dwelt in wigwams with a house for the chief of similar construction but of oblong shape and much bigger. Grass or rush curtains divided the interior. All their land was held in common, with a plot for each family and an extra share for the chief, to enable him to entertain guests and to lay by a reserve in case of famine. Their villages were fortified with stockades.

They buried their dead and, after allowing the corpses to lie in the earth for some months, they exhumed them, cleaned the bones, and placed them in a sort of shrine they called "manito-kump," meaning "place of the mystery-spirit." They greatly revered these relics and when they migrated, carried them with them.

They called their important men "cockarouses," and the white settlers quickly adopted this expressive word for their own. Their medicine men exerted a powerful interest in the tribe. These Indians appeared to have possessed the art of making bark canoes, as well as the universal dugouts. For currency, the Nanticokes used "roanoke" and "peake," sometimes called "wampum-peake," two kinds of shell. Roanoke was made out of conch shell and was dark purple in color, while peake, white in color, was made of cockleshell. The bits of shell were strung like beads. Captain John Smith shrewdly observed that this currency caused "as much dissention among the Salvages as gold and silver amongst the Christians."

There is no shell to be found along the shores of Chesapeake Bay or its tributaries. It all came from the ocean beaches which were readily accessible to the Nanticokes; hence they were in a good position to trade. One of the earlier traders dubbed them the "best Merchants of all the Salvages." The value of peake and roanoke varied with the times. During the earlier days of the colony at St. Marys, an arm's length of roanoke was valued at from five to ten pounds of tobacco. As tobacco averaged about twopence a pound, roanoke was worth a shilling an arm's length, and up. Peake, the white kind, was much more valuable.

The story of the relations of the Nanticokes with the whites is a troubled one and far from creditable to our side. Captain John Smith visited them; he called their river the Kuskarawaok, and named several tribes as living along its banks. One he called "Nantiquake," the first time the name appears. None of the other pioneers ever distinguished between the people of these villages; to them they were all Nanticokes. These were the Indians, it will be remembered, who hid from Captain John Smith in the reeds. After the white men had discharged their firearms into the hiding place, they found "much blood" there.

For many years after this bad beginning, the Nanticokes were suspicious of the whites. Yet they were reasonable, on the whole. During the 1660's, when white men began coming into their country from Accomac, a treaty was concluded with their "emperor," Unnacokasimmon, who, in token of his fealty, agreed to make an annual tribute of four Indian arrows. Before this, settlers in the northern part of the Eastern Shore had had a lot of trouble with the Nanticokes and two armed expeditions had been sent against them.

From time to time the Indians were accused of various "insolencyes" and affronts, but they considered themselves allied with the whites. They had been instructed by their emperor to tie a white cloth around their left arms in token of amity, and to distinguish them from the savages who were hostile. Also, they had been instructed, upon approaching a white man in the woods, to throw down whatever weapons they were carrying. What more could be asked of them?

In the course of time, Unnacokasimmon died. It was said that his people had considered him too friendly toward the whites and that he had been poisoned. His successor, Ohopperoon, was therefore held a usurper, by the whites. The situation was further complicated by the murder of an Indian by three white men. Whatever Ohopperoon's rights to rule might be, the proprietary officials decided to send a mission to renew the old treaty, and our old acquaintance, Colonel William Stevens, was chosen to head it.

He was allowed to choose his own associates, and he was told to take a good party of horse and a company or two of foot in order to appear in a good manner before the Indians—if he thought that advisable. His instructions continued:

You are forthwith to repair to the present Emperour of Nanticoke and him and his great men in the name of his Lordship and us, his deputyes, kindly salute. You shall lett the Emperour know that you are come to renew the peace that his Lordship, the Right Honourable the Lord Proprietor and Unnacokasimmon, their old

Emperour concluded, which we on our sides have kept most firm and inviolable, and are desirous to continue, confirm and preserve the same if soe be he and his great men are willing.

Ohopperoon was further to be told that orders had been given for the apprehension of the three alleged murderers and that they would receive a fair trial with the Indians' case fully presented. The emperor was urged to come to the trial with his great men. Ample provision for their entertainment was promised. In any case, they wanted him to come to St. Marys to renew the old treaty.

Colonel Stevens's mission was successful, and Ohopperoon and some of his warriors presently appeared at St. Marys before the governor and the Council. "Very good expressions" were exchanged. The unfortunate Nanticokes had to be satisfied with that. They did not get what they asked for, a guarantee that they would be left undisturbed in their lands along the river, and a promise of free trade with the English. However, the old treaty was renewed and the governor presented the emperor with "a laced Coat, a Shirt and Hatt which he very thankfully accepted, and with great satisfaction the Indians then took their leaves and departed."

When Ohopperoon died the great question was, who should succeed him? By this time Maryland had passed from proprietary administration to royal administration. A man named Asquas was the choice of the Indians themselves, but Governor Copley refused to acquiesce on the ground that Asquas was "an Enemy to their Sacred Majesties." He appointed one Panquas as "Captain General and Commander in Chief" of the Nanticokes, with Announghtought as "his Second and Assistant in the Rule," and the Indians had to take it and like it. On the occasion of this conference the Indian envoys were presented with two matchcoats, two pairs of worsted stockings, and two of "the King's guns."

After a few years the Nanticokes deposed Panquas and took an emperor of their own choice, one Felton. It was further reported in St. Marys, "that they [the Nanticokes] entertain and receive strange Indians." Rumors like this could always be set in motion by interested parties against the hapless redskins. Colonel Charles Hutchins, sent to look into the situation, reported that "their behavior seems to be more sturdy than formerly & they doe forbeare coming among the inhabitants"—i.e., the white settlers. A refusal to trade was of course the unforgivable sin, and they were sternly warned to throw out their new emperor, Felton.

Meanwhile the white men were continually encroaching on the Indians' land. The Nanticokes complained that such settlers created "great annoyance and Dissatisfaction among the Indians who Desire to live among themselves without Disturbance." Reasonable enough! New orders were issued from St. Marys that nobody should settle "where any of our Neighbour Indians are actually seated, or soe neare to them as to annoy or Disturb them." The orders were not enforced. In some cases the Indians were deprived of their land without even receiving, as one of them complained, "coats for it" (as provided by the treaty).

The Assembly, finally stirred into action, deeded land forever to the tribe along the northern bank of the river in the neighborhood of Chicacone (now Chicone) Creek "under the Yearly rent of one Beaver Skin." This was in 1698. It was found inadequate, and ten years later three thousand acres was added on Broad Creek, a tributary of the Nanticoke that now lies in the state of Delaware.

By this time the tribe was much reduced in numbers.

It is the old bad story. Their complaints were numerous and pitiful. They were prevented from cultivating their land; they were robbed by the Negro slaves of the settlers; "the English bring strong Drinke to their Towns and sell it among their Indians to their great Prejudice." Hearing this, the Council authorized "the Great men at the Indian Towns upon such Liquors being Brought thither to break & Stave the Bottles, Casqs and Barrells, or oversett and Spill such other Vessels wherein such Liquors may be." However, the traffic went on.

Here, in part, is one of their pitiful appeals to the Governor of Maryland:

> As a scattered Remnant of a confused Nation We Come to see you once more, our Brother, before we are all Dead or Dispersd out of this Nation. . . . for as there is but few of us remaining, nay even But a handfull of us and but few Young men and Women, and as we love to Travel the Roads and other Places to seek the Support of Life, and as you are our Brother therefore beg and hope and beg you will not Suffer us to be trodden down quite, for we are as a child Just beginning to Walk.
>
> . . . .
>
> We now present several Belts of Peak as a Pledge of our Trust and Confidence in you our beloved Brother. We of this Nation are now in a Sorrowfull and Deploreable Condition by being hindered of the Previledges and Benefits of our Lands which is our Total living, and as wee the poor Indians . . . go out in the woods a Hunting and build Cabbins to Defend us . . . some of the White People . . . will set them on fire and burn them down to the ground and leave us Destitute of any Cover to Shelter us from the weather.

In 1742 Panquas, still the ruler of the Nanticokes, got into serious trouble with the provincial authorities. The usual crop of rumors had been set afoot that the miserable remnant of Nanticokes were plotting with the Shawnees to massacre the English. It was said that all the Indians had disappeared into the marshes, that war dances were being held, drums beaten; that the Indians were preparing a great store of poisoned arrows and the Indian doctors were getting ready to poison the wells of the English, etc., etc. All this put the white settlements in a dither. Panquas was captured and fetched to Annapolis (which had become the capital) for trial.

There is no record of what finally happened to him. He must have been a very old man by now. As for the Nanticokes, despairing of getting justice, they packed up the precious bones of their ancestors and migrated north. They had asked and obtained permission to join with the Six Nations, the Iroquois. A few remained in Maryland. In the end the government allowed these the sum of $666.75 for quitting their claims to the lands allotted them. Thus was the Anglo-Saxon conscience soothed!

Near the end of the eighteenth century William Vans Murray, sent at the instance of Thomas Jefferson to make a vocabulary of the Nanticoke language, reported:

> The tribe has dwindled almost to extinction. . . . The little town where they live consists of but four genuine wigwams, thatched over with the bark of cedar—very old—and two framed houses—in one of which lives the Queen, Mrs. Mulberry, relict of the Colonel who was the last chief. They are not more than nine in number. The others of the tribe, which in this century were at least five hundred in number, having died or removed towards the frontiers, generally to the Six Nations.

Of the Nanticokes who went north, some settled along the banks of the Susquehanna near Conestoga Creek; some went to the Wyoming valley in northern Pennsylvania; others to branches of the Susquehanna River rising in New York State; still others got as far as Canada in the neighborhood of what is now Brantford, Ontario. In Pennsylvania they have given their name to a city. Wherever they went, they became absorbed in the surrounding tribes and lost their own customs and speech. The Canadian lot still call themselves Nanticokes, but that is all they have left.

The wide Nanticoke River, swinging in immense curves through the marshes under an unobstructed dome of blue, is very beautiful—but something monotonous. Far up from the mouth, Barren Creek comes twisting in from the east through the vivid sea grass. This was one of the favorite haunts of the Nanticokes.

At the end of the next reach of the river, the town of Vienna (local pronunciation: vee-anna) is seated on the west bank. The main north and south highway is carried over here on a handsome new bridge. Since the broad and deep river affords such easy communication with the bay, Vienna has been a port of entry ever since it was founded in 1706. Some of the byways in the town are still paved with the cobblestones brought here as ballast by the ships which came to load tobacco or white oak timber. In the days of the Nanticokes, the spot was called Emperor's Landing. Five thousand pounds of tobacco were paid the Indians for one hundred acres on which to found the town—a better price than they usually got. For a while the new town was called Baltimore.

A mile above Vienna, Chicone Creek comes in from the north, called by the Nanticokes Chicacone. This until the end continued to be their Main Street, and upon it stood their town of the same name. A stretch of fast land, where creek and river come together, would have made a fine site for it, but the village is said to have been higher up the creek and on the other side.

At the end of a long, straight reach of the river, its principal tributary, Marshyhope Creek, comes in from the north. Marshyhope is almost a river in its own right; narrow and deep, it is navigable all the way up to Federalsburg in Caroline County and beyond. About five miles up from its mouth, twin villages face each other across the stream, Brookview on the left, Eldorado on the right, and half a mile farther, in sight of both, one unexpectedly comes on a fine eighteenth century mansion on a bold bank to the right. This is another Rehoboth—spelled a little differently.

The land was taken up in 1673 by John Lee, a son of Colonel Richard Lee, the founder of that famous family in Virginia. The present house was built in 1723 by that Thomas Lee who fathered two signers of the Declaration of Independence, Richard Henry Lee and Francis Lightfoot Lee, and it has been preserved almost unchanged from the day it was built. Standing on a high bank washed by the charming little river at its foot and shaded by ancient trees, it is one of the most enchanting retreats the heart of man could desire.

Walnut Landing lies on the Marshyhope near its mouth, a place of two houses at the end of a dirt road. This is one of the spots associated with the infamous name of Patty Cannon; here she is said to have brought her kidnaped Negroes by wagon and loaded them aboard her vessel to be sold south. Here is her story:

She was born Lucretia Hanly. Her father is said to have been the son of a wealthy nobleman of Yorkshire, who was entrapped into a low marriage and cast off by his family. He emigrated to Montreal and soon joined a gang at St. Johns, who were engaged in smuggling goods across the United States border. He was convicted of the murder of an old friend, Payne, who had discovered his crimes, and his career was brought to an end by the noose.

His widow turned her home into a "house of entertainment." One Alonzo Cannon, a respectable wheelright of Delaware, happened to be taken sick while stopping there, and it fell to the task of Lucretia to care for him. So agreeable did she make herself, so tenderly did she wait on him, that Alonzo took her back to Delaware with him when he left. It is likely that young Lucretia was willing to do anything to escape that "house of entertainment." This was in the last years of the eighteenth century.

She was sixteen then, "and by no means bad-looking, though rather large." Lucretia—or Patty, as they called her —was described as being fond of music and dancing, also witty and a great talker. The young couple settled on the Nanticoke River about ten miles below Laurel, Delaware, near the Maryland line. They established a ferry, called Cannon's Ferry, and did very well with it.

But Patty was an out-and-out bad one; "very sensual in her pleasures," the story has it. After three years of marriage, the discovery of his wife's real character so preyed on Cannon's mind that he died. That was one explanation of his death; another was that Patty poisoned him. After his death, she became one of the most abandoned and notorious of women. She moved down near Johnson's Crossroads on the Delaware-Maryland state line, and set up a low tavern.

Slave dealers were her particular prey, because they carried large sums of money. She used all kinds of tricks to induce them to lodge at her house. By degrees she got a great reputation among them for hospitality, because she rarely charged them anything for lodging. Her house became a sort of headquarters for the slave dealers. Meanwhile, she was gathering around her a gang of ruffians who were absolutely obedient to her will.

At this time Patty was described as a big, dark, gypsy-like woman with flashing eyes. Her glance and her voice could be terrifying, yet she was able to make herself very feminine and winning when she chose. She had the courage and the strength of a man, and was perfectly capable of taking on any of her victims by herself if need be.

The first murder that she was to acknowledge in the end was that of a gentleman from Richmond, who was fired at through the window while eating his dinner in her house. His body was secreted in the cellar until nightfall, then buried in a side hill. Next on the list came two slave dealers who had only stopped in for a drink and were detained all afternoon by her fascinating conversation. After dark they were put on their way for Laurel via Cannon's Ferry. Patty and three of her gang set off immediately afterward at a gallop. They were familiar with every inch of the country. Crossing the river above the ferry, they rode around to intercept the travelers, and threw logs across the road at the top of the hill where it came up from the ferry. There they hid themselves to await their coming.

When the travelers paused at the road block, the bandits fired, wounding one of them. The horses bolted and both escaped, but the wounded man died later. One of Patty's gang, Griffin, paid on the scaffold in Cambridge, Maryland, for his share in this crime.

Before death he made a full confession of this and other murders, implicating Patty, and she found it expedient to disappear for a time. It is most likely that she went to Philadelphia to organize her new business. When she reappeared in Delaware and Maryland it was ostensibly as a slave dealer, buying and selling her human merchandise in a lawful manner. It was at this time that Joe Johnson, the bloodiest ruffian of them all, appeared as her right-hand man. He was her son-in-law. Nothing is said about that doubly unfortunate woman, Patty's daughter.

They built a much larger house in the same neighborhood. In this enterprise Patty kept in the background as far as she could, and the house was advertised as Joe Johnson's tavern. By placing it so that it overlapped the borders of three counties in two states, Sussex in Delaware, Caroline and Dorchester in Maryland, they cunningly prepared to outwit any of the local authorities who might try to interfere with them. A building known as the Smith House stands on the spot today. It is supposed to include the timbers of Joe Johnson's tavern.

Meanwhile in Philadelphia, Patty had left behind her a villainous Negro called Ransom to act as her agent. That this man was educated and intelligent made him all the more dangerous. It was his job to prowl along the waterfront with plenty of money, treating Negroes until he had made them drunk. For his accomplice, Ransom had an old wench who kept an infamous house in a low street near the Navy Yard. Here the unlucky Negroes were doped with liquor and held until Patty's vessel came into port. If they were free Negroes, so much the better; there was less chance of a search for them.

Loaded aboard, sometimes a dozen at a clip, they were carried to some obscure landing place on the lower Delaware and transported by wagon to Patty's house. After having been kept prisoner there for a while in order to confuse any search that might be made, they were carried by wagon again to Walnut Landing on the Marshyhope (or to some other secret rendezvous; Patty had all the rivers of the Eastern Shore to choose from), where they were put aboard another vessel and carried south to be sold. Sick or decrepit Negroes were coolly cast overboard; troublesome children cracked over the head with a rattan that had a piece of lead fastened to the end. Patty seized one crying child and threw it on the fire, afterward burying its body in the cellar. There are old prints depicting this horror.

Once, in her dining room, she was in the very act of stabbing a traveler in the back when she heard other travelers entering the front door. She flung the body on the table, caught up the corners of the tablecloth with dishes, food and all, and, dropping the bundle in a big chest, turned to greet the newcomers with her best smile. One of the murders she afterward confessed to was that of a slave dealer who came to her house to spend the night with two valuable slaves. He was beaten to death in his bed and buried in the back garden. The slaves, of course, were added to those shipped south.

Patty had a Negro boy working for her, aged fifteen, who was kept in ignorance of her crimes up to a certain point. But in the end he saw or was told something about the child who was burned and, overcome with horror, he ran away, meaning to give information. Patty caught him and brought him back. He was beaten, starved and confined in the cellar among the gruesome evidences of previous crimes, but Patty could not break his spirit and she finally beat him to death with a stone.

In 1828 she received news of the hanging of her only brother, James, in the penitentiary at Kingston, Ontario. He was a counterfeiter and horse thief—a romantic family, the

Hanlys! Soon afterward she was informed of the death of her mother, perhaps from a broken heart. After that Patty appeared to cast all restraint to the winds—she hadn't exhibited much before. She became utterly reckless, and when a traveler, who was known to be carrying a large sum in cash, was discovered to be missing, suspicion was excited at last among her neighbors.

One of them came to Patty and asked to be shown through her house, saying that he wanted to build one on the same plan. Patty good-humoredly led him from room to room —but avoided attic and cellar! She was called away for a moment while the man was in the house, and he asked her old Negro servant what was in the cellar. The old woman, with manifest terror, said she dared not tell. The neighbor promised to see that she was protected; however, before the servant could tell him anything, Patty came back.

Nevertheless, the neighbor decided to lay information before the authorities, and on the following day the sheriff of Sussex County came to Patty's house with a dozen men to apprehend her. Patty and her gang put up a desperate fight, but in the end they surrendered and were carried to Georgetown, Delaware, where they were cast in jail. Joe Johnson was never caught.

One of the gang turned state's evidence and told the officers all he knew. They took him back to the house and he pointed out the spots in the garden where they should dig. Several skeletons were recovered. In the attic the searchers found a cell constructed of great timbers spiked together. Here they found twenty-one Negroes shackled and chained to the timbers. They were set free.

At the trial Patty denied everything. She and two of her accomplices were sentenced to death; three others got off with seven years apiece. Later, Patty asked for a priest and confessed that she had killed eleven persons with her own hands, and had assisted at the killing of more than twelve others. She had poisoned her husband and had strangled one of her own babes at three days old. Three weeks before the date set for her execution, she poisoned herself and died in agony. This happened in 1829.

CHAPTER 10

The Dorchester Marshes

IN sailing north along the Eastern Shore, after passing the wide mouths of the Wicomico and Nanticoke rivers, you would find yourself in Fishing Bay, a shallow inlet from three to four miles wide and about fifteen miles in length, entirely surrounded by the immense Dorchester marshes, except for an island of fast land here and there. The first of these islands lies inside Bishop's Head fronting on a creek aptly named Tedious. Here stands a waterman's hamlet called Crocheron, at the end of one of the interminable marsh roads leading from island to island and eventually to the main.

Fishing Bay has no features; there is nothing but endless blue water and endless green marsh, laced with creeks and ponds, invisible until you come to the edge. The creeks bear the usual common names: Thorofare Creek, Cedar Creek, Raccoon Creek; some have no names, and one bears the odd appellation of Backgarden Creek, given it in a spirit of levity perhaps, since there is no garden back or front within miles. The steamboat used to come into Fishing Bay as far as Elliott's Island on the east side, which supports a populous village, amphibious in character. It is connected with the world of landsmen by a lonely marsh road to the town of Vienna, more than twenty miles away.

Two rivers empty side by side at the head of Fishing Bay, the Transquaking and the Big Blackwater. A short distance above its mouth, the Transquaking receives a tributary as big as itself, the Chicamacomico, and the Big Blackwater is joined by the Little Blackwater. The four streams comprise a system of drainage for the marshes different from anything else on the Shore. They pursue their sluggish courses in such a fantastic series of wriggles and whorls that it may be only a few hundred yards across from reach to reach, yet miles around. This country should be viewed from an airplane; indeed, it is the only way it can be viewed. The four rivers are so precisely alike throughout their courses that I would defy anybody, brought blindfold to a spot upon them, to tell where he was upon regaining his sight. Yet, come to think of it, I have never heard of a fisherman or a trapper getting lost among them.

Marshlands in Dorchester used to be assessed at twenty-five cents an acre and the actual value per acre, in a saying of the day, was less than an acre of blue sky. All that is changed now, owing to the growth in popular favor of Hudson Bay seal—in other words, the humble muskrat. Muskrat pelts which used to sell for eight cents are now bringing as much as four dollars; the trappers are growing rich, and mashlands, having risen to one hundred and fifty dollars an acre, are profitable at that.

The little creature is protected under the laws of Maryland; the open season for trapping extends only from January 1st to March 15th, yet in that brief time a skillful trapper can make from nine hundred to twelve hundred dollars. A farmer who rented his marshland to a trapper for one-half the proceeds of the pelts made 130 per cent on the value of his land. Forty acres of marsh in another place yielded six hundred dollars per annum in pelts for several years. The total catch in Dorchester County is said to be about a million skins annually.

The muskrat, like his big cousin the beaver, is very handy with his paws. For his dwelling he builds a workmanlike mound of sticks and mud about three feet in diameter and the same height. The entrance is always underwater to discourage his land enemies, but it is warm and dry within. These are his winter quarters; for summer he makes burrows

in the banks of the streams and the young are raised here. These burrows are very destructive to the built-up marsh roads; some go so far as to ascribe the slow sinking of the whole Eastern Shore littoral to the indefatigable muskrat. He feeds exclusively on vegetable matter, the stems and roots of water plants and the like; the fleshy roots of the tuckahoe are much esteemed by him, and the dainty creature insists on washing his food before he eats it. He is an inveterate night prowler, and is rarely seen except on those occasions when he raids a cornpatch or a vegetable garden for a change of diet.

The muskrat has always been eaten in any district where

he abounds. To save the susceptibilities of the customers, he often appears on the menus of Eastern Shore hotels as "marsh rabbit." His flesh has even been likened in flavor to that of terrapin. Others assert that it tastes like the flesh of the wild duck which shares the same habitat. Here is an old Dorchester recipe for cooking muskrat:

> Let them soak in salted water one day and night. Put them on and parboil for about fifteen minutes. Change the water and cut up. Add onion, red pepper and salt to taste and a small piece of fat-back [home-cured hog meat]. Add just enough water to keep them from burning, add a little thickening to make gravy, and cook until very tender.

The muskrat's coinheritor of the Dorchester marshes, the wild duck, is no longer seen in such "multitudinous millions" as were reported by the first settlers; still, having been watchfully protected for some years, the ducks are fairly plentiful. Shooting clubs for wealthy sportsmen have pre-empted acreage in several parts of the marshes and on some of the bay islands. There are said to be forty-one varieties of wild duck in Maryland. Of these, all but a dozen winter in Dorchester. The most highly prized is of course the canvasback; the most plentiful the black duck, no mean substitute.

This recipe for cooking black duck, from the chatelaine of a famous Eastern Shore family, shows an attention to detail that reveals the artist:

> Do not draw the ducks more than three hours before you will use them. The less time the better. They bleed freely and should be washed in as little water as possible and with a rag, as otherwise you lose much of the blood, which of course is the flavor. Do not stuff with anything as it is important the heat should strike inside the duck to prevent the loss of juices there. Have an old-time baking-pan not higher than two inches on the sides, so the heat can sear the duck at once and does not steam them, causing

loss of juices. Have a very hot oven, hot enough to sear them all over at once. Rub the breasts with butter. Put them in the low baking-dish with as little water as possible, baste three times, adding boiling water to the baking dish each time so that it will not dry. Bake twenty-two minutes if you can have a very, very hot oven, or twenty-five if your oven isn't so good.

As it was impracticable in summer to explore these meandering rivers by boat (for a reason which will appear), I invited an old riverman who knew them well to visit them with me at such points as we could reach by car. We set out from Cambridge and, during the drive south, my companion entertained me with tall tales of rivers. We had been talking about the deep, unexpected holes that are to be found in all Eastern Shore rivers, due to some obscure action of the tide. My friend said, with a perfectly grave face:

"There is such a hole near the mouth of Watts' Creek that is ninety feet deep. It is called Jake's Hole. Its exact depth is known because it's been sounded often enough, and I'll tell you why. There was aplenty pirates round here in the old time. The one that mostly cruised in these waters was Blackbeard; Edward Teach was his right name. Well, Blackbeard picked Jake's Hole for one of his caches, and dropped an oaken chest bound round with copper bands in there. It's still there. God knows what's inside it!

"Many knew about this and aimed to recover the treasure, but Blackbeard had left a school of man-eating red herring to guard the place and none could come near. Well, there was an Englishman called Lord Longbow bought a fine place on the river and his cousin, Prince Fakir, came to spend the summer with him. Lord Longbow took him out in a boat to show him the river, and as they passed by Jake's Hole he was trying to teach Prince Fakir to sing 'Yankee Doodle.'

This tickled the man-eating red herring so that they laughed theirselves to death.

"Those that knew about it thought it would be a cinch, then, to recover Blackbeard's treasure, so they proceeded to Jake's Hole with their ropes and grappling irons and so forth. But it turned out that Blackbeard had left another spell on the chest. It was easy enough to catch holt of it, but as soon as they histed it near the surface, the ropes bust into flame and burned through with an awful stink of sulphur, and the chest dropped to the bottom of the hole again. Many have tried it, but it was always the same. They only lost their grappling irons for their trouble. So the chest is there yet, if you want to have a try for it. . . .

"That famous beard of his," the storyteller continued, "started growing right under his eyes and would have hung down over his chest, only he used to plait it in many little tails which he tied with different colored ribbons and caught behind his ears. . . . I suppose you've heard how Blackbeard came to his end?"

I said I had not.

"Well, that was off Sharp's Island out in the bay. Blackbeard was lying in wait under the island at the edge of Dick's Hole for a richly laden East Indiaman that was expected down from Baltimore. He was so intent upon it, he failed to notice the tops'l schooner *Julia Harlow* lying inside the hook. Young Joshua Covey was her master. Covey was able to creep up on Blackbeard in a yawl boat, and to board him before he was discovered. Covey cut off Blackbeard's head with one mighty sweep of his saber.

"But a pirate, you know, prided himself on never losing his head. Blackbeard threw the copper plate that showed the location of all his caches into Dick's Hole and jumped in after it. He swam around the vessel three times without his head before he disappeared from sight."

From the frequency with which one meets with his name on the Eastern Shore, one would think that Blackbeard must have sailed up here, but the facts of his brief piratical career are known, and he never sailed north of the Carolinas. The truth is, he laid a spell of horror on the whole Atlantic seaboard.

Meanwhile, we were descending the long neck between the Transquaking and Little Blackwater rivers, through Aireys and Bucktown, dusty hamlets sunk in Sabbath torpor. The flat lowlands adjacent to the marshes are wonderfully rich; the farmers boast of raising seventy bushels of corn to the acre. Our destination was White House Farm on the Transquaking, but in the effort to take advantage of every strip of fast land, the road made so many turns that we lost our sense of direction and suddenly came out on Best Pitch Ferry. Best Pitch it is written on the map, but everybody calls it Base Bridge. There was never a bridge here.

A little rope ferry was pulled up on our side, with a young Negro in his Sunday clothes perched on the rail. The river (Transquaking) was hardly wider than twice the length of the ferry; on the other side the road lost itself in the endless marsh. This road would eventually bring you to Vienna on the Nanticoke, after twenty miles more or less. At the sight of prospective passengers, the ferryman leaped down joyfully; his face fell when we told him we were looking for White House Farm. He was minding the ferry for his uncle this Sunday, and so far he had not had a customer.

The scene before us was one of great beauty under the hot summer sun. It had the thrilling quality of boundless space; it was without a single break; on one hand the deep, narrow, yellow river came curving out of the marsh, and on the other hand it immediately curved out of sight again; in front a vast empty sea of green domed by a sea of blue without a fleck of cloud.

After receiving new directions, we turned about and soon came to White House Farm. This comprises a rich stretch of fast land with the river curving around it. The house is a gentleman's residence with brick walls two feet thick and, I was told, fine interior woodwork. It was built by the Ecclestone whose name often appears in the early county annals. At the time of our visit it was untenanted.

When we got out of the car and started up the avenue leading to the house, a cloud of what my companion called "square-winged" sheep flies rose from the tall grass and descended upon us. Little branches of leaves were quite ineffective in keeping them off; they hadn't tasted human blood for a good while, I suppose, and it drove them crazy. We fled back to the car and started the engine. That explains why any extended exploration of the Dorchester marshes is out of the question in the summer.

It would be a paradisaical spot if it weren't for the damned sheep flies. My friend pointed out the spot on the river where the little tops'l schooner *J. B. Meredith* was built, and drew me a neat sketch of her, topmast and rigging complete. He was proud of her as being the only vessel ever built hereabouts. For many years she made money for her owners by carrying out the farmers' corn and bringing in their fertilizer.

"How could they ever sail a vessel up that winding ditch?" I asked.

"They didn't try to sail her when they got into the river," he answered. "They put the men ashore to track her with a line."

"In the marsh?"

"It isn't often covered with water," he said, "but only

spongy-like. And they had boots. In those days a man would do anything for nine dollars a month and his board."

He showed me a spot on the map where, by digging a short ditch from one reach to another across the marsh, they had saved themselves going around over five miles.

Since the Chicamacomico River joins the Transquaking between White House Farm and Best Pitch Ferry, I did not actually set eyes on that river, but I am sure it is no different from the others.

Returning then to sleepy Bucktown, lying parched in the heat, we struck off to the west and in due course came to the Little Blackwater, as much like the Transquaking as one pea to another. So crooked was it that we kept coming on it again after we thought we had left it behind us. There was a bridge here. At this point we were skirting the upper edge of the salt marshes, and to the north rich farms stretched along both sides of the river.

After crossing the bridge, we passed alongside the Blackwater Migratory Bird Refuge, a federal project established in 1931. Here many kinds of wild duck are bred in security. Ducks with their wings clipped are used as decoys to attract their wild brothers to the spot.

In another mile or two we came to the main highway to Hooper's Island, and a short diversion here brought us to a modern bridge over the Big Blackwater River. The view to the right and left of the bridge is very pleasing. We were back in the middle of the salt marshes, but here the endless expanse is broken by a number of tiny islands of fast land, each supporting a few pine trees. Each of a different size and shape, the whole collection looks comically like trimmed hats in a milliner's window.

On the way down to Hooper's Island, by turning off to the left on Route 336 and taking the first side road across the marsh to the right, one comes to a little freshly whitewashed wooden house overlooking Honga River which is completely charming. A narrow door and two windows; two big dormers in the steep roof with neat, pointed arches; a huge, freestanding chimney; that is all, but one remembers it. The house is called Lake Cove.

One Henry Lake lived here during the American Revolution; he was a captain in the Dorchester militia. Among other children, he had a handsome daughter, Lavinia, or, as she was known far and wide, Lovey Lake. One day when Lovey was alone in the house, a party of Tory picaroons came up the Honga looking for her father to carry him off to the British ships. While ransacking the house, they tried to remove Lovey's silver shoe buckles, but she resisted so stoutly that they gave up the attempt and, thrusting her into an inner room, locked the door, set fire to the house and decamped. Lovey escaped by a window and, after putting out the fire, ran across the fields to get some men together. The picaroons were still in the neighborhood, and the Americans chased them back to their boat.

Near the house stands one of Dorchester County's greatest curiosities, the old windmill. Up to within recent times, it was still grinding grain; the millstones and the ratchet wheel are still there.

Hooper's Island, as mentioned before, is really three, Upper, Middle and Lower. The sprawling villages which cover them are of much the same character as those of Deal's Island, but much more extensive, for Hooper's Island stretches down between the Honga River and Chesapeake Bay for a good ten miles. It is never more than a half-mile wide, and sometimes only a causeway to carry the road.

The villages, Honga, Fishing Creek and Hoopersville, are comprised of the same newly painted, wooden houses with red roofs, and there are boats, boats everywhere on the river side. Such swarms of waterfowl used to fly over these islands that you will find many of the old houses with bars outside the windows to keep the birds from breaking the glass at night when there are lights within. Applegarth was the name of the village on the lower island. Its inhabitants were tempted away by the high industrial wages paid during the first World War, and they never came back. The bridge was washed out in the great storm of 1933, and has not been rebuilt. Applegarth is a completely deserted village except for a gun club.

The people of Hooper's, too, are like those of Deal's Island, stalwart, friendly, yet with a hint of mockery toward city slickers; very religious, yet at the same time full of the salt of humor. One could fill a book with the stories of the Hooper's Islanders; I shall relate only one anecdote.

On Goose Creek in olden times lived an old chief of the Wiwash (!) tribe who had taken the English name of Billy Rumley and married a white woman. His tribe migrated to other parts, but he chose to remain on Goose Creek. He used to punish his wife by tying her to the lubber-pole in his big chimney and smoking her over a smoldering fire below. This was done, he explained, "to make her sweet." Billy was of a highly procreative disposition, and individuals in the neighborhood with a tinge of copper in their skins are still pointed out as his descendants.

There are many odd misnomers in this part of Dorchester County: for instance, Golden Hill, where there is neither a hill nor any gold; the Hunger River in a land where nobody ever need go hungry; and Blackwater River, which is a kind of yellowish color. There are also Lakesville, Woodlandtown, etc., where no towns ever even started.

CHAPTER 11

The Little Choptank

FROM Hooper's Strait northward, the Eastern Shore shows an entirely different character; except for a little cove here and there, the salt marsh disappears; all is fast land, fantastically contorted by rivers, bays, inlets and creeks. The first wide opening is the Little Choptank River, and that is the crookedest and the raggedest of all. Somebody has likened its shape on the map to that of a writhing octopus.

Between James' Point and Hill's Point at the mouth is a distance of about three miles, and the river widens out within. James' Point is at the end of James' Island, which used to be a long peninsula jutting from the southerly shore. Though a channel washed through long ago, that part of the mainland where James' Island was broken off is still, with Eastern Shore pertinacity, called James' Island too.

Between Hooper's Point and Ragged Point the river narrows down to two miles. Just inside Hooper's Point on the south is Slaughter Creek, a deep, wide inlet extending for several miles. The steamboat used to run in here as far as Taylor's Island, a populous oystering and fishing village like Hooper's Island. The next inlet on this side is Parson's Creek. By following that to its head, it would be an easy portage to the head of the Big Blackwater. No doubt, the Indians went this way. Then comes Woolford's Creek and Madison Bay, formerly Tobacco-stick Bay.

In 1814, a tender from H.M.S. *Dauntless,* under command of a Lieutenant Phipps, came raiding into the Little Choptank and commandeered whatever provisions could be found. They set fire to a schooner in Tobacco-stick Bay. On the way back to their ship, they ran aground off the mouth of Parson's Creek. Here they were attacked by a detachment of the Dorchester militia under Captain Joseph Stewart, who captured the whole party consisting of two officers, seventeen men and one colored woman. A gun captured in this engagement is still preserved on Taylor's Island. They call it Becca Phipps.

It was not often the hard-marching militia were able to get their hands on men-of-warsmen like this. The prisoners were carried to Cambridge to be exhibited in triumph, and afterward to Easton. The two young enemy officers with their good looks and charming manners created a great flutter in the dovecotes of Easton, and one of them, when they were finally exchanged, left a memento behind him in the shape of a little Britisher.

Another raiding party, which got away, cleaned out the smokehouse of Gabriel McNamara and also took one of his slaves. The unkindest cut of all was that the slave snatched up his master's new hat and wore it away when he was taken.

It is the northern shore of the Little Choptank that shows the most fantastic convolutions. One after another, the wide, deep creeks wriggle inland, Brooks' Creek, Hudson Creek, Back Creek, Philipps' Creek, Beckwith's, and Garey's. And the shores of each creek in turn are broken with countless bays, inlets and coves. The banks are low, but well out of reach of the tide, and for the most part lined with beautiful trees; there is no marsh. These intimate, indented, peaceful waterways, clean and deep to the head, have created a country of unique charm. They call for houses, and the houses are there, but not enough of them to be crowded. A man has room to breathe.

About eight miles from its mouth, the Little Choptank divides into two equal branches; Fishing Creek wriggles on

to the east with scores more of points and inlets, while the main stream verges a little to the north.

On Garey's Creek stands Spocot, one of the most picturesque old houses in Dorchester, and usually termed the oldest. Certainly part of it was built soon after the land was patented to Stephen Garey in 1662. The place is farmed today by a descendant of Garey's. The house is a T-shaped frame dwelling with five broad chimneys and no less than thirteen dormer windows. It was once the center of a self-contained community with a shipyard, gristmill, general store, smithy and large slave quarters. A couple of the quaint slave houses have survived. The surrounding trees are fine. One tree on the land, the Indian Council Oak, is said to be more than four hundred years old. In the view from the lawn at Spocot, with the quiet creeks stealing away on two sides, there is nothing grand or magnificent, but it would be very easy to live with.

At the point where Garey's Creek comes to a head near a hamlet called Lloyd's, it is only about half a mile across to LeCompte's Creek, which empties into the Great Choptank. Naturally, it has been proposed to cut a canal here, but now that these waters have such a little traffic to bear, it is not likely that it will ever be carried through.

On little Lee Creek beyond, rises Windmere. While not an ancient house, it enjoys an enchanting view, and has several interesting features. It occupies the site of the original home of the Radcliffe family. The east wing, built on Taylor's Island in 1700 and moved here, is still called Aunt Polly Critchett's House. During the War of 1812, Aunt Polly had one of her slaves row her out into the bay, where she boarded the flagship of the British fleet and demanded and obtained the release of her husband's vessel. Her house still has its original exposed rafters, paneled fireplace, and mantel. On the lawn at Windmere stands a one-room schoolhouse built more than a century ago at Castle Haven by one of the Radcliffes.

Fishing Creek and its tributary, Church Creek, with all their inlets and coves, offer countless more fine sites, and many of them are occupied by old houses. Near the head of Church Creek lies the village to which it gave its name, a small place, ancient and rich in character. There are so many hoary old houses with gambrel roofs and dormer windows that nobody pays any attention to them. The oldest and the quaintest one, with a gable roof, tiny windows, and an immense chimney, is called simply Old House. Records show that it was standing here two hundred and fifty years ago.

The people of Church Creek are very set in their ways, and in the neighboring city of Cambridge they are looked upon as a little "quare." As in other country villages, many of the young men go away to make a living; those of Church Creek always come back as soon as they have raked a few

dollars together. In Church Creek, they say in Cambridge, all a man needs for his living is three hens and a barlow knife. He pawns his knife at the store on Saturday night and redeems it during the week with his eggs. They also say that repairs to the old houses are so unusual that once, when a man was seen walking along with a bundle of shingles and a small bucket of tar, the village council met to inquire into the matter.

It is not a tidy village, but this is less the fault of the old houses than of Sam Jones's store. Unfortunately, since it was Sunday when I was there, I could not enter this remarkable emporium; I had to be satisfied with gazing in the show windows. Some of the panes were broken and casually mended with strips of paper. Each window revealed a great heap of miscellaneous articles, bottles of pop, shoes old and new, extremely secondhand clothing, odd tins of vegetables, and job lots of china and hardware. I could picture the scene inside! An old-timer said that Sam Jones never forgot where anything was, that he had an instinct that always led him direct to the spot.

Under a broken shed roof at one side of the store was piled Sam Jones's stock of secondhand furniture. After having been exposed to wind and weather for some years, the upholstered chairs and sofas had acquired a strange, shredded appearance. The old-timer said there was a piano at the bottom of the heap, but I couldn't make it out. Sam Jones has made money out of his store. It is true he went broke in 1929; that was because he contracted to buy too much land; but now he is doing well again.

Church Creek was founded in the middle of a forest of white oak, and did considerable shipbuilding until the white oak was depleted. One glorious specimen, the Treaty Oak, still mounts guard at the entrance to the village. That tree in itself is worth journeying to see. The church which gives village and creek its name is Old Trinity at the other side of the village. It is believed to have been built before 1680; in the course of improvements, the old high pews and the pulpit with its sounding board have been lost, but still the charm of antiquity envelops the little brick structure.

One of its greatest treasures was a red velvet cushion presented by Good Queen Anne, and said to have been the very cushion on which she kneeled to receive the crown of England. So highly was it regarded by the congregation that once, they say, a visiting church dignitary found it reposing on the altar. He threw it angrily on the ground, crying: "If Queen Anne were here, would you place her on God's altar?" After surviving for nearly two centuries and a half, the red cushion was burned up in a fire which destroyed the house of the parishioner who had it in her care.

The churchyard, with its ancient trees occupying a point of land washed all around by the wide, still creek, is completely satisfying. This is how a churchyard ought to look. Here are the graves of Thomas King Carroll, the former governor of Maryland, and his daughter whose services to the nation were so great and unrequited, Anna Ella Carroll. On her stone is written: "A woman rarely gifted; an able and accomplished writer." In another place, a miller of long ago has the upper and nether stone of his mill to mark his grave. They bear no inscription, and need none.

CHAPTER 12

The Choptank River, Part One

THE Choptank is the longest and best known of Eastern Shore rivers. It is more than a geographical feature, for it draws a spiritual line between the people who dwell to the south of it and those to the north. They are all Americans, of course, all Marylanders, all Eastern Shoremen, but with a difference. Several observers of the scene have called attention to this difference, and have ascribed various reasons for it. Whatever the reasons, it is clear that they go back to the beginning of the white settlement.

I suggest that it is a larger infusion of the spirit of nonconformity that makes the southern Shoremen differ from their northerly neighbors. This results on the credit side in an increased independence; on the debit side, in a greater lawlessness. It will be remembered that the first white settlers on the lower Shore were such men as Stephen Horsey, William Stevens, Ambrose Dixon and George Johnson, Quakers and other nonconformists, who had left their homes in Virginia rather than submit to the rule of the Anglican Church.

In the beginning there were many Quakers north of the Choptank also, but it is curious to note how quickly they fell away from the Society of Friends when they discovered that, according to their ideas, it narrowed their lives. Such people were naturally of the Established Church; they went to church on Sundays and dutifully paid their tithes, but they had no notion of letting religion interfere with their daily lives. The northerners were people who liked to live according to rule, who established an ordered society and a code of manners. On the debit side, they were apt to live *too* well and to squander their substance.

It may be objected, against this theory, that the Tory picaroons—in other words, the upholders of the old regime during the American Revolution—were almost exclusively recruited from the southern counties, but the briefest examination will show that they were not Tories for England's sake, but because it provided opportunities for pillage. They were in rebellion against the dominant party of that day; in other words, nonconformists.

During the eighteenth century the great Calvinist preachers toured the Eastern Shore, first Makemie, the Presbyterian, and his successors, then Francis Asbury, Lorenzo Dow and a host of other Methodists, not forgetting the native product, Joshua Thomas. Such preachers had only a moderate success north of Choptank, but they swept the southern counties, and a great religious awakening took place down there, the effect of which is not yet entirely spent. Such preaching as Joshua Thomas's arouses men's passions; the camp meetings provided a vent. Now that camp meetings have gone out of fashion (except among the colored people), Calvinism is apt to strike in. That, I submit, is why the southern Shoreman, while ordinarily just as good a citizen as his easygoing brother north of Choptank, is nevertheless more liable to startling outbursts of lawlessness.

The lower course of the Great Choptank exhibits the

same broken outlines as the Little Choptank, but of course on a larger scale. Off the mouth of the river lies little Sharp's Island, a spot that has been mentioned in this narrative, and will come into it again. In an early transfer deed the island is stated to have comprised about seven hundred acres. After the winds and tides of two hundred years have worked on it, it now has scarcely seventy acres.

Cooke's Point bounds the mouth of the river on the south. It was called for Sir Andrew Cooke, who took up this land in 1661 and called it Maulden. His son, Ebenezer Cooke, was Maryland's first recognized poet. Since he wrote "Laureate" after his name and had it printed so, it may be that he held some sort of poetical appointment in addition to his official job, which was deputy receiver-general to the Right Honorable Charles, Fifth Lord Baltimore.

Ebenezer's two principal works are *The Sot-Weed Factor,* published in London, 1708, and *Sot-Weed Redivivus,* or *The Planters Looking-Glass,* 1730. Sotweed, of course, was slang for the tobacco plant. They are long rhymed extravaganzas revealing a good deal of humor in describing the misadventures of an English merchant while sojourning in Maryland. Here is a quotation describing dinner at a planter's house:

Wild Fowl and Fish, delicious Meats,
As good as Neptune's doxy eats,
Began our Hospitable treat;
Fat Venison followed in the Rear,
And Turkies wild luxurious Chear:
But what the Feast did most commend,
Was hearty welcome from my Friend.
Thus having made a noble Feast
And eat as well as pamper'd Priest,
Madera strong in flowing Bowls

Fill'd with extream delight our Souls;
Till wearied with a purple Flood
Of generous Wine (the Giant's blood
As Poets feign) away I made,
For some refreshing verdant Shade;
I slumbered long . . .

The point corresponding to Cooke's across the mouth of the Choptank is Blackwalnut Point, at the end of Tilghman's Island. Inside the river opens, firstly, Harris Creek, more than a mile wide at its mouth; secondly, Broad Creek, with innumerable creeks of its own inside; and thirdly, the mouth of the Tred Avon, a considerable river in itself, which will be treated in a separate chapter. This is Talbot County on this side. I pity any school child of Talbot who has to draw a map of its fantastic outline.

There is a pleasant book in which an old-timer describes the Elysian days of his childhood on Harris Creek. He and his brothers wore pinafores to their knees and walked two miles every morning to a red schoolhouse facing the bay. The teacher's name was Absolom Americus Vespucius Christopher Columbus Thompson. Every boy in the family had a gun, and after school hours the mother would issue one charge of powder and shot to each boy. If he brought in game he would get another charge; no game, no more powder and shot that day. It taught them how to shoot.

The greatest wonder in the lives of those boys came in 1860, when the steamship *Great Eastern* came steaming up the bay, an incredible sight. She was of 22,500 tons, 680 feet long, and had accommodations for 1,000 passengers. She could do seventeen knots an hour and she sailed clean away from all the steamers who came down the bay to meet her.

Before 1850 every landowner farmed his own land.

There were no investments but land, and a farmer had no other interests. If he made money he increased his holdings of land. Then corporations began to be formed and farmers speculated in shares. When the Civil War robbed the land of labor, and the old proprietors began to rent their farms to landless men and move to the towns, the old places quickly ran down.

Emancipation did odd things to the colored people. There was one freedman who was fond of marching along the road singing lustily:

> My name's Perry Denby and Bay Side's my station
> Mr. Seth's is my stopping-place; Christ's my salvation!

This man's father was Uncle Perry, the faithful old family coachman, who stayed on after the war. Emancipation made no change in him except for one day in the year, Election Day. Then for twelve hours Uncle Perry had to be called Mr. Denby. Year after year, until he died, he insisted on walking seven miles to the polls, rather than share the carriage with a Democrat—his former owner.

In addition to gunning, the boys' recreations included fishing, fox hunting and tournaments. When they ran the fox to earth, they dug him out with care not to injure him, and popped him into a bag to be saved for the next hunt! Tournaments, of course, were the great occasions of the year. The principal man of the neighborhood acted as marshal of the field, and chose another for herald. The young fellows, dressed up in ribbands and scarves and assuming fancy names such as Knight of Woodland Creek, Knight of Royal Oak, Knight of Probasco, jousted for rings. The winner was privileged to choose and crown the Queen of Love and Beauty.

There was always a band and much flowery speechmaking; the riding was followed by a supper out of doors, and a ball. After the ball the boys would change their clothes and start plowing.

On the south, or Dorchester, side of the river, the next point to Cooke's is Todd's and the next to that Castle Haven,

which, by its bold outlook far across Chesapeake Bay, was predestined to be the site of a great house. A little island lies off the point forming a natural harbor, much appreciated by watermen in a squall. The first to appreciate this site was Anthony LeCompte, a Huguenot refugee and a grand gentleman who, after serving with distinction in the English Army for eleven years, emigrated to Maryland about 1655 and settled first on the Patuxent River of the western shore. According to tradition, three seagoing vessels were required to transport his retainers and his household goods.

Whether he built his house on the point or, as some say, beside LeCompte's Creek which runs behind it, eight hundred acres here were patented to him in 1659. He called it Antonine; later it was known as St. Anthony's. A tradition survives that "Monsieur's" house was of brick with very narrow, small windows set high in the walls as a protection from the Indians; in other words, a veritable castle. Monsieur died in 1673. His descendants in Dorchester are legion.

The present house was built in 1730 by a friend or relation of the LeCompte family. It has been rebuilt, added to, and "improved" so many times that little if anything of the original remains. Since the days of the LeComptes, it seems to have brought bad luck to its owners. Several wealthy families have lavished money on it and gone broke. For a while, it was the summer home of the magnificent Governor Thomas King Carroll, and several generations later, of another magnificent politician, Mark Hanna of Ohio. It was offered to President Herbert Hoover for a summer White House, but he declined it. It was once a fashionable girls' school. Now it is untenanted and forlorn.

Adjoining Castle Haven and looking across wide Le Compte Bay is Pokety Lodge, the great modern estate of the late Walter P. Chrysler. On the other side of LeCompte Bay is Horn's Point, the estate of the late Coleman duPont, but this is an old house. For many years it was the home of a branch of the Goldsborough family, and William L. Goldsborough, a nabob of befo' the war, has left his stamp on it. An officious neighbor once informed him that his Negroes were stealing his corn and selling it in Cambridge on Saturday night.

"Whose Negroes did you say, sir?" asked the towering colonel.

"Yours, sir."

"And whose corn?"

"Yours, sir."

"Very well, sir, than I will trouble you to mind your own business."

On the smaller creeks of the Talbot shore, across the river from Castle Haven, stand many old houses, each once the seat of an important family. This was the place of the first settlement in Talbot County. The whole stretch was part of a huge grant made in 1659 to Edward Lloyd, the first of his name in Maryland, of whom we shall hear more. He called it Hîr Dîr Lloyd, which is said to signify in Welsh, Lloyd's Long Line. Edward Lloyd was one of the leaders of the Puritan rebellion against Lord Baltimore, but he had made his peace with the proprietary and became, even earlier than Colonel Stevens, a highly successful real estate operator on the Eastern Shore.

The first of these inlets is Boone Creek, just around the corner from the Tred Avon River. At its head stands Bonfield, an old seat of the Chamberlaine family. The original house burned in 1927, but that which has replaced it agrees well with the surrounding scene. It is built on a little rise, which, according to tradition, was constructed by slaves who carried the earth up from the creek shore in baskets on their backs. Bonfield is now the home of Hervey Allen, the author of *Anthony Adverse*.

On Island Creek, at the end of a long lane with a magnificent poplar tree filling the vista, is Island Creek House, highly modernized, yet charming still, with its brick ends and corners and clapboarded sides. This was a Martin house, and the graves of the Martins fill the old burial ground close by.

On Chlora's Point, not far away, stands a fine house of the same name, another Chamberlaine homestead. The simple lines of the original building have been somewhat obscured, but the site, among all these lovely sites, stands out in the memory. In front of the house spreads a little creek, or, more properly, a lagoon, protected from the broad river by a sand spit with a narrow opening, thus creating a private harbor for small boats. The original name of the Chamberlaine family was Tankerville, probably an Anglicization of de Tanqueville. The Tankervilles in England had been hereditary chamberlains to the crown since the time of Henry II, and the first of that name to emigrate to America chose to call himself Chamberlaine.

Next door to Chlora's Point, and perhaps a mile away is the Wilderness, which faces the open river, another house of the Martin family. Daniel Martin, twice governor of Maryland in the early nineteenth century, lived here. Incidentally, it has been pointed out that, from a boat out in the middle of the Choptank at this point, the homes of seven governors of Maryland would be in sight. The Wilderness has a ghost. It appears that one of the early Martin proprietors, upon returning home from a ride to inspect his farms, found that his young wife had died suddenly during his absence. The poor woman cannot rest quietly because she was deprived of an opportunity to bid her husband farewell, and any man who sleeps in the chamber where her husband used to lie, will be awakened in the night by the soft kiss of a beautiful young woman.

On Trappe Creek rises Compton, which to one observer is the most satisfying of all these houses. Somehow the patina of age has been preserved unmarred. One lover of the house has compared the rose color of the ancient bricks to the tints in the depths of the Grand Canyon. I remember it as having been whitewashed long ago, and that the flecks of old whitewash mixed with the red of the bricks give it a delicate frosty look; but however you describe it, the color affords a peculiar satisfaction. This house has fallen into the hands of owners who are in love with it and who have taken infinite pains to preserve and restore it. Inside, coat upon coat of paint has been removed to reveal the grain of the woodwork. No innovations are permitted here.

Compton was built in 1760 by John Stevens, who left a tradition of princely hospitality behind him. The story-and-a-half kitchen wing looks older. Samuel Stevens, grandson of John, was an able and colorful figure in early Maryland politics. In 1824 he became the first Democratic governor of that Federalist stronghold. Naturally, in their campaign literature, the Federalists tried to make Samuel Stevens out an ignorant, uncouth figure, but in truth he was a man of excellent breeding and education. The greatest accomplishment of his administration was the enfranchisement of the Jews.

Governor Stevens always took a cow with him on the sailing vessel that carried him to and from Annapolis, and "old Sam Stevens' cow" was the mainstay of the political humor of the day. Another Federalist story was to the effect that when Governor Stevens had to welcome the Marquis de Lafayette to Maryland on his famous return visit in 1824, he greeted him with the question: "General, have you ever been in America before?"

Trappe Creek heads in a lovely deep pool, ringed round with green and having a road coming down at one side to an old steamboat wharf. This is Trappe Landing, a port for the village of Trappe a couple of miles inland. The state highway has bypassed the village, and it seems to sleep in eternal peace. Very suitable to such a spot is the Old Dickinson House, a rambling, gambrel-roofed structure of many dormers and angles.

A mile or two up the road is a hamlet called Hole-in-the-Wall, in spite of efforts to change the name to Hambleton. There are several stories to account for its name. Some say there was once a real hole in the wall where sailors passed in smuggled goods. A more likely explanation is that there was an ordinary here which had been called after a favorite public house in England, Hole-in-the-Wall.

Close by under a grove of fine trees stand the ruins of White Marsh Church, which may have been built as early as 1685. A mutilated parish record shows that it had an acting rector of the Church of England in 1690. The church was abandoned during the Civil War and it finally burned in 1896. In the churchyard many of the broken gravestones lie in heaps. The grave of Robert Morris, father of him who became the financier of the American Revolution, is in good condition.

The oddest story in connection with the old church concerns the wife of the Reverend David Maynadier, an early rector. He was a Huguenot who had fled France when the Edict of Nantes was revoked. It was said of him that he was "a Whig of the first rank and reputed a good liver but a horrid preacher." While he served at White Marsh Church his wife died and was buried in the churchyard. With her was buried a handsome ring that was widely known in the country. The night after she was buried, two strangers opened her grave to steal the ring. As it resisted their efforts to pull it off, they cut off her finger. According to the story, the lady was not dead but in a trance. The shock of losing her finger revived her, and the terrified thieves fled while she climbed out of her coffin, gathered up her shroud, and made her way back to the rectory. There her husband found her lying in a swoon against the door. He carried her in and she survived for several years more.

Returning to the Choptank, on a little creek next to Trappe Creek stands Crosiadore, the ancestral home of the Dickinson family. The name is said to be a corruption of Croix d'Or, but I wonder if it might not have been Crozier d'Or. The little island lying in front of the house was once a peninsula, and it may have been likened by somebody to a bishop's crook.

The first Dickinson was Walter, one of a group of planters from Virginia recruited by Edward Lloyd for his new settlement on the Choptank. At the same time Dickinson bought a large tract in Jones' Creek Neck, Delaware. The family prospered and went on accumulating land in Talbot, Dorchester, Caroline and Queen Anne counties, Maryland, and in Kent County, Delaware. The eldest son of the third generation was Samuel. His first wife, Judith Troth, and two small children were carried off by an epidemic in 1729, and the old graveyard at Crosiadore still bears testimony to that pitiful event.

Samuel Dickinson's oldest son by his second wife, Mary Cadwalader, was the famous John Dickinson of pre-Revolutionary fame. While John was still a child, Samuel moved permanently to his lands in Delaware, leaving Crosiadore to his oldest son, Henry. John Dickinson, therefore, is usually referred to as a son of Delaware, but he was born at Crosiadore.

He studied law at the Middle Temple in London, and afterward practiced in Philadelphia. He had one of the best minds in the colonies. His *Letters from a Pennsylvania Farmer*, as much as any single factor, prepared the people for a rupture with the mother country. Yet, when the Declaration of Independence came before the Continental Congress, of which Dickinson was a member, he would not sign it. At that juncture, he felt that the colonists were moving too fast. But afterward he strove with all his power for the success of the American cause. Already the author of the famous Declaration upon Taking Up Arms, for Congress, he drew up the Articles of Confederation in 1781, and was a member of the Convention of 1787 which framed the Constitution.

The elder branch of the Dickinson family has continued to live at Crosiadore ever since. Having maintained their position throughout the generations, they have altered, enlarged and redecorated the house according to the taste of their own day, and it now bears no resemblance to the original structure except in the steep roof of the main block. But the alterations have been carried out in good taste, and Crosiadore is one of the first houses of the Shore.

About three miles upstream from Crosiadore, the mile-and-a-half Emerson C. Harrington bridge crosses to Cambridge, second city of the Eastern Shore and seat of Dorchester County. Before the bridge, there was a ferry here from time immemorial, and the former inn for the accommodation of travelers still stands on the Talbot shore. Now known as Perry Farm, it was built about 1687.

Dorchester County was organized about 1669. Some of

the old-fashioned people speak of it as "Dorset," which is of course correct, since the word Dorchester refers to a city. Cambridge is a most comfortable-appearing town; everybody seems to be doing pretty well there. It was laid out on the shore of a small, deep, curving creek, which forms an admirable harbor. It has one noble street, High Street, so named in the foundation of the town. Facing it are half a dozen gracious old houses and many more, the homes of later great men, which are not so gracious. After the Civil War the people of the Eastern Shore were no longer willing to take the trouble to build their houses of brick. The wooden houses are big and comfortable enough but sadly lacking in the beauty of the older homes. Town after town on the Shore bears the stamp of the General Grant style of architecture. It is the old trees which save them. At the foot of High Street is a grassy little peninsula extending into the broad river and forming a unique park open to all the winds of heaven, like the deck of a ship.

Christ Church, Episcopal, is the center of Cambridge in the best sense. The parish was one of the original thirty established in 1692 when the Church of England became the established church of Maryland. The present church, the third on the site, is a modern Gothic building of conventional design, but it is distinguished by some fine modern glass. The churchyard is an epitome of the life of Cambridge and Dorchester for two centuries and a half. Its ancient wall of rosy bricks still surrounds it.

The house of my friend the antiquary, whom I have mentioned, looks over the wall, and the churchyard is one of the favorite objects of his research. He has on several occasions recovered the gravestones of old worthies of Dorchester from lost family burial grounds, and has brought them here.

He has written a brochure which lists the name of every person known to be buried here. The names include three former governors of Maryland—to which two more will someday be added—and a host of generals, judges and other men honored by their townsfolk. Soldiers of the Revolution and of the War of 1812 rest here, and wearers of the Blue and of the Gray lie side by side.

The oldest building in Cambridge is the large wooden mansion called The Point, which stands where creek and river meet. The main part was erected in 1706-1710 by Colonel John Kirk, who was Lord Baltimore's land agent for Dorchester. The house is now a sad ruin, the grounds a jungle. It is difficult to understand why the prosperous little city has not secured this perfect site as a park for its people, and preserved the old house as a memento of its past.

In the western environs of Cambridge, two fine old houses face the river, the first, Glasgow, once the home of William Vans Murray, who served the infant republic in The Hague and Paris; the second, Hambrook, on a noble point ending in a hook of sand, which encloses a good harbor. Ill-considered improvements have defaced but have not succeeded in destroying the dignity of this fine house.

CHAPTER 13

The Choptank River, Part Two

IN Cambridge I engaged a motor fishing boat to view the upper Choptank, and early one Sunday in May we set out from the yacht basin with lunch basket and thermos jug. Rain threatened and we watched the sky anxiously, for there was no shelter aboard. The shores were revealed through a light mist in successively deepening gray planes like a Japanese print. The sun glinted through thin places in the cloud ceiling, and finally broke through gloriously. Before the day was out, we would have been glad of a few clouds.

In order that we might not miss anything of interest alongshore, we decided to hug the Dorchester bank going up, and come back on the Talbot side. We passed the town with its crowded creek, and soon afterward ducked under the long bridge. A humane State Roads Commission permits fishing from this bridge, and already the patient anglers were lined up along the rail. It is a godsend for queasy fishermen (or fisherwomen) who don't enjoy going out in small boats. The captain said they used to drive all the way from Pennsylvania.

There was a strong south wind in our faces, and little waves were slapping the starboard bow. It was the time of locust blooming, and the spicy fragrance came off the shore in gusts. Upon putting the town behind us, we settled back to enjoy the combination of hot sun and cooling wind and the changing prospects of the immense river. It was not long before we became pleasantly drugged with ozone. An immense effort was required to rouse oneself to make notes.

The creeks that opened in the Dorchester shore along here were small. Each had a house mounting guard over it. The first was Shoal Creek; the tall, whitewashed brick house on its bank is said to have been one of Patty Cannon's way stations. It was built about 1750 by Joseph Ennals, and passed in the early nineteenth century to that Charles Goldsborough who was a governor of Maryland, and a splendid host.

The next is Hurst Creek. Here the old house called Eldon has been destroyed by fire, but the box garden remains intact, one of the most extensive and beautiful on the Eastern Shore. The box gave off a delicious scent in the hot sun. The next creek is White Hall, with a characteristic eighteenth century mansion of the same name beside it, standing out boldly in a fresh coat of white paint. After rounding long, low Oystershell Point backed by pines, the next narrow opening was that of Indian Creek, which spreads out to the right and left inside.

This name brought to mind the unhappy Choptank Indians whose story is much the same as that of the Nanticokes. Captain Claiborne traded with them in this river before the Marylanders came, and reported them dangerous and tricky. But in later years they gave the proprietary government little trouble—too little for their own good.

The great George Fox, founder of the Society of Friends, stopped here in 1672 and addressed a meeting of the Choptank Indians. He says in his *Journal:* "To give them their due they sate very grave and sober and were all very attentive, beyond many that are called Christians." Fox had an interpreter to explain his doctrines to the Indians. "We had a very good Meeting with them," he goes on, "and a very good Service it was, for it gave them a good Esteem of Truth and Friends, Blessed be the Lord!"

When assured of the friendship of the Choptanks, the

proprietary officials did what they could to protect these gentle allies from the neighboring tribes. The rulers of the Assateagues and the Nanticokes were forced to sign agreements setting forth that if any of their subjects killed a Choptank "it would be esteemed as great an offense as killing an Englishman."

The most dangerous enemies of the Choptanks were the Senecas, a tribe of the Five Nations or Iroquois far to the north. One year great uneasiness was caused on the Eastern Shore by the appearance of small parties of the Senecas. Tequassino, king of the Choptanks, sent word to St. Mary's that "not long since there came down tenn Senecas as spies and have taken a view of the townes of all the Eastern Shore Indians." Tequassino believed that the Senecas, instigated by the Delaware Indians, were preparing to fall on the Choptanks and their neighbors. A troop of militia was called out and sent to range through the country, but there is no evidence that they found any Senecas. Soon afterward, the proprietary government dealt effectively with this danger by sending a commission to Abany to make a treaty with the Five Nations.

The original reserve for the Choptanks included all the land along this shore from Cambridge eastward. From time to time it was narrowed down until at last they were limited to a strip barely three miles wide between Indian Creek and Secretary, or Warwick, Creek above. And even for this pitiful allotment they, the original proprietors of all the land, were forced to pay a nominal rent at St. Marys.

There was no bloodshed but continual quarreling. The Indians complained that they were obliged to build fences to protect their crops from the roving cattle and hogs of the white men, and that the owners of the stock then destroyed the fences. The white men accused the Indians of shooting their stock. There was some truth in this, for it was difficult to teach the Indians that cattle and hogs were not just other kinds of game. The sad part is that, while the Indians were frequently punished for shooting the white men's beasts, there is no record that a white man was ever punished for destroying an Indian's fences or crops.

By the end of the eighteenth century there were but four Choptank Indians left on the river which bears their name. They were confined to the use of eighty acres of land, which they finally exchanged for small annuities. That is the end of their story.

Upon leaving Cambridge, our course upriver had been to the southeast. Gradually we had been rounding the outside of an immense bend until now we were heading north and the wind was on our backs. Above the mouth of Indian Creek I knew there were two fine old houses on the shore, but we looked for them in vain. They were completely hidden among their trees. The first is Vue de Leau, a rambling structure dating from many periods. Near-by is an Indian mound which has yielded much ethnological data to excavators from the Smithsonian Institution. These experts are able to tell from the examination of a man's bones what he died of centuries before.

The other house is Goose Creek Farm, a tall brick building of 1750 with an unusual floor plan. An indenture on file in the Cambridge courthouse sets forth that the land on which it stands was purchased from the Choptank Indians in 1693 by Frances Taylor, wife of Thomas Taylor. The document bears the totem marks of Chief Hachwop, his queen and five of his "greate men."

Secretary Creek, now called Warwick River, is navigable for a mile or so to the village of Secretary, a typical faded, dilapidated, bowery village of the Shore. What a background such a village would supply for a motion picture of rural scenes! No scene painted could reproduce its down-at-the-heel and completely charming aspect. It asks to be photographed.

Creek and village were named for Henry Sewall, who was secretary of the province under Charles Calvert, governor of Maryland and eventually third Lord Baltimore. Sewall was granted two thousand acres here in 1661, and the house he built about that time is still standing—or a part of it. As Sewall soon passed out of the picture, it has always been known as My Lady Sewall's Manor. What remains is a small brick house in the earliest style; it is in a sad state of neglect, but like all the houses of its era, is irresistibly charming.

After Sewall died, Jane Sewall, his widow, married Charles Calvert and passed to larger scenes. They met on shipboard coming from England. Her son, Major Nicholas Sewall, continued to live here, and in 1720 or thereabouts he richly embellished his mother's house with carved paneling. That is now to be seen in the Brooklyn Museum of Art. Major Sewall was appointed to the Governor's Council and played an important part in provincial affairs. It was he, by the way, who was sent to search for the Seneca Indians with a troop of horse, but failed to find any.

Above Warwick River the shores of the main stream begin to grow marshy on the inside of each bend. We passed the mouth of Cabin Creek, a fine wide stream winding inland until it was lost in the haze. On each of the two river points stood an old farmhouse, making an effective composition with its trees. Occasionally we had to make a detour far out in the river to round the end of a pound net hanging from its long row of poles. At the end of each net hung a lantern and a little board with the name of the owner crookedly painted on it: Bill Wheatley, Jake Sanders, etc. On the poles around the trap sat the gulls, gorged and unwilling to take to wing. They believed, no doubt, that the fish trap had been established for them.

The Choptank swings sharply back to the east at a point where big Hunting Creek comes in from the west. The effect is of two streams colliding head on; Hunting Creek, winding away in hairpin curves between its marshy shores, would be a river in any other country. It would make six of the little streams that pass for rivers in England. The pleasant village of Choptank stands at the joining of the rivers, looking straight down the united stream. Choptank serves as a port for the town of Preston not far away.

In Preston there is a newspaper, the *News*, which prints every week a contribution from my friend the riverman, he who showed me the Transquaking River. He signs his articles "Minnie Wheeler's Boy-Friend." The *Minnie Wheeler* was a quaint steamboat which plied up and down the Choptank during the eighties and nineties, and my friend served on her as a youth in various capacities from deck boy to mate. One day they were run down and sunk in the Patapsco by an Old Bay liner. A suit followed to fix responsibility for the accident, and Captain Perry of the *Minnie Wheeler* was put on the stand. The slick lawyer for the Old Bay Line asked him if he kept a log, and when the captain was forced to admit that he did not, the lawyer had him dead to rights. "A menace to navigation!" he called him—and other things. So the *Minnie Wheeler* lost her case.

As they left the courthouse, Captain Caleb Wheeler, the owner of the line, handed his boy half a dollar and, with picturesque profanity, told him to go buy an exercise book and keep one of them logs hereafter. "And by the power of the Holy Ghost and All Angels, let me see you put down

MINNIE WHEELER

everything that happens." One exercise book succeeded another until, after eight years, when the steamboat line sold out to a railroad, there was a great pile of them. It is these logbooks which supply the matter for Minnie Wheeler's Boy-Friend's contributions to the Preston *News*. I shall quote from them.

Hunting Creek marks the northern boundary of Dorchester and beyond it we had Caroline County on our right. The river narrows above its big tributary, though it still averages half a mile in width. We cut across from one marshy point to another, with a washed bank on the outside of each bend, and occasionally a glimpse of an ancient house under its trees. I remember a tall, eighteenth century, wooden house beside Skeleton Creek that looked as if it had never been painted in all its two hundred years. We passed and saluted the *Mamie Doolittle*, the only power vessel we saw all day.

The river finally straightens out to the north again, and we saw Dover Bridge in the distance. This reach is famous for its fishing, and I saw a method that was new to me. A gill net about seventy-five feet long was paid out from a small boat in midstream. Weighted at the bottom and buoyed at the top to keep it perpendicular, it was allowed to float away with the tide. After a while the men in the boat picked up an end of it and, rowing around, took in the other end. It was then drawn into the boat like a purse with its finny spoils.

A couple of miles below the bridge on the Caroline side, stands Franzier's Flats House, but I missed it. It is described as one of the finest formal Georgian houses on the Eastern Shore. Captain William Frazier, who built it, served throughout the Revolution but is better known as a leader of Methodism in this region. The famous Francis Asbury, circuit-riding preacher and afterward first bishop, mentions many visits to this house in his *Journal*. The second-story front room, where he held his meetings, is still called the "church room." This house was once surrounded by a moat.

Above the bridge, the river tends to the northeastward. The next spot of interest is Gilpin's Point, opposite the mouth of Tuckahoe Creek, Choptank's biggest tributary. Tuckahoe forms the boundary of Talbot County, and above it both shores of the river are in Caroline. Colonel William Richardson lived at Gilpin's Point. He was Caroline County's Revolutionary hero. All that remains of his extensive establishment are some bits of an old coral wall (the coral was brought from the West Indies as ballast in Richardson's ships), an ancient dairy, and the colonel's fast-crumbling tomb. A colonel first of the Maryland Flying Camp and later of the Fifth Regiment of the Maryland Line, Richardson fought through all the early campaigns. In 1781, while on a mission to France, he and Dr. William Hindman were captured by the English. While prisoners in England, they helped the famous Joshua Barney to escape from Mill Prison. When the British threatened Philadelphia, Colonel Richardson was delegated to move the Continental treasury to Baltimore. He died in 1825, full of years and honors, treasurer of the Eastern Shore and a county judge of Caroline.

Above the mouth of Tuckahoe, the much narrower river takes on an intimate aspect that was lacking below. One would have liked to drift along here, watching the beautiful wooded shores reflected in the glassy surface of the water and looking into the winding creeks, but the day was half gone and we still had far to go. However, we took time to land at a ruined wharf which bears the strange name of the

Two Johns. It commemorates a quaint story of the recent past.

John Stewart and John Crossey were two vaudeville actors who had gravitated together as a team because they looked as much alike as twins. They called their act "The Two Johns"; their combined weight is said to have been seven hundred pounds; in their day they were almost as famous as that other team of Weber and Fields. In order to call attention to their absurd likeness, they scrambled their names thus: John Stewart Crossey and John Crossey Stewart.

How they came to discover Caroline, most remote and unsophisticated of Eastern Shore counties, nobody can explain, but discover it they did, and during the 1880's, at the height of their prosperity, they bought a farm here on the loveliest part of the Choptank River and christened it the Two Johns. They "improved" the plain old Caroline farmhouse in accordance with the flamboyant taste of the day, and built a wharf which they leased to the steamboat company in order to assure communication with the outside world. They also had a pavilion at the water's edge for dancing and theatrical performances.

All summer, while the theaters were closed, the Two Johns held high revel beside the Choptank. Swarms of their friends from the great world came and went by steamboat. Among their associates were Paul Dresser, author of "The Banks of the Wabash," Louise Dresser, his sister, and the famous Ada Kline. The good people of Caroline were amazed by the goings-on at the Two Johns; not understanding it at all, they naturally thought the worst. In order to win their good will, the Two Johns chartered a steamboat one Sunday and invited the whole town of Denton to come to one of their shows. I have not been able to find anybody who attended that show, but I am sure a good time was had by all.

Minnie Wheeler's Boy-Friend tells me that the crew of the steamboat were all agog at the pretty actresses who went and came on the river. They were forced to alter some of their ideas about actresses, these were so ladylike. Of Miss Kline they were somewhat in awe. After all these years, the old riverman speaks of "her nice discernment and delicate skill" in dealing with people. She had a girl friend whose name the boys never learned, who used to stand on the bank and wave to the *Minnie Wheeler*. Captain Perry always brought her as close to the shore as he could. They used to speak of this charming lady as "Captain Perry's girl," "but," said my friend, "she was tactful enough to make each man aboard feel that she was his girl."

After a few years the Two Johns, like all such jolly Bohemians, went broke and disappeared from these scenes, leaving only the memory of scarlet threads in the sober texture of Caroline life.

We climbed the bank to see what their house was like. It was perfect. On the front of the uncompromising old Caroline farmhouse they had built a dizzy façade, like an extravaganza of 1885, with its bay windows, fancy porches, gingerbread work, and an absurd little wooden tower topping all. This structure is already fast going to pieces; only the back part, the original farmhouse, is habitable. There is something touching in the decay of such a gimcrack toy. One hears echoes of the laughter that sounded within those broken walls. I picked my way through the fallen plaster of the rooms. When I tried to push open a precariously hung door, it fell on me. I failed to find even the smallest memento of the vanished players.

There was no vestige of the roundhouse or pavilion that had been described to me as standing on the water's edge, and I don't think it ever existed. Still there, is a big rectangular building that may have been built for a mill or a warehouse, and this I believe is where they danced and put on their shows. The Two Johns are gone, but they have left their name on the maps of Caroline County. Out on the main highway there is a sign at a crossroads: "The Two Johns 2 Miles."

Potter Hall stands on a low grassy rise sloping to the river's edge a mile above. There is another decaying wharf here. The kitchen wing of the foursquare brick house was built in 1730 by Captain Zabdiel Potter, whose name is on the brass door knocker. Zeb Potter was a notable mariner whose ships sailed from the edge of his front lawn to all the seven seas. In 1760 he sailed away, never to return. The main block of the house was built in 1808 by his grandson, William Potter, whose name is on *his* brass knocker. William became a brigadier general in the Maryland militia and was three times a member of the Governor's Council.

After five more enchanting miles of the narrow river, quiet and lonely up here except for a little group of buildings at Pealiquor Landing, we came to the town of Denton, county seat of Caroline. This was where the steamboats turned around and went back, though Greensboro, ten miles higher up, was known as Head of Choptank or Choptank Bridge. This last ten miles I am sure is the most beautiful of all, but our gasoline was running low and it was doubtful if we could obtain a fresh supply on Sunday.

Denton has a fine site on high ground above the river. It was originally called Edenton after the last royal governor of Maryland; his wife was the sixth Lord Baltimore's sister. When Governor Eden was sent home, the townspeople dropped the initial E. This is the place I referred to as the most characteristic town on the Eastern Shore. There has been but little influx of new blood here. Caroline, though the Choptank River flows right through it, is called the inland county of the Shore because no part of it touches broad

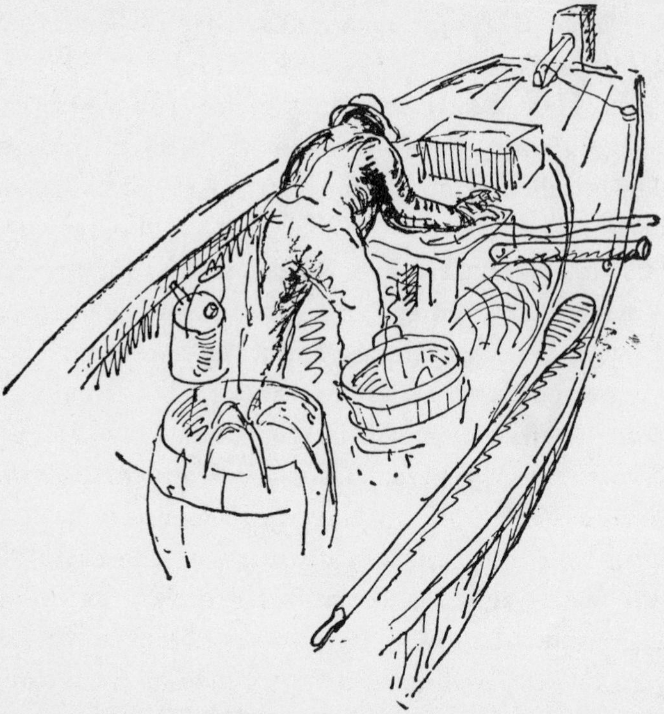

water. People from outside are always looking for places on broad water, so Caroline gets almost none of them. Caroline looks down with mingled scorn and envy on the station-wagon set of its neighbor Talbot.

Denton, like the other towns, has had disastrous fires, and little of the past survives except the Old Brick Hotel, which was doing business as early as 1775. In that year the

County Court ruled that "the tavern keeper maintain good rules and order and do not suffer loose, idle or disorderly persons to tipple, game or commit any disorders or other irregularities in his ordinary." Across the road stands the early Victorian courthouse in its green square, old enough now to have acquired a pleasing quaintness. A great illuminated clock in its tower gives Courthouse Square quite a metropolitan appearance at night. The streets of Denton present almost uninterrupted tunnels of green, lined with the big, comfortable, white-painted houses that are associated with all old American villages. You get glimpses of spacious back yards with old-fashioned shrubbery, well designed for games of hide-and-seek.

Denton, even more than Princess Anne, has an intense concentration upon local affairs. Politics is a man's meat there; I mean county politics. Life is anything but dull, because the town is nearly always furiously agitated by some local issue, such as the choice of a site for a new post office, or the appointment of a deputy county clerk. The way of a Republican is hard in Caroline, though they do exist there, and sometimes even slip into office when the fight among the Democratic factions becomes suicidal in its bitterness. To sum up, in Denton the spirit of the Eastern Shore with all its faults and all its charms flourishes in perfection.

On the way back, we found the mouth of Tuckahoe Creek so much obstructed with the weed from which it takes its name as to seem not much more than a ditch, though its source is far up in Delaware and it is navigable for good-sized vessels as high up as Wayman's Landing, the port for Hillsboro. The *Minnie Wheeler* used to run up to Wayman's, and what a pretty trip it must have been! The Tuckahoe winds like a snake.

"Captain Perry," said a young lady passenger of long years ago, "what makes the Tuckahoe so crooked?"

"Well, miss," was the answer, "reckon it's to show off our new steamboat."

In Tuckahoe Neck is the Daffin, or Thawley, House, where Charles Dickinson and Andrew Jackson met for the first time on the occasion of a house party. Mrs. Daffin was Dickinson's sister. Jackson is said to have persuaded Dickinson to emigrate to the West. In 1806 the two men quarreled over a horse race, and after long, ugly recriminations, met in a duel on the banks of the Red River in Kentucky. Dickinson shot first; Jackson, though wounded, then took deliberate aim and shot his adversary dead. He was much criticized by Dickinson's friends, and by his own enemies, but impartial men held that he was justified.

At a hamlet called Marydel, at the head of Tuckahoe, there was another duel fought in 1877 that caused a terrific noise at the time on account of the social prominence of the adversaries. James Gordon Bennett, editor and proprietor of the New York *Herald*, had been engaged to Miss May of Baltimore. Bennett, being accused of misbehavior in the May home, was horsewhipped by the young lady's brother, Fred May, one of the most famous viveurs of his day. Later the two met with pistols at Marydel. Bennett lost a lock of hair. There was no further damage, but, as a result of the affair, Bennett exiled himself to Paris for the rest of his life, whence he conducted his newspaper by cable.

Below Tuckahoe we had Talbot County on our right. The next considerable opening was that of another King's Creek, with Kingston Landing beside it and a half dozen old houses. This was one of the points where Lord Baltimore desired to found a town in 1683, but it never grew. Over the treetops we could see the "cupalow" of a great house of post-Civil War design, already disintegrating. It looked interesting, but there was not time to investigate.

A mile above Dover bridge, Troth's Fortune came into view, a delightful little hip-roofed dwelling of 1676, with a curious projection from one side which contains the stairway. Architects call it a stair tower. In 1682 William Troth, the builder, was attacked here by a Choptank Indian called Poh Poh Caquis. The report of the trial that followed has survived.

It was conducted by Colonels Philemon Lloyd and Henry Coursey (of whom we shall hear further), and all the "greate men" of the Indians were summoned to attend. One John Shepard was a witness. He described how he admitted Poh Poh Caquis to warm himself by the fire in Troth's house. By and by, Troth came home and Thomas told him Poh Poh Caquis had said there were two hundred "Sinniquois" [Senecas] near by. "Pish!" said Troth, "dost thou believe him what he talks of, for he Lyes!"

Troth takes up the tale. "The Indian," he said, "then fell ahollowing. Thomas Bussey comes to the doore and as I turned to speak to the said Thomas, the Indian made ready his gunn. I tried to take it, she went off, and with the bending of my body to gett hold of the said gunn, the shott mist me. Poh Poh Caquis took his Tomahawk and followed me 8 yards. I called for my gunn and he ran, and when he was about thirty yards from me I discharged my gunn at his &c."

In his own defense the prisoner acknowledged that he was drunk, otherwise he would not have shot at William Troth or have done any mischief.

A discussion of old grievances on both sides followed. The commissioners ruled that they must be forgotten. Poh

Poh Caquis deserved death, they said, but they let him off with twenty lashes. Wewoquap, a fellow Indian, administered the lashes on the spot. King Ababco and King Tequassino then offered to pledge their words for Poh Poh Caquis's future good behavior. Would they lock him up? asked the commissioners. They didn't see how they could do that, so Poh Poh Caquis was ordered "banished into some remote part beyond the sea." Rather a hard sentence, since nobody seems to have been hurt but Poh Poh Caquis "in his &c." However, he was not sent out of the country.

At the Talbot end of Dover Bridge, the ancient ferry-house is still standing. It is sad to see it disintegrating, because it represents an early type of wooden house of which, so far as I know, there is no other example surviving on the Shore. From the front of the steep roof projects an upper chamber built out over a porch below. This structure is balanced by a kitchen wing behind, so that the house is really built in the form of a cross. It has another amusing feature. Though the kitchen is attached to the main building, there is no door between! All the food had to be carried out into the yard and back into the dining room, until in recent years it occurred to somebody to build a little penthouse, linking the two rooms.

About three miles below the bridge, on a fine site on a sweeping bend of the broad river, once stood the town of Dover, a real town with dwellings, warehouses and wharves. Seagoing ships used to come up here and lie at the wharves long enough for the fresh water to kill the barnacles on their bottoms. In 1778 the Maryland legislature made Dover the seat of Talbot County and authorized the building of a courthouse here, but nothing came of it. Easton got the courthouse. Now not a stick or a stone survives of Dover.

Soon afterward, we passed what was left of Lloyd's Landing, with the mouth of Miles' Creek winding through a marsh beyond. Near the shore of this creek, but out of sight of the river, stands Saulsbury House, another one of the quaint structures in Talbot. This is a brick house supposed to date from about 1663. The builder had the original notion of placing his gambrel roof from end to end of his house instead of across it. Thus the roof soars high enough in the air to give him a third story, and the chimney rises yet higher. This house preserves the legend of one Jesse Cryer, a hermit who was living here in 1871. He made himself a pair of wings and attempted to fly from the roof of an outhouse. Since his death is not recorded, it may be presumed that he lived to make other inventions.

The question of gasoline on this unfrequented river was momentarily becoming more serious. We were now reduced to a couple of inches in the bottom of the tank, and nearly twenty miles to go! It was with great relief that we saw the village of Choptank looming around a bend. Upon tying up at the basin of the Preston Yacht Club, we found that our captain had no can; however, he was fortunate enough to obtain the loan of one from a glittering yacht tied up near-by. We watched him disappearing along the village road in no little anxiety. However, he proved to be a man of resource. In due time he hove into view weighed down by a full can. I asked no questions.

Back along the Talbot shore we chugged happily onward. Rounding Jamaica Point I was intrigued by a tall, rather splendid old house, rosy against its green background. It was exactly the right sort of house to find on that bold point. The captain could not tell me its name or history, so on the following day I drove back by car to have a look at it.

It bears the same name as its site, Jamaica Point. It was built by a Hughlett about the time of the Revolution and has not been changed at all. A nobly proportioned house of three stories and attic, with a big service wing, it contains fourteen rooms. A graceful stairway winds up for three flights to the attic; the rest of the interior woodwork and the plaster moldings are simple and fine. Each of the doors leading to the big twin parlors has a little circle of glass let in at eye level. An interesting feature is a big, square, enclosed porch occupying the angle between main block and kitchen wing. Paved with brick laid on edge in a herringbone pattern, five generations of farmers have found this sheltered space indispensable in performing their chores.

On the river we passed Goose Point and long Chancellor's Point, which marks the abrupt change of the river's course from south to west. Chancellor's Point got its name from Philip Calvert, brother of his lordship and chancellor of the province, who received a large grant here but never built a house.

Then back across the river and under the long bridge, where the same fishermen were still lined up at the rail—or others indistinguishable from them—and so to a landing.

CHAPTER 14

The Town of Oxford

UPON rounding Benoni Point in the estuary of the Choptank and heading north into the Tred Avon River, the village of Oxford lies upon one's right. Among the countless fine sites for a town in the neighborhood, this one is pre-eminent. Our forefathers had an unerring eye for a site. Oxford is built on a peninsula about a mile long, which presents its long side to broad water and has an irregular creek stealing behind it deep enough to float the seagoing ships of a former day. In that harbor, ships could anchor within twenty yards of the beach.

There is nothing in the present aspect of the village to suggest its age and its former importance except the magnificence of the trees that line its two principal streets. Morris Street, called after the town's greatest citizen, runs the length of the peninsula, and at the north end the Strand branches off, facing the upper reach of the Tred Avon. All the old houses have disappeared; the most ancient survival in Oxford is a grapevine planted nearly a hundred and fifty years ago and still bearing. In its palmy days, it is said to have produced twenty-four thousand bunches of grapes in a single year. The figure sounds romantic.

The first mention of the place is in 1658, when the ship

Golden Fortune, Captain Samuel Tilghman, loaded tobacco here. Lord Baltimore created Captain Tilghman the first admiral of Maryland to "use and Enjoy the powers, dignities, Privileges, benefits and Immunityes of right due and belonging to him as Admirall." Captain Tilghman was granted a thousand acres at the head of Tred Avon that he called Tilghman's Fortune, but he never settled there. It was another Tilghman who founded the great family of that name on the Eastern Shore.

Oxford was one of the thirty towns ordained by Lord Baltimore in 1683 which really got started. It was laid out in the following year and a number of lots sold. Owing to the Protestant revolution and the accession of William and Mary, which ousted Lord Baltimore from the government of the province, it all had to be done over ten years later. Oxford was then christened Williamstadt after the king. Williamstadt and Annapolis were created towns and ports by the same act of the legislature. They were the only ports of entry in the province. In spite of the act, the name Oxford persisted, and Williamstadt was soon dropped. For many years after that, Oxford and Annapolis grew and prospered equally.

One of the firms of London merchants to establish a "factory" at Oxford was Foster, Cunliffe and Company. A factory in those days was a warehouse, a center for trade. About 1738 this firm sent out Robert Morris to be their chief factor at Oxford. He left his son, that other Robert Morris who was to play so great a part in the American Revolution, an infant of three, in London. Robert Morris the elder was a man of humble birth and scant education. His father was a sailor, his own trade that of nailmaker. But by sheer power of personality in twelve short years he made himself one of the greatest figures in Maryland.

This was the time of the flowering of Oxford, when private carriages were introduced and the planters and their wives began to vie with London in the magnificence of their dress and their household appointments. Horse racing was introduced and the "Comedians from Virginia" gave at least one season of performances at Oxford. When the governor and his lady came over from Annapolis to attend the races, the summit of the social season was reached.

Soon there were eight firms of British merchants established at Oxford, of which Foster, Cunliffe and Company was the chief, besides an equal number of provincial firms, of whom one at least, Samuel Chamberlaine and Company, was on an equal footing with the Britishers. Many of these merchants had their ships built at Skillington's yard up the river. There were other shipyards, too, all of whom were among Mr. Morris's most profitable customers. There were said to be more than two hundred ships trading to Oxford. Captain Jeremiah Banning, who kept a diary, writes of that time:

> The storekeepers and other retailers both on the western and the eastern side of the Chesapeake, repaired there to lay in their supplies. Oxford streets and Strand were covered with busy crowds ushering in commerce from almost every quarter of the globe. . . . Seven or eight large ships at the same time were frequently seen at Oxford, delivering goods and completing their lading; nor was it uncommon to despatch a ship with 500 hogsheads of tobacco within twelve days of its arrival.

Tobacco was the principal article of export; then skins, wheat, pork and lumber. In return, Cunliffe's brought everything the Marylanders could be induced to buy.

Robert Morris was at the head and front of all this. He made Cunliffe's the greatest factory in Maryland. He was also a partner in other stores and factories at Cambridge and at Dover on the Choptank, at the Head of Wye, and at a place called Townside on the Chester River. It is doubtful if the Messrs. Cunliffe were informed of all these enterprises of their factor, but in any case they had no reason to complain of the returns that Morris made on their investment.

He instituted two important reforms in the province. With the passage of time the planters had become careless and in some cases downright dishonest in packing their tobacco. Failing in his attempt to get a law providing for government inspection of tobacco, Morris instituted a system of inspection on his own account, and the other buyers quickly followed suit. The inspectors they hired were called "receivers," and it was their duty to view the growing tobacco and view it again after it was cured. They rejected about one-third of the crop. That Morris was able to carry through such a reform in the face of the powerful planters is eloquent testimony to his force of character.

His second reform, the introduction of a government currency, was made necessary by his first. Heretofore, tobacco was the currency of Maryland; everything was reckoned in pounds of tobacco. As both the price and the quality of tobacco were subject to the widest fluctuations, there could hardly have been a more unsatisfactory medium of exchange. Finally, when the planters undertook to pay their debts with tobacco that had been rejected by the receivers, it brought matters to a crisis, and money, as we know it, was introduced.

In addition to being a shrewd merchant who made money for his employers and for himself, Morris became one of the first gentlemen in a community of gentlemen. His natural qualities completely overcame the handicaps of his humble birth and lack of education. Jeremiah Banning says: "As companion and bon vivant, he was incomparable. . . . He was a steady, sincere and warm friend where he made professions, and had a hand ever open and ready to relieve real distress. At repartee he bore down all before him."

Captain Banning was not blind to his faults, either. He goes on: "His greatest foibles were that of a haughty and overbearing carriage, perhaps a too vindictive spirit, and to this may be added an extreme severity to his servants—and which indeed might have been reckoned the greatest reflection on the times, for it was not uncommon, when people of the first class met together at each other's houses, to hear them boast of the new invented ways of whipping and punishing negroes and servants; and I am sorry to say that the ladies would too often mingle in the conversation and seem to enjoy it."

To Robert Morris in 1742, Messrs. Cunliffe sent out young Henry Callister as an assistant. Callister was wellborn, well-educated, and of an extremely lively and sociable disposition. He had a weakness for both the bottle and the girls. His relations with Morris were somewhat troubled in the beginning, which is not surprising, but before Morris died, he had won Callister's respect and even his affection.

Callister was a diverting correspondent, and he kept copies of the letters he wrote. It is to this source that we owe most of our information about the great days of Oxford. In his first letter home, he draws an unflattering picture of Maryland.

> The country being altogether wild and savage . . . an immense forest full of vermin of various sorts and sizes. European merchants have found it to their Interest to introduce new broods of

vermin which they keep the country supplied with, viz. Cats, Dogs, Negroes and Convicts.

> Our Fires are Wood, our Houses as good,
> Our diet is sawng and homine;
> Drinke juice of the Apple, Tobacco's our Staple
> Gloria tibi Domine.

Cunliffe's, naturally, trafficked in Negro slaves; that was no reproach in 1740. They also dealt in convicts and in indentured servants—or redemptioners, as they were sometimes called. The Marylanders were very averse to the importation of convicts. Upon arrival they were sold for the term to which they had been sentenced. It was difficult to find buyers, and the traffic was never very great. True, in 1747 the ship *Johnston* arrived at Oxford with a cargo of Scots rebels taken at the battle of Culloden; but the only crime of these men was in being on the wrong side in politics, and they were eagerly bought up at Oxford and Annapolis.

The business of importing and selling indentured servants continued up to the Revolution and even later. These men and women were in thrall only for the value of their passage money, which in the early days used to average £6. Their lot was a hard one, for they were scandalously ill-fed and ill-lodged aboard ship. They were usually sold upon arrival for a five-year term, and the profit would be great on a useful man such as a carpenter, blacksmith or tailor. Children were sold for a longer term, that they might be capable of caring for themselves when freed.

Sick, worthless or rebellious servants were likely to be left on the captain's hands. Sometimes the captain would take the leftovers on tour in the effort to sell them, but more often he would sell them off cheap to a speculator, who would carry them from tavern to tavern in a search for buyers. A favorite story in Maryland which crops up everywhere is that of the smart redemptioner who, at the end of such a journey, being the last one left, made his master drunk in an inn and traded him to the landlord in exchange for a good horse.

At the expiration of the servant's term, his master under the law had to furnish him with tools, clothing and corn to help him set up for himself. He received fifty acres of land from his lordship, and thereafter enjoyed all the privileges of a freeman. No stigma was attached to such a condition of servitude. Several of the proudest families in Maryland are descended from such a one.

The agreement or indenture was made out in duplicate, one for the master, one for the servant. The two sheets were then placed together, and a jagged piece (or indent) torn out of the margin. The document could then be proved in court only when the two torn places fitted exactly. This was the origin of the term "indentured," or, as it is sometimes written, indented servants.

When a ship arrived with servants to sell, a gun was fired to bring down the planters. This scene might take place in any river on the Eastern Shore, but every ship trading there had to call first at Oxford to enter her cargo at the custom-house. She might have a hundred prisoners to dispose of—prisoners they were, until they had worked out their indenture. Sometimes they were auctioned off, but more often the sale was by private agreement.

The men were close-shaved and the women ordered to put on their best headdresses. A keg of rum was broached for the customers. The planters' first concern was for letters and news from England. That disposed of, the prisoners were inspected like cattle. Interviews between a prospective buyer and his chattel took place all over the deck. Then offers were made to the captain and bargains concluded.

Returning to young Henry Callister, as time passed he began to think better of Maryland. His salary was increased to £35 a year, he was permitted to trade to a certain extent on his own account, and he was allowed free carriage on four hogsheads of tobacco annually. A musician and a versifier, he became a favorite with the young bloods of Talbot County. Here is a letter he wrote to young Henry Hollyday:

June 27th 1748

Extempore

My dear, my good & generous Friend
You do not need to apprehend
That Clöe has discarded you
For any other Youth in view.
If you are serious, so am I,
I'd have you once again to try,
I've reason that I can't disclose } good poetry
For thinking you the Man she chose;
As to that foolish secret Lye
We'll find the truth on't bye & bye.

I'm tired of foolish rhyming [some words missing]. You have no rival. My dear Friend shew your Courage, at it again. I have not seen any of them since, but I intend soon to do so & it is very probable I shall privately enough learn something to your advantage; but nothing will do without your resolution; consider the Sex; consider how fearfull they are to give Encouragement. Pray mind these few things I tell you & visit Miss Nancy & allow her all the airs she chooses to put on; this time of Courtship they will make much of, they know they lose their authority when married. I have not time to write with Elegance upon this matter, your man wants to go home & I think will say something to you. When I send back your paper I may write to you again.

My compliments to the Sheriffe.

Dear Hall

Your affectionate Friend and Servant,
H. Callister.

The Hollydays were among the greatest people in the county. Colonel James Hollyday, the lad's father, who had died the previous year, had been treasurer of the Eastern Shore, naval officer at the Port of Oxford, and a member of His Lordship's Council. Henry's mother was the famous Sarah Covington, a great beauty of whom we shall hear again. The "Nancy" of the letter was Anna Maria Robins, daughter of George Robins of Peachblossom. The advice given in the letter was taken, because Henry Hollyday and Anna Maria Robins were married during the following year, and Henry built Ratcliffe Manor for his bride, still one of the most elegant mansions on the Shore.

In 1750, before he reached his fortieth birthday, Robert Morris was cut off in mid-career by an accident. Captain Samuel Matthews, of the ship *Liverpool Merchant*, a Cunliffe vessel, having arrived from sea, gave a small party aboard for Mr. Morris and other gentlemen, as was the custom. Upon leaving the ship, Mr. Morris, who was under some apprehension of danger because of an ugly dream he had had, suggested to Captain Matthews that the usual salute of honor should not be fired until the boat was well astern of the ship.

The captain, who was accompanying his guests ashore, thereupon ordered his men to hold fire until he gave them a signal. While the small boat was still abreast of the ship and only twenty yards distant, something caused the captain to fling up his hand, and the guns were fired. Even so, the waddings would have passed safely over the small boat had not the breeching of one gun been carelessly left under it, thus depressing the muzzle. The wadding from this gun struck Mr. Morris's arm, shattering it above the elbow. Six days later he died.

He had brought out his son and namesake a few years

before and placed the boy at school in Philadelphia. Writing to the younger Robert Morris some years later, Henry Callister describes his father's last hours. Callister was the last to be with him; he was reading to him from Plato's *Phaedo* at the end, and thought it eased the dying man's pain. In his will Morris left Callister six books of his own choosing, £10 sterling, a mourning ring, and "one of my mahogany arm'd chairs."

After Morris's death, Callister wrote Cunliffe's to inform them of their factor's various private trading ventures. This has the look of rather a shabby act; poor Callister was no hero. He had high hopes of succeeding Morris as chief factor, but the place went to one Hanmer, another employee, and Callister remained in charge of the branch on the Chester River. In 1754 he got the coveted place and returned to Oxford. He loved the fine air and the oysters of that port. He worked hard and faithfully, but he was playing a losing game, for the decay of Oxford had begun, though few as yet suspected it.

The decay was not solely due to the death of Robert Morris, of course. The tobacco trade had suffered much by the war between England and France—King George's War, they called it in Maryland. Eastern Shore tobacco was a dark, rank Orinoco, and the English would have none of it. France took the crop. During the war, there was only one French tobacco buyer in London, and by playing off one importer against another he was able to buy tobacco at his own price. Furthermore, having discovered that they could not grow the best tobacco, Eastern Shore planters were turning to wheat. Lastly, the swift rise of the port of Baltimore was sucking the life from Oxford.

The declining trade caused hard feelings between Callister and his employers. He left them in 1759 and set up for himself on the Chester River. For a while he appears to have done a large business, with several branch stores in charge of clerks, but luck was against him and in 1763 he was a bankrupt. He retired to a farm that he owned at Crumpton on the Chester. The gay young spark, the affectionate friend, lover of music and flowers, was turning into a querulous old man, who no longer cared to move out of the smoke of his own chimney. He died at Crumpton about 1765 before he was fifty.

Messrs. Cunliffe do not appear to have engaged another factor when Henry Callister left them; their business in Oxford became extinct about 1760. When the merchants shut up shop, the decline of the port was accelerated. The last seagoing ship called there in 1775. In 1793, only forty-three years after Robert Morris's death, Jeremiah Banning could write in his diary:

> The once well-worn streets are now grown up in grass, save a few narrow tracks made by sheep and swine; and the strands have more the appearance of an uninhabited island than where human feet had ever trod. . . . Bereft of all former greatness, nothing remains to console her but the salubrious air and fine navigation which may anticipate better times.

Oxford is still a quiet, umbrageous village, one of the most ingratiating on the Shore, but something is stirring there, and it is conceivable that Jeremiah Banning's prophecy may yet be fulfilled. The boatbuilding business has been revived; there is a flourishing oyster industry, and the fame of its lovely site and fine air brings many summer visitors.

CHAPTER 15

The Tred Avon River

THE Tred Avon River, a mile wide at its mouth, is only about ten miles long, but it is crowded with old lore. For more than two centuries there has been a discussion as to the proper spelling of its name, and what it means anyhow. In the oldest records I have found a dozen different spellings: Third Haven, Thread Haven, Trade Haven, etc. The preponderance of evidence appears to be in favor of Third Haven, so called because it afforded seamen the third haven in the mouth of the boisterous Choptank—but I shall not undertake to settle the matter.

Many winding creeks, small and large, all different and all beautiful, empty into Tred Avon, and nearly every creek bears one and sometimes several famous houses on its shores. The first big creek on the left, as one ascends, is Plaindealing. The fine house which gave it its name, the second house on that site, was lately destroyed by fire; only the graveyard is left. Susanna Robins of Peachblossom (a sister of Anna Maria) married Colonel Thomas Chamberlaine and went to live at Plaindealing. The colonel died while still a young man and, according to the story, the faithful Susanna sat at a window for seven years watching his grave. Every night she had a lantern placed upon it so that she could still turn her eyes to the spot. But in the eighth year, her handsome young cousin, Robert Lloyd Nicols, came riding by and the lantern burned no longer.

Old Plaindealing was full of stories. There was Squire Ungle, a riproaring old fellow according to tradition, though the county records reveal him as a worthy citizen and certainly no worse than his neighbors. He was speaker of the House of Delegates. However that may be, while drunk he toppled over the banisters of the top landing at Plaindealing and fell to the ground floor, breaking his neck. He bled, and the stains remained on the floor of the great hall, in spite of all scrubbings, as long as the house stood. This happened in 1727.

Then there is the story of the friendly ghost who directed a little boy where to dig for gold. Most of the descriptive books on Maryland aver that an immense sum was recovered, but this is not so. It was only a hundred years ago, and the little boy, who lived until recent times, has told the story. Boy and man, he was a sober, unimaginative fellow without the least desire to impress anybody.

Every time the little boy (he was the son of a tenant) walked past the graveyard at Plaindealing, he saw an old man standing by a broken vault and gradually he lost his fear of him. When the boy's mother was with him, she couldn't see the old man but the boy could. Having conquered fear, he began to talk to the old man and was answered. Finally the old man, telling the boy there was gold on the place and that his folks might as well have it, described where to dig. He would find the gold under some stones that were arranged in a certain manner. The boy told his father, who dug like so many other gold-seekers on the Eastern Shore. The stones were found as described, but no gold. Crowds visited the scene of the excavation and the story became wondrously embellished. It is almost a shame to strip it bare.

Jeremiah Banning's place, the Isthmus, was also in Plaindealing Creek. His house has given place to a modern dwell-

ing, but his grave is here and his quaint office still stands on the creek shore, where it commands one of the sweetest water views in Talbot. Every Eastern Shore gentleman in the eighteenth century had an office somewhere about the grounds, and behind the decorous lawbooks on its shelves, a bottle.

Here toward the end of his life the old seaman set down his *Narrative*. He begins it in a formal, gentlemanly style, but the man's native humor and humanity soon break through, and the story becomes thrilling in its accounts of tempests, imprisonment, and other misadventures. The seaman had the art of turning a graphic phrase.

He was attacked by gout during his forties and left the sea. He protests that it was not due to overeating or drinking; he ate sparingly and when he drank, it was necessitated by his business in order to procure "good consignments." It was his great hardships and anxieties at sea that brought on the gout. An ardent patriot, he was made a colonel in the Revolution. His active service was confined to battling the Tories of Dorchester and Somerset. His command drove off the raiders who had taken the *Mayflower* at Castle Haven.

As he grew old, Colonel Banning's fellow citizens loaded him with honors. He delighted to keep up the old customs of the Shore, such as the burning of the yule log. As long as it burned, no slave was forced to work. It was a practice of the slaves (winked at by the masters) to bury the chosen log for months beforehand in a swamp, so that it would become thoroughly water-soaked. Colonel Banning died in 1798, leaving a good fortune to his three children and setting free his slaves. He loved the English box, and four little bushes were set out around his grave. They have now grown together, and to a great height, his only monument.

The first principal creek on the east side of Tred Avon is Goldsboro', a deep, narrow inlet lined with intriguing indentations and subcreeks. On the south bank stand two quaint old houses, Anderton and Jena. The latter used to be one of Jacob Gibson's farms, named, like all his places, for the victories of Napoleon, whom he greatly admired. His

Friedland was also on this creek, but the original house is gone. Jacob Gibson will be dealt with in the next chapter.

On the north side of Goldsboro' Creek stands Otwell, an ancient house of singular charm. Unfortunately, it is so very old that many of the original trees have died and the grounds have rather a bleak aspect. The first building here was the familiar story-and-a-half plantation house with a hip roof, and the usual irregular and picturesque appendages attached to one end. A long addition in the same style was then built across the other end, making it a T-shaped house. All the bricks used in the building were baked on the spot; they were whitewashed long ago, and have weathered to various tints, the whole very mellow and satisfying. Otwell has been the seat of a branch of the numerous Goldsborough family for more than two centuries, and Goldsboroughs still live there. The house is full of old family treasures.

It will be noted how often the same family names crop up in the story of the Eastern Shore. There were not so many of these first families, and of course they are all intricately related. A member of one of the most ancient, which we may call the A family, was describing to me how the A's and the B's, another house of equal age and pride, had been intermarrying back and forth for nearly three hundred years "until," said my sprightly informant, "it is a wonder that we of the present generation can even crawl!" When I related this anecdote to another sprightly Eastern Shore lady, not related to the A's or B's, she remarked acidly: "Some of them can't!"

The next creek on this side is Trippe's, broad and beautiful, and with many a fine house on its inveigling coves. Next comes Peachblossom, which is no less charming than its name. It was George Robins, the father of two girls who have been mentioned, who planted the first peaches grown on the Eastern Shore. The beauty of the blossoms created such a sensation in the neighborhood that the name Peachblossom came to be applied both to the Robins house and to the creek. The house no longer stands.

Between the two creeks, Ship's Point, sometimes called Turner's Point, juts out into the river. In the latter part of the seventeenth century, this was the site of Thomas Skillington's shipyard, which bore a very invidious reputation. In those days, this was a remote spot and rumor had it that shipbuilder Skillington had chosen it because his best customers were the "brethren," a euphemism for the pirates who preyed up and down the coast. One of Skillington's customers, a Captain Martin, not a pirate, however, was said to have poured out sufficient coin on the Skillington dining table to cover it to the depth of a foot.

The business of fitting out pirates is said to have lasted under Thomas's son, Percy, until about 1730, by which time most of the brethren, including Stede Bonnet, Blackbeard Teach and Captain Kidd, had either died in battle or had had their necks stretched. Whatever may be the truth in these stories, it is a fact that as late as 1750 gold pieces of eight, chequins and pistoles were found among the subscriptions to the Talbot County free school.

Ship's Point belonged to Jeremiah Banning at one time, and the big house, Avondale, now modernized, which stands there, was built for one of his sons.

A couple of miles above the mouth of Peachblossom, the Tred Avon divides into three branches and comes to an end rather suddenly.

On one of the points, with a noble view down the main river, I found Ratcliffe Manor, basking in grace and dignity under the late afternoon sun. There is nothing "quaint" about this house; the design (*circa* 1750) is so right, the style so good, as to appeal to men of any era. Such a house is ageless. It was built, it will be remembered, by young Henry (Hal) Hollyday for his Nancy that he won after so much trouble. They lived here in great happiness and had nine children.

The house is a characteristic Georgian structure of mellow brick, two stories and a half in height. It has a jerkinhead roof, as architects term it, graceful pedimented dormers, and four satisfying big chimneys. The many-paned windows winked at the setting sun. Inside, the stairway, mantels, paneling and other woodwork are all of a piece in reflecting the best workmanship of a good period. One of the finest features of the place is the avenue of approach, a mile long, two hundred feet wide, and set out with a double row of catalpas, planted when the house was built. The catalpa when young is a commonplace tree; after two hundred years it becomes incredibly gnarled and broken, decorative in the highest degree.

The easternmost of the three branches of the river divides again in another mile, and the point thus formed is Easton Point, head of navigation and a landing for the city of Easton, a mile away. I sat on the ruined wharf and tried to picture a trim white steamboat coming up the smooth stream between unbroken green banks. The narrow, navigable waterway cried out for a steamboat to complete the picture.

On the wharf an old fellow joined me in mourning the passing of the steamboat. He, it turned out, had been the wharfbuilder. "Not much room in this quiet pool for the steamboats to turn around in," I suggested. "Just, and no more," he said. He went on to tell me how one evening the "*Joppie*" (*Joppa*), Captain Wolfert, was bearing down on the wharf "loaded with fertilize' to the beam" when, just at the critical moment the engine-room bell failed, there was a hideous crash, and the wharf folded up.

The steamboat was towed away for repairs and the wharfbuilder did his job. Two weeks after the *Joppa* was put in service again, she smashed up the wharf a second time. "The cap'n tried save his face by claimin' she hadn't been fixed right, but I could prove it." The wharfbuilder thereupon went into detailed specifications of the timbers and the spikes he had employed in his repairs, and pointed out some of the very spikes.

The first steamboat came up the Tred Avon as long ago as 1819. That was the *Maryland,* and her captain was that Clement Vickers who had played a worthy part in the defense of St. Michaels, as shall presently be related. Two years before that, the steamboat *Surprise* had made a few trips up the Miles River with passengers for Easton. She had engines "on a new rotary principle," but they were not satisfactory, and after tinkering with her for a long while her owners retired her.

But the *Maryland* was a success and apparently served for a number of years. She is described as being broad and flat-bottomed, like a schooner with full bows and a square stern, no joiner work above decks and no masts. Certainly no beauty. Her passengers shared the hull along with freight, machinery, boiler and fuel for the same. She left Easton Point at 8:00 A.M. on Mondays and Thursdays, and after calling at Annapolis was due in Baltimore at 6:00 P.M.

In 1838 Tred Avon landings were served by the steamboat *Paul Jones,* a narrow, sharp-prowed, and for the times, a speedy vessel. The *Hugh Jenkins* followed, and remained in service until she was requisitioned during the Civil War. Then the *Osiris,* the *Cambridge* (1846), the fastest thing on the bay. She burned up five years later. The *Champion* followed, a new vessel purchased by Captain Stranbery with the proceeds of a lottery prize, and the *Kent,* which became a great favorite and ran for nearly thirty years.

Later vessels were requisitioned by the federal government or taken by the Confederates, and during the Civil War steamboating languished on the bay. Later it was revived with larger and more luxurious vessels, *Ida, Joppa, Avalon, Tred Avon,* etc. At one period there were as many as three lines serving the Choptank and its tributaries, all doing a good business. The *Minnie Wheeler* came up here; she was the first vessel to have a searchlight, invaluable aid in making a wharf at night. Finally, in 1912, an order was placed for the *Dorchester* and the *Talbot,* big vessels representing the last word in comfort—they even had a few staterooms with baths—but they are not remembered with the same affection as the *Joppa.* Most of these vessels made their last trip in 1932.

One who was a boy over fifty years ago has left an account of taking the steamboat at Easton Point. In the late afternoon, Trump Gale circulated slowly through the leafy streets of Easton in his battered bus, drawn by two swayback bays. "All aboard for the boat!" he sang out. After boarding the bus, you made various stops around town to pick up other passengers, Trump pleading, just as he might today, "Please move up in front!"—and then at last rattled down to the point at a trot over the shell road.

There was always a crowd on the wharf at evening, perfectly contented to wait until any hour if the steamboat was late; farmers' sons, all newly washed and combed, the more sophisticated white-collar town boys, and all the neighborhood girls in freshly starched dresses; Negroes with their shining teeth, indulging in rough horseplay but careful to avoid jostling white folks. One of them would have a mouth organ, and a group would start dancing and clapping juba.

The intending passenger had the choice of several lines: it might be the *Ida* of the Maryland line that night, or the *Tred Avon* of the Choptank line, or the *Minnie Wheeler,* all superb vessels as remembered from boyhood, resplendent with Brussels carpets and easy chairs; everything as clean as a pin. The fare to Baltimore was fifty cents, which included a clean berth and extra-polite attention. A private stateroom cost extra.

The word would run through the crowd: "She just left Oxford; be here in half an hour." Soon every eye would be fixed on the bend. If it was still light, a wisp of smoke might be seen in the sky; if darkness had fallen, the reflection of her searchlight could be seen a long way off. At last she swims into view and her deep-throated whistle sounds for the wharf. Here she is! What a moment! She drifts slowly alongside with engines stopped. How big she is! What majesty! What grandeur!

The light coiled lines are flung ashore; the wharf tender ducks, catches a line, and hauls in the hawser, drops the heavy loop over a wharf post. The captain up on the hurricane deck signals to the engineroom to reverse speed, while every face on the wharf turns up in admiring regard of that superman in blue and gold. In those days, every small boy on the Shore dreamed of becoming a steamboat captain.

The gangplank was run ashore and a scene of noisy activity took place. The passengers did not go aboard yet; that would have been to miss half the fun. Jazz had not yet been named, but the Negro roustabouts with their banging hand trucks conducted all their operations to the rhythm of jazz, prancing, shaking their shoulders, whirling their empty trucks on one wheel, and singing in time. The racket was terrific.

After the dead freight was all on—or off—the cattle were loaded. If the beast had horns, two grabbed him in front and pulled while a third followed behind, twisting his tail. Calves were hauled on by their forequarters, while another hand shoved behind. An animal would often escape, whereupon a mad chase took place, everybody hollering together. The calves were loaded forward under the best staterooms, and they used to bawl uninterruptedly all the way to Baltimore. At the very last, the boy strode on board, greatly uplifted by the envious glances of the stay-at-homes.

These steamboats that came up to Easton Point also served Cambridge and other Choptank landings, back and forth across the river as far north as Denton. The round trip from Baltimore back to Baltimore occupied about thirty-six hours. Time was no great object on the Eastern Shore in steamboat days. Thus these lines performed a useful service in bringing the people of several counties in contact and making them acquainted with each other. The Eastern Shore has always been somewhat like a congeries of nine little nations, each jealous of its own notions.

The service had traditions that helped to make each trip on the steamboat a festive occasion. For one thing, it was an unwritten law that the captain should be of good family; in other words, a gentleman as well as a navigator. He was expected to play host to his passengers, to see that everybody had a good time. Naturally, the captains became outstanding men; it was a point of pride with them, as with a good bishop, to remember everybody who used the line.

The leading men in each community were frequent patrons; the governor himself and his henchmen; the United States senator (it is the rule in Maryland that one of the two senators must always be an Eastern Shore man), besides state senators, assemblymen, the circuit judges with their train of attorneys, big landholders. Important conferences were held and deals made during the leisurely journeys from wharf to wharf. Naturally, the captain consorted with all such men on an equal footing. *Minnie Wheeler's* Boy-Friend asserts that he obtained his whole education from listening to the conversation of "big men" in the pilothouse during his tricks at the wheel.

Another tradition of the bay steamboats ordained that the passengers must be well-fed. The food was simple, and as far as possible of the country, but it was cooked according to the best Eastern Shore standards. Supper at half a dollar included steak or country-cured ham, fish or crabs (sometimes both), oysters always, a choice of hot biscuits, homemade rolls or corn bread, also vegetables and fruits from the local gardens. Who that has ever known it will forget the array of little white birdbaths that were spread around his plate? The smiling waiters were of the best class of Negro servants. It was a job that was much sought after. As the old-timer I have quoted said, "They would break their necks for a nickel tip."

Easton, the county seat of Talbot, is usually referred to as a "pretty" town. This means no more than that the streets are lined with old trees, and with comfortable houses set back far enough to leave pleasant lawns in front. In this respect, Easton is very like Cambridge (though it has not the noble Choptank out in front), but there is a subtle difference in the spirit of these two towns only sixteen miles apart. Cambridge has gone in for industry and Easton has not; Cambridge has forged ahead in population and Easton doesn't care; Cambridge, in spite of its growth, is still almost pure Maryland, while Easton has become sophisticated through contact with the great world.

An officer of the bank in Easton said to me with a grin, "Talbot's principal industry is Pittsburgh and New York millionaires." He did not expect to be taken too seriously. There is much more to Easton—and Talbot—than the station-wagon set. With their big taxes and their generous benefactions, the wealthy newcomers have brought prosperity to the county, but it is not too much to say that Talbot has changed the millionaires more than the millionaires have changed Talbot.

The coming of the rich has not been an unalloyed benefit to the county. One of the newcomers said to me, "I have noticed that nearly all the men who come to the Eastern Shore to start a new life, start it with a new wife—just like me!" Sometimes the new marriage does not take, and the fine new place then quickly goes to seed. In other cases, men with princely incomes establish magnificent homes on the Shore and die. Their heirs either do not have the means to keep up the paternal magnificence, or else they don't care for the Eastern Shore, and so the showplace comes into the market again.

It is only when the sons and daughters of the newcomers intermarry with the daughters and sons of Talbot (which happens very often) that the new family becomes fixed to the Shore. Each strain benefits from the other, and the consequence is that in Talbot County the simplicity of country life is neatly balanced with knowledge of the world. There is no better society.

Talbot County was created so long ago that the date cannot be established. It was about 1661 but the act has been lost. It was named for another sister of Cecil Calvert's, Grace, who was married to a Sir Robert Talbot. Easton is not an old town as Maryland towns go; it was made the county seat in 1710 and the courthouse was built during the following year, but for many years afterward it had no name but Courthouse, or Talbot Courthouse, and there was little else there. Not until 1788 was the village that had grown up around the county buildings organized, first as Talboton, then Easton. Jeremiah Banning was one of the commissioners appointed to survey the town and name the streets.

The present courthouse, the second on this site, opened for business in 1794. It was rebuilt in 1878 and the Victorian additions are not so good. But the shell of a dignified, well-proportioned building is there, and at comparatively small expense it could be brought to harmonize with the really fine county building that has lately been put up next door. If only the ugly red paint were scraped off the bricks of the old courthouse, the people of Talbot would be astonished to see what they had.

Washington Street in the neighborhood of the courthouse green has a pleasing old-time air, and it is possible that some of the little brick houses with dormers in their steep roofs may have looked down on the stirring scenes of the Revolution.

Talbot, unlike Dorchester and Somerset, was ardently patriotic. What Tories they had were of the meeker sort. The Stamp Act was hung from a gibbet in Easton, and left hanging until it was repealed. An active Committee of Observation was formed and a company of minute men. Their own Matthew Tilghman was elected president of the Maryland Convention, which was the government pro tem. The administration was divided into two, a separate Council of Safety, and state officers being appointed for the Eastern Shore in order to expedite business. William Hindman became the treasurer, while James Hindman, his brother, was elected captain of the first company of regulars raised for General Smallwood's Maryland Flying Camp. Other companies of regulars followed, and two whole battalions of militia.

There was no fighting on the Eastern Shore except what was necessary to keep the Tories in order and to repel raiding parties. But the soldiers of Smallwood's Flying Camp, subsequently the Maryland Line, gave a fine account of themselves in almost every battle of the Revolution from Long Island to Cowpens. They were good in defeat, too, the supreme test. The Eastern Shore performed one special little service to the country that has generally been overlooked. At a time when the Continental Army was in desperate need of flints, it was discovered that much of the ballast brought over in the tobacco ships, and tossed overboard without a thought in the Choptank and Wye rivers, actually consisted of flintstones. They were joyfully fished up and there was no more shortage.

The War of 1812 hardly touched Easton, and it will be dealt with in the stories of Miles River and the Sassafras.

Neither in the Civil War was there any fighting on the Eastern Shore; the scarcity of references to the war in the county records strikes the investigator as rather odd. As a matter of fact, it was an exceedingly unhappy time, because the sympathies of all the counties were overwhelmingly southern. Their towns were garrisoned throughout by federal troops, and any demonstrations for the South were sternly suppressed.

Down in Pocomoke, they tell how the Union soldiers strung a great flag across the main street, and how the natives thereafter refused to use the street. They went around by the alleys sooner than pass under the hated flag. When Union soldiers passed by, housewives went out and vigorously swept the sidewalks to remove the contamination.

An incident that occurred in the old courthouse at Easton will serve to illustrate the extraordinary bitterness prevailing at that time. The story was reported by a southern sympathizer.

Judge Richard Bennett Carmichael was on the circuit comprising Kent, Queen Anne, Talbot and Caroline counties. At the elections of 1861, it was charged that squads of Union soldiers were sent to the polling places of Queen Anne's and Talbot for the purpose of intimidating the voters. It was alleged that many voters were arrested by the soldiers to keep them from voting the Democratic ticket. Judge Carmichael, sitting in Kent County, charged the grand jury that such acts were unlawful and that it was their duty to take cognizance of them. The grand jury, however, did not act.

Six months later, Judge Carmichael was trying a case in Easton. The hotel dinner bell had just rung and the courtroom was almost empty. Several rough-looking fellows ran in. They were not in uniform and showed no badges or other credentials. Their leader, crying "Come out of here!" seized Judge Carmichael by his beard and dragged him from the bench. The astonished judge managed to kick the fellow off the platform, whereupon the whole party attacked him, beating his bare, bald head with the hammers of their pistols until he sank to the floor drenched in blood. He called loudly for the sheriff, but that worthy and his deputy had decamped.

The fainting judge was then informed that he was under arrest. A surgeon dressed his wounds, but he was not permitted to send for a change of clothes and was taken away all bloody as he was. He was confined in Fort McHenry, Baltimore, for six weeks, then transferred to Fort Lafayette in New York harbor for two months longer. As a result of being kept in damp casemates, he was permanently lamed by rheumatism. He spent a final two months in Fort Delaware and was released on December 4, 1862.

He returned to the bench, and while sitting in Kent for the spring term, 1863, he renewed his charge to the grand jury concerning the lawless acts of the military. When this grand jury refused to take action, Judge Carmichael resigned from the bench and retired to his farm.

During his whole term of imprisonment, he was never charged with any offense, nor brought to trial.

A curious phenomenon in the early history of Talbot is seen in the rise and decline of the Quakers. For some years after the coming of the first settlers, there was no house of worship of any sort within the confines of the county. The good George Fox, in his tours of the Eastern Shore, was the first to bring them religion, and there were other eloquent preachers of that faith. Consequently, most of the families joined the Society of Friends.

But it was not long before these people of Cavalier traditions began to resent the interference of the stern Quaker discipline in their private lives. For instance, there was William Stevens of Compton who, upon his meeting with Lady Baltimore when she landed at Oxford, doffed his hat to her and kissed her hand. Upon being rebuked for it by the leaders of the Meeting, the whole Stevens connection left. There were other such incidents, with the result that, when the Act of 1692 was passed establishing the Church of England throughout the province, most of the first families hastened to join that church, and with its successor, the Episcopal Church, it has been pre-eminent in Talbot ever since. Three of the original thirty parishes were organized in Talbot: White Marsh in the south, St. Michael's in the middle part, and Wye Mills in the north.

Today the most appealing survival of the past in Easton is the Quaker Third Haven Meeting House, built in 1683, the oldest surviving house of worship on the Shore. In 1700 William Penn himself conducted a meeting under one of the great oaks in the yard, and it is said that Lord and Lady Baltimore attended it. Freedom of worship was a guiding maxim with the Baltimores, though they were out of power at that moment. The simple wooden meetinghouse with its straight-backed benches and the green yard with its rows of identical little gravestones like those of soldiers, under ancient cedar and oaks, have a moving charm. A remarkable thing is that the records of Third Haven have been preserved intact from the date of the first meeting in 1683.

CHAPTER 16

St. Michaels

THE Miles River, like the Tred Avon, is entirely included within the boundaries of watery Talbot. It was first called the St. Michaels. The Quakers, they say, objected to the sanctification, so it became Michael's River, and that was finally corrupted to Miles. At Miles River bridge, the course of its windings brings it within a couple of miles of the town of Easton, and some of the old steamboat lines used to serve Easton by this route. The Miles is a much bigger body of water than the Tred Avon. It is all of three miles wide, where it empties into Eastern Bay behind Kent Island.

In sailing north up the coast from Blackwalnut Point at the mouth of Choptank, you have the long stretch of Tilghman's Island and Tilghman's Neck on your right, and midway you will pass the smaller Poplar Island on your left. The peninsula on the main has been called Bay Hundred since the earliest times. Harris Creek lies on the other side. In England long ago, the "hundred" was applied to a district containing ten families, ten estates, or a hundred fighting men, but in Maryland it never had that significance. Here it was merely a convenient political division; in other words, an election district.

Tilghman's Island, like Hooper's and Deal's to the south,

is the abode of oystermen and other followers of the water. The inhabitants of such remote places are reputed to be inhospitable, if not downright rude to strangers, but the reverse is true of Tilghman's. On each visit I have been struck by the politeness of the people. Every face lights up at the sight of a strange car; all pause, expecting you to converse and explain yourself. The old Negroes touch their caps and murmur, "Gemmen!" Of course, very few strange cars visit Tilghman's, and the coming of one is an event.

This island is really a part of the long neck above that has broken off. There is a bridge over the deep narrows where the tide courses swiftly. The long shore of Bay Hundred above was familiarly known as Bayside, and will call for frequent mention in this narrative.

Along here is an old house now called Webley, though its former name of Mary's Delight was much prettier. During the 1830's, it was the home of Dr. Absolom Thompson, who made his professional rounds riding bareback and barefoot on a mule. His kit was limited to a jar of calomel, a lancet, and a syringe with a nozzle like a twelvebore shotgun. Nevertheless, his practice became so great that he had to establish a hospital in his home. It was the first on the Eastern Shore.

At the top of Bay Hundred stands Rich Neck Manor, which was Matthew Tilghman's home during the Revolution. He referred to it as Bayside. The whole country hereabouts is associated with his name. Tilghman's Island, then called Choptank Island, was his. The present manor house includes a part of the gambrel-roofed original; the rest was built in Matthew Tilghman's lifetime after a fire. Nearby stands the strangest piece of architecture in Talbot: a tiny, archaic structure of brick whose use can only be guessed at. It may have been a chapel. It was already old in Matthew Tilghman's day.

Matthew Tilghman, known affectionately as the patriarch of Maryland, was perhaps the most valuable man given by the state to the service of the Revolution, though some others are more widely known. At the outbreak of hostilities he was elected president of the Maryland Convention, which at that moment was tantamount to being governor. When the state was organized, he was elected president of the Senate and held that office until he died. He was a delegate to the great Congress of 1776 also, and would have been a signer had he not been detained in Annapolis by the business of Maryland. While the administration was divided, he was president of the Council for the Eastern Shore. He fathered Maryland's first constitution and her Bill of Rights.

Besides being a great administrator, Matthew Tilghman was a very human individual, as evinced by the following delightful letter about Commodore Grason and the picaroons. It was written August 3, 1781, to his daughter, Anna Maria, who was visiting her sister, the wife of Charles Carroll, the barrister (so-called to distinguish him from his famous cousin of Carrollton) at Mount Clare near Baltimore. Anna Maria subsequently married her cousin, the famous Lieutenant Colonel Tench Tilghman.

. . . I am vexed with myself for missing the opportunity of our Barges to Annapolis, of boasting of the doings of the Eastern Shore, I won't say of the Council. [The writer was president of the Council.] Our three Barges having been fully manned and fitted out, and the Commodore having in form received his instructions, sealed up and not to be opened until they all met at Sharpe's Island, put out on his cruise last Saturday evening. On Monday they fell in with two barges and a whale boat—the barges, one commanded by Robinson that robbed my island [Choptank] the other by McMullen that hung up Henry Gale and the whale boat by Whaland. McMullen was taken and the other two put to flight, and on Wednesday morning the Commodore with his captured barge and two small boats retaken, which were prizes taken by the barges, came in triumph to the ferry [Miles River ferry]. The novelty drew numbers all day.

The event has given general joy, and if we cannot flatter ourselves with peace, we begin to think we have a chance of remaining safe from the plunderers that have of late infested us. The great barge [Zedekiah Walley's *Protector* building at Pocomoke] is also fitted out and commissions gone down, and by this time I expect Walley with his 24-pounder is on a cruise. The barge, Mr. Polk says [state senator from Somerset] bears the 24-pounder well, and it has been fired several times. We will not attack the British fleet, but as for anything else, we shall make nothing of 'em. The Commodore has taken a recruit of provisions and stores, and is gone off for Annapolis with the prisoners, and then goes down the Bay to cruise until Wednesday or Thursday next, when we are to have a meeting of the Council. The commanders are all to attend, and I expect some grand expedition will be formed. You will show this to Charles Carroll. I think it is nearly as pompous as he could write.

Upon rounding Tilghman's Point, a vessel comes all the way about and heads *south* up the Miles River. There is no accounting for the vagaries of an Eastern Shore river! Bennett's Point lies opposite Tilghman's, with the Wye River coming in just this side of it. All the land on that side is known as Miles River Neck.

Proceeding upriver, one leaves Deepwater Point to starboard, and the village of St. Michaels comes into view within its pretty harbor. At St. Michaels the two main elements of the Shore, the aristocratic planter and the waterman, meet and fuse. The broad reaches of the river out in front ask for boat races, and boat races they have. The annual regatta at St. Michaels in August is a rendezvous for the whole of Chesapeake Bay. And the workboat races are just as much of a feature as the yachts. The liveliest event used to be the log-canoe race, which was started with the boats pulled up on shore with sails furled. It had to be given up because it led to so many fights.

Naturally, St. Michaels has been a great boatbuilding place since the earliest days. Here, more than in any other one spot, the beautiful models of the bay craft were evolved and fashioned—canoes, bugeyes and pungies; also some of the most famous Baltimore clippers. At the very time of which I am about to tell—the War of 1812—there were three barges for Commodore Barney's flotilla on the ways.

There has been a St. Michael's Church at this spot since the earliest days. St. Michael has been called the patron saint of Maryland because Lord Baltimore's rents fell due on Michaelmas Day. With all the waterways of Miles and Wye leading to its door, and the Choptank with its tributaries only a few hundred yards distant, it was the natural spot for a church in the days when everybody traveled by water. The great families went to church in a six- or eight-oared barge rowed by slaves in livery. Religion was followed by trade, and the settlement grew up around the church.

St. Michaels is forever associated with the name of Jacob Gibson. He didn't live in the village but at his place, Marengo, across the river. Gibson was the man who so admired Napoleon that he called all his numerous farms after Napoleon's victories: Austerlitz, Jena, Friedland, etc. When he was defeated for some office or other, his successful adversary called *his* place Waterloo.

Gibson was a magnificent character, swaggering, truculent, warmhearted and humorous. He was incessantly engaged in quarreling with his neighbors. There is an abundance of material for a sketch of him, since he was an inveterate letterwriter to the newspapers. When his letters were refused by the paper as being *too* abusive, he paid to have them printed and circulated as handbills.

Here is the beginning of a long advertisement that he inserted in the *Republican Star* of Easton in 1804:

> Boasters of sheep-raising and sheep-shearing; stop your gasconading and behold two animals like their owner [Jacob Gibson] who astonishes while he excels, and puzzles the inquisitive why and how they do so.

Appended to the advertisement was an affidavit that the two sheep weighed 333½ pounds, and their fleeces 39 pounds. This was merino wool worth two dollars a pound.

A sample of his correspondence: He is girding at the members of the Agricultural Society lately formed in Easton, who would not admit him to membership.

> Mr. Smith:
>
> I am sick, tired, sunburnt and mad. The run-fever and backache among my *legion of honor* and their *invincibles* [his farm hands] have left me (after six days dashing) twelve twentieths of my wheat yet to cut. Please let the little farmers know that as soon as their lots are secured, I hope they will reinforce me to help down with my continent and colonies, or the eating world may be put on short rations. To prevent mistakes, I want aid at Marengo, Ulm, Austerlitz and Trafalgar [*sic!*]. [Here was one case where Napoleon's side slipped up!]
>
> J. Gibson
>
> Saturday Night, 6th day of harvest.
> N.B. Tell the bankers I shall want a basket full of dollar notes.

In 1798, when Jacob Gibson's man, Joshua Seney, was elected to Congress, Gibson won $3,000, and put this in the *Maryland Herald:*

To the poor and virtuous widows of Talbot County:

Having been particularly favored through life by Providence in worldly affairs and particularly in the late election, wherein I have won a considerable sum of money, I conceive it a duty indispensably incumbent on me to bestow some of this improper got wealth to a useful purpose.

He goes on to allot one hundred barrels of corn to the widows to be distributed at several convenient points. In addition, the widows of his own neighborhood "From Three Bridges to Potts' Mill and to the bottom of Miles River Neck" were to have "a free corn house for twelve months." I take it this meant they were to have leave to help themselves from Gibson's own store of corn.

This called forth a sneer from one of the opposite party, who signed himself "No Boaster." He was rebuked by "A Friend of J.G."—or very likely J.G. himself, as follows:

When Mr. No Boaster will distribute among the widows and orphans in the same liberal manner that Mr. Gibson has done, then he shall have the liberty to boast as much as he pleases.

In 1801 the *Herald* published a political satire called "The Grand Caucus," signed "Peter Calomel," who was soon identified as Dr. Ennals Martin of Easton. Everybody was lampooned in it, but chiefly Jacob Gibson. As soon as he learned who the author was, Gibson attacked Dr. Martin on the street. Martin was a man of size, weight and courage, and no less brusque than Gibson himself; in short, a worthy antagonist. The contest which followed was a Homeric one, catch-as-catch-can, and without benefit of Marquis of Queensberry rules. On this occasion Jacob was badly beaten up and, as a crowning irony, had to call in Dr. Martin to dress his wounds!

In spite of all foibles, Gibson was well thought of by his neighbors. In 1802 he was appointed an associate judge of the Talbot County court, and upon resigning that office in 1806, was elected a state senator for the Eastern Shore. Gibson, it need hardly be said, was an ardent Democrat and all his fights were with Federalists. From a handbill published January 8, 1809, upon being challenged by a Federalist to a duel:

> I hope it will not be considered a wanton egotism to say that I am the only *stump orator* in the district who confronts this faction [the Federalists] and beards it in its teeth. That for the last ten or twelve years I have been compelled to talk all, to write all, to flog all and to pay all; and now I must die for all. This dying is unseasonable at this time as my services may be wanted to my county for I see the clouds arising that may require all the energies the county possesses to support its government and our National rights. To die in such a contest would be honorable and pleasing to me because it would give me a sure passport to future bliss. But to be nibbled to death by rats and mice, that reflection is worse than hell.

No duel was fought.

When a rumor was circulated that Jacob Gibson was about to turn Federalist, he issued a furious blast. In a postscript he added:

> If any person after this notice hears a Federalist say that I have turned Federal and will break his mouth, I will pay all costs.

Gibson was an extraordinarily ingenious man. He evolved a plan for paying off the British national debt without adding a penny to taxes. Nobody ever listened to that, but he had another plan for the founding of a farmers' bank at home that almost went through. He intended that this bank, through the increment of its funds, should eventually manumit all the slaves in the county. He had it figured out to the last digit, and offered to put up the necessary capital ($30,000) himself. After the slaves had been freed, he proposed that the profits of the bank should be applied to "the support of the clergy who are the worst paid people in this country and whose functions are indisputably necessary." This illustrates the other side of Jacob Gibson's character. In the end nothing came of the scheme, and the slaves had to wait sixty years for their freedom, and then their owners didn't get a penny for them.

In addition to other properties, Jacob Gibson owned Sharp's Island in the mouth of Choptank. In 1813, when the British fleet was in the bay, he set out for the island to save what he could of his stock. It should be explained that the village of St. Michaels is built on a neck of land less than half a mile wide, separating the waters of the Choptank from the Miles. Gibson, therefore, in order to lessen the risk of capture, crossed this neck and went down Back Creek and Broad Creek to reach his island.

Before he could remove any of his property, the British arrived. Gibson was made prisoner and some of his cattle were carried aboard the ships. Gibson, with characteristic boldness, demanded to be brought before the admiral, to whom he talked with such good effect that he was released on parole and given permission to remove certain property that the British didn't want. Furthermore, he was paid $225 in notes and orders on the British treasury for what they had taken. He was detained on the island for several days.

Meanwhile, the people of St. Michaels, expecting an attack, had been in a dither since the first approach of the British. Some French volunteers in the fleet had committed ugly outrages down at Hampton, and these reports, greatly exaggerated, had reached the village. Earthworks were thrown up at the mouth of the harbor, guard vessels stationed downriver, an infantry company organized under Captain Joseph Kemp, and an existing troop of cavalry under Captain Robert Banning, reorganized as scouts. Jacob Gibson had observed what he regarded as the excessive fears of the village with a sardonic humor.

On April 18, 1813, a bargelike vessel with sails and oars was discovered coming up Back Creek toward the village. A drum was beating on deck in martial fashion, and a red flag flew from the masthead. Naturally the villagers took this for the vanguard of the British and were thrown into wild consternation. Only two men could be seen on the deck of the approaching vessel, but it was supposed that the redcoats were hidden below. Messengers were dispatched in several directions to bring in Captain Banning's scouts; women and children were sent inland out of reach of a supposedly brutal soldiery; cattle were hidden in the woods; Captain Kemp's St. Michael's Patriot Blues flew to arms and gathered on the shore.

In a town like St. Michaels, all the local craft are well-known, and as the enemy vessel drew closer it was recognized as one belonging to Captain Richard Spencer of Beverly. She tacked at that moment and the waiting soldiers saw a ragged Negro in the waist thumping an empty rum barrel; the red flag began to look suspiciously like a bandanna handkerchief. A moment or two later they could make out the burly form and hear the uproarious laugh of Jacob Gibson. He was on his way back from Sharp's Island.

The rage of the soldiers knew no bounds, and Jacob, upon landing, was received with a chorus of curses and a hun-

MARINE PRODUC

13E948
Aaron Sopher

dred shaken fists. The most violent was Captain Banning of the mounted troop, who was a Federalist, hence a political enemy. His men were less excited; but the foot soldiers actually presented their muskets at Gibson's breast and he owed his life to the coolness and good sense of Captain Kemp. A contemporary account says that Gibson "apologized," but I doubt it. I cannot see Jacob Gibson humbling himself before a crowd of men even if they had guns in their hands. I believe he talked himself out of this jam. At any rate, he was allowed to depart for his home at Marengo unharmed.

He immediately proceeded to Baltimore to inform the authorities of what had happened at Sharp's Island. He was an astute man, as well as a brave one, and he drew up a statement setting forth exactly what had passed between himself and the British admiral, Sir John Borlase Warren. He enclosed copies of the two communications he had had from the admiral. He sent this statement to James Monroe, secretary of state, and a copy to Governor Winder of Maryland. He was holding the money, Gibson said, at the disposal of the United States government.

There is no doubt that he regretted the trick he had played on the people of St. Michaels, though he was never the one to admit it. In Baltimore he purchased two cannon for the defense of St. Michaels, and shipped them around the head of the bay to avoid the British. Truly a magnificent peace offering. For the time being the cannon were mounted on wagon wheels, and when St. Michaels *was* attacked, they did good service.

Upon his return to Talbot, Gibson found that the story of his dealings with the British admiral had aroused a storm of criticism and abuse throughout the county. Even the members of his own party were ready to accuse him of dishonorable dealings with the enemy. The people refused to believe that the admiral would have granted such favors unless he had received a corresponding benefit in return.

Gibson issued two broadsides in his own defense. The first repeated what he had written to the secretary of state and the governor. When this failed to allay the storm, he published a highly characteristic handbill, of which the following is part:

> . . . I had no right to expect to be favored [by the Admiral] but on the contrary to be the first victim of British vengeance. Fortunately God has made me of strong nerves, that I can shine, when I please, in a church, a drawing-room, a grog-shop or a brothel; and if through my address and urbanity of manners I softened the roaring lion to a kind lamb and obtained papers that helped my country, and rendered no aid to the enemy, was I not justifiable? . . . The Federalists I could persuade myself to forgive . . . but for Democrats cowardly to shrink from the support of their first main pillar! From the Federalists I had nothing to expect. They forced me to ride them rough shod. I have never spared them nor ever will when I see them err. I have given them whip and spur. I rolled them in this county, from high political standing to the bottom of the valley. I took Democracy from its slumbering ashes. Yes, I—Jacob Gibson did it. With my zeal, perseverance, justice of the cause, and my purse (and I dare contradiction) raised you Democrats from the bottom of the political valley to the top of the political hill. I placed your feet on the neck of Federalism, and when you got there you forgot how it happened . . .

In the end Jacob Gibson was completely exonerated both by the authorities and by the more intelligent of his neighbors.

Meanwhile, the British fleet had been reinforced and had moved up to Poplar Island, even closer to St. Michaels.

Avoiding that village for the moment, they proceeded up to the head of the bay, where they burned Frenchtown, then Havre de Grace on the western shore, and back to set torch to Georgetown in Kent County. The fears of St. Michaels increased as the successive reports came in. The British boasted: "We will ship the Democrats for being enemies to the British Government and drub the Federalists for being enemies to their own." On August 10th, twenty-five British vessels were reported in Eastern Bay and the people of St. Michaels knew they could not much longer escape. There were six vessels in all on the ways at St. Michaels.

They had done what they could to make ready. Several other militia companies had been assembled, bearing such names as the Easton Fencibles, Mechanic Volunteers, Hearts of Oak, Independent Volunteers, etc. Their first care was to provide themselves with handsome uniforms. The ladies of the village had worked a fine silk flag, which was presented with appropriate ceremonies to Brigadier General Perry Benson, who was in command. By August there were five hundred men under arms.

Four guns, six-pounders and nines, were mounted behind the breastworks on Parrott's Point on the southerly side of the harbor, and according to tradition there was a boom across the mouth. Captain William Dodson was in command here. Lieutenant Clement Vickers, with two guns, was stationed on the Bayside road just below the town, in case the British should attack by land. Gibson's two guns, in charge of Lieutenant John Graham, were mounted on Impey Dawson's shipyard wharf within the town.

On August 9th the townspeople were warned of an impending attack by a British deserter who came ashore at Bayside. The night fell wet and drizzly. The enemy, in eleven barges, with three hundred soldiers and marines, stole up close to the opposite shore of the river escaping videttes posted at Ashcroft's and other points. They passed beyond the village and crossed just above the fort on Parrott's Point.

The Britishers waded ashore through shallow water. They were discovered by a sentry on the flank of the breast-works, who gave the alarm. A farcical scene succeeded, for the defenders of the fort, excepting three, flung down their arms without firing a shot and ran pell-mell for the village through a field of corn. The British sent a volley after them but no damage was done except to the corn. Only Captain Dodson with a white man and a Negro stuck to the guns. One gun only could be trained on the advancing British. Though it was already loaded, Captain Dodson thrust into the muzzle a twenty-seven-pound bundle of old scrap iron, nails, etc., wrapped with rope yarn, and fired it. At the moment of discharge the gun leaped over the parapet into the ditch. But that one shot did fearful execution among the British. It was enough. They turned and fled back to their barges.

Each barge was mounted with one or more cannon, and the British lay to out in the river and bombarded the town at their leisure. Their fire was returned with spirit from the two guns on Dawson's wharf; Vickers's guns were fetched up from the Bayside road to help. On account of the fog, perhaps, the British fire did little damage to the town. One cannon ball is said to have gone through the roof of a house and bounced down the stairs, passing the terrified wife of the householder on its way. From this circumstance, perhaps, has grown the story that the townspeople hung lights in their upper stories and in trees to deceive the aim of the British. No contemporary account speaks of such a ruse.

The Talbot artillerists showed better aim. One barge at least was hit, and had to be lashed between two others to keep it afloat. Not a drop of Talbot blood was spilt, but the British (as subsequently reported by a deserter) lost a captain, a lieutenant of marines, and twenty-seven men. Most of these were killed in the first and last awful discharge of that gun which leaped the parapet. According to tradition, the dead naval officer was a nephew of Admiral Cockburn himself, who, on the eve of his return to England, had begged permission for "one last frolic against the Yankees." Upon seeing his dead body, the admiral is said to have exclaimed, "He was worth more than the whole damned town!" Jacob Gibson's two guns directed by Lieutenant Graham, were given the credit of finally driving the British back to their ships.

The booty captured by the Americans consisted of one pair of boarding pistols, two boarding cutlasses, and a pair of dancing pumps! After the British retired, there were violent recriminations among the town's defenders, and Talbot blood then began to flow from punched noses! One company had never paused in its flight until it reached Royal Oak, four miles distant. There, when the roll was called, every man answered to his name! This was quoted, sarcastically, as a wonderful example of militia discipline.

The fleet sailed north to attack Queenstown in Queen Anne County. They were unsuccessful here also. On August 26th, they were reported off Bayside, where they put ashore 1,800 soldiers and 300 sailors. General Benson had only 600 militia hidden in the woods to bar the way of this formidable force. An observer reported that "the number of small boats was so great it was like chips thrown on the water from a basket." However, it was only for shore exercise. After burning a couple of small boats and plundering some houses, the British re-embarked, the ships presently stood down the bay, and the Talbot militia was disbanded.

The following year, 1814, saw the burning of Washington and the attack of the British on Baltimore. Captain Sir Peter Parker, to create a diversion, landed in Kent County but was defeated at Caulk's Field and killed. Easton and St. Michaels were in expectation of an attack, but none materialized. Having suffered a repulse at Baltimore, the enemy abandoned his bases in the bay and sailed south. But petty privateering continued.

After the war, age softened the asperities of Jacob Gibson's character. The war taught him the lesson that even a Federalist might love his country. He contented himself now with being a spectator of the political scene, but his high spirit was never subdued. He died in 1818 and was buried at Marengo. His house there was destroyed by fire in 1847.

Frederick Douglass, the eloquent Negro slave, spent a part of his servitude at Bayside, and he has left an unflattttering picture of St. Michaels as it was in 1833. Yet one recognizes the truth of it; this is the Eastern Shore at its worst. At this period the business of shipbuilding was declining and the oystering trade was rising. "Every boat carried a jug of rum against the cold," remarks Douglass. In his somewhat flowery style, he speaks of St. Michaels' "indolent disregard for social improvement" and calls the village "an unsaintly as well as unsightly place."

Douglass, quite naturally a refractory slave, had been hired out by his owner to a slave breaker named Covey to be tamed. Thus Covey obtained ample labor to till his fields at little or no expense. Douglass has drawn a devastating portrait of this mean, sly man, whom the Negroes christened the Snake. He was a coward too, and when Douglass, a magnificent physical specimen, finally dared to fight him back and beat him, Covey never laid hands on him again.

Slave traders, slave breakers, overseers and all such cattle were very offensive to the genteel white people of the Eastern Shore, Douglass explains, but were held to be necessary evils. Since they were universally detested, naturally they acted detestably. It was the poor white man who had just acquired his first slave that made the most brutal master.

CHAPTER 17

The Miles River

ABOUT four miles above St. Michaels, the Miles River executes a right-angled bend and heads toward the northeast. The view from the southerly shore at this point is a never-to-be-forgotten one. You look down one long reach to the horizon, and far up the other between tree-bordered, deeply indented shores. This 12-mile river, so insignificant among the rivers of earth, nevertheless sweeps out to the bay with all the majesty of another Amazon.

A few miles farther upstream, Miles River bridge crosses. Before the bridge was built, this was Miles River ferry, the point whence Commodore Grason departed on his cruise, and to which he returned with his prizes. It is less than three miles by road from here to Easton. The little *Surprise,* first steamboat to visit the Eastern Shore, tied up here in 1817. I am sure she was well-named. The *Emma Giles* was the best-known of later steamboats to serve this wharf.

At the left-hand end of the bridge, as one faces upstream, is a comfortable old house called the Anchorage. Its most famous proprietor in bygone times was the Reverend John Gordon, rector of St. Michael's Church downriver during the later eighteenth century. Behind his church he maintained a race track where he and his parishioners bet on each other's horses after service.

Across the road from the Anchorage stands a crumbling stone church covered with creepers. This is St. John's. It is not ancient, having been built as recently as 1833, but it was abandoned for lack of support in 1900 and is fast be-

coming an interesting ruin. It stands close enough to the water to be pleasantly reflected in its surface on still days; indeed, the bank is washing on that side, and the whole structure threatens to slide in.

At the other end of the bridge, hidden among trees, is the modern house which replaces the Rest, home of Admiral Buchanan, the distinguished naval officer who commanded the ironclad *Virginia* (or *Merrimac*) during the Civil War.

He and Admiral Farragut were friends in youth and became adversaries at the Battle of Mobile Bay.

The view looking upstream from the bridge is fine and characteristic. The river divides into three deep prongs which wind away out of sight between their tree-bordered banks. They are Glebe Creek (formerly Fausley), another Goldsborough Creek, and the upper reach of the Miles.

On the first point, but hidden among its trees, stands the Villa, a modern house of no architectural value, but having a strange and fateful history. It was built just before the Civil War by Richard France, known as Maryland's "Lottery King." Licensed by the state, he became so scandalously rich that the authorities were forced by the better element in politics to rescind his license. He then undertook to operate in Delaware. Outlawed there, robbed by his partner, seized for debt in Delaware, he died penniless in jail.

The next owner was Henry May, of the celebrated Baltimore family. Throughout his regime the Villa was a scene of abounding hospitality and luxury. In the troubles that followed the Civil War, May was involved in a financial scandal. It was charged that his broker became a bankrupt through May's failure to meet his obligations. As a result, May was ostracized socially and finally died at the Villa out of pure chagrin.

The Villa was then purchased by a young Randall, of whom nothing has been recorded except that he ran through a great fortune at breathless speed, and sold out to a mysterious "Mr. Brady." No one on the Shore ever knew who or what Mr. Brady was. He was a very plain man. He came and went silently in a magnificent yacht. This was during the late seventies before the migration of millionaries to the Eastern Shore, and nothing like this yacht had ever been seen in those waters. Later, after certain disclosures had been made, the county people became convinced that the Villa had been the hide-out of Boss Tweed, New York City's famous boodler, while the police were looking for him. They now believe that "Brady" was his butler.

A little farther up Glebe Creek stands a modernized dwelling that is said to include within its walls a part of Wenlock Christison's house. Christison was one of the great Quaker preachers. He suffered repeated persecutions in Massachusetts—"twenty-seven cruel stripes on his naked body at one time laid on with deliberation (so was the order of the Magistrates who stood to see it) in the cold winter season, who bid the Jaylor lay it on; who did as hard as he could and then robbed him of his wastcoat." He came to Maryland in middle life, about 1670, and was presented with some land on Glebe by a well-to-do Quaker. Another presented him with a servant. Here he lived in peace with his family "without fear of pillory, jail, or constable's whip," and he called his place "Ending of Controversy."

At the head of the creek is Fausley Wood Farm, a quaint old house, chiefly notable for having been the birthplace of Tench Tilghman, the chevalier sans reproche of the American Revolution. He was born in 1744. After having made a competency in business in Philadelphia, he joined Washington's "family" in 1776 and remained with the commander in chief as aide-de-camp or secretary until the end. He devoted every penny of his private fortune to the Continental cause. The reticent Washington, judging from his letters, loved the young man better than any other of his officers.

Tench Tilghman is the Paul Revere of the Eastern Shore. His popular fame rests on his journey from Yorktown to Philadelphia with the news of Cornwallis's surrender. The event has inspired no less than three poets to write lengthy ballads, but their sentiments are better than their poetry. Colonel Tilghman, a modest man, left no account of his exploit, and the poets had to make it up out of their heads. Only a tradition of galloping hoofs in the night and demands for a fresh horse persists on the Eastern Shore.

The best of the three poems is by Howard Pyle, the artist, who was no mean balladist when his fancy inclined him that way. With a grand disregard for historical fact, Pyle assumes that Tench Tilghman rode the whole way from Yorktown, Virginia, to Philadelphia, whereas in reality he took ship from Yorktown to Annapolis, another vessel across to Rock Hall, in Kent County, and by horse from Rock Hall to Philadelphia.

Arriving in Philadelphia in the middle of the night, Colonel Tilghman narrowly escaped arrest by the watch for making a racket at the door of the president of Congress. But the words "Cornwallis, Yorktown" ensured him a great welcome. Lights flashed everywhere; all Philadelphia got out of bed and spent the rest of the night in the streets; the Liberty bell was rung.

In the last year of the war, Tench Tilghman married his cousin, Anna Maria, daughter of Matthew Tilghman, the patriarch. General Washington wrote him reproachfully: "Why have you been so niggardly in communicating your condition to us? By dint of inquiries we have heard of your marriage; but have scarcely got a confirmation of it yet." Colonel Tilghman lived only three years longer, dying in 1786 from an abscess of the liver contracted at Valley Forge. Washington wrote: "He left as fair a reputation as ever belonged to a human character." His young wife retired to

Aaron Sopher

Plinhimmon on the Tred Avon River. Her widowhood lasted for fifty-seven years.

Samuel Hambleton, purser of the *Lawrence,* Boss Tweed, the boodler, Gordon, the racing parson, Admiral Buchanan of the Confederate Navy, Wenlock Christison, the Quaker, and Tench Tilghman, of General Washington's family—what an oddly assorted company to be associated with the banks of one small river!

On Goldsborough Creek stands Myrtle Grove, one of the most satisfying of all the old houses on the Shore, because it strikes a true balance between neglect and ostentation. It is not in the least run down; on the other hand, it exhibits nothing of the distressing polish of some of the millionaires' homes. It is still possessed by descendants of the builder; the lovely old house is in their blood, and all their care is to conserve its true character.

It was built in 1741 by Judge Robert Goldsborough, a solid citizen and one of the innumerable descendants of Madam Jenckins-Henry-Hampton of proud memory. A portrait of Judge Goldsborough with his wife and two children by Charles Willson Peale is the chief treasure of the house today. The judge's son, Robert Henry Goldsborough, was an even worthier descendant of his regal great-great-grandmother. A cultivated, vivacious, elegant gentleman, they called him the Chesterfield of the Eastern Shore, and give him credit, more than any other, for establishing the code of polite behavior which persists more or less to this day. He was twice appointed to the United States Senate, and left behind him a tradition of unfailing courtesy to an opponent, which can hardly be said to have survived in that august chamber.

Beside the Miles River lives a delightful old lady, unmarried, whose conversation better illustrates life on the Eastern Shore than any description of mine.

"My house," she said, "is in the unique case of having descended through the female line for five generations. I remember an English visitor who asked what the Goldsboroughs were so famous for on the Eastern Shore and my mother replied tartly, 'For propagating males.' My people were not gifted that way. There was an eighteenth century proprietor, Jacob Hindman, who had five sons and he left this property to whichever one of them was willing to assume his debts of honor to Colonel Lloyd. The eldest son turned it down, but the second son, William Hindman took over. However, he presently sold the place to his brother-in-law, my ancestor. Then came the five generations of women.

"My mother had only nine ancestors. My sister, when she wished to join the Colonial Dames, managed to dig up eighteen, but when she learned that the Colonial Dames charged five dollars a head for ancestors, she concentrated on one.

"There's supposed to be buried treasure on this place. My great-great-grandfather became president of the Maryland Senate, and before leaving for Annapolis, he buried all the family valuables for safekeeping. He died and was buried in Annapolis before he could describe the hiding place to anybody. His daughter searched for it with a hazel twig, followed by a servant with a spade. You see, everybody had to bury things when they went away from home. It was usually in a truck patch, but his daughter never found it. Every generation has searched for it since, without any better success. Once there was a young man came here with earphones to search. It was his idea that when he heard a singing in his ears, he was to stop and dig. All he found was a plow point and a few rusty nails. He's in an asylum now.

"In my grandmother's time, some spiritualists were called in to locate the treasure, and we had a table-rapping séance. The answer came, to measure off so many feet from the corner of the office in a southeasterly direction, then so many feet in another direction, and dig down five feet. Before they got to five feet a terrible thunderstorm came up and Grandmother made them fill up the hole for fear the colts would break their legs in it. They never did get down to five feet.

"The only treasure I ever found around the place were some George I coins, some French coins of Louis XVIII, and some Spanish silver coins.

"In the old days the white gentlemen didn't do much, you know. They left the work to the slaves and the overseer while they rode around and dined with each other. They had a sort of club. One gentleman named Bracco lost everything he possessed at cards. He was a very agreeable man, and Great-grandmother let him have a farm rent-free. At Gross' Coate there was a little darky that the gentlemen planted on a stool in the middle of the table to fiddle for them while they drank and played cards. One night Great-grandmother's husband brought him home without a word of explanation, and he lived here during the rest of his long life. His name was Ned. He was the most trusted servant on the place. He was always loaned out with the silver and the cut glass for county weddings. He is buried here in the colored graveyard.

"When Great-grandmother's first husband died, she had to sell fourteen farms to pay his gambling debts. Later she married again—that was my great-grandfather, but when he died it cost her only ten thousand dollars. Afterwards, one of Great-grandmother's economies was to insist on having everything they used made in the house. All the nice things they had had from Baltimore were raveled out and rewoven with wool to make a cloth just a little better than that used for the Negroes. Five Negro women used to sit in the dining room at night, knitting, raveling and sewing. Great-grandmother kept a sharp eye on them. If a piece of sewing didn't suit her, 'Hm!' she would say, 'that was sewed with a hot needle and a burning thread!'

"'Sally-go-naked' was the name of the rough cloth for the field hands made of flax fibers. It had to be beaten on a wooden block before it could be cut and sewn. The hands ate 'shovey,' which was corn meal fried in the pan after meat.

"Barney, one of the slaves, came to Great-grandmother. 'Mistus, I want you to sell me. I don't want to cheat you, mistus. I want yo' put me in yo' pocket.' You see, he had made up his mind to run away. Barney was the only slave that Great-grandmother ever sold.

"One night Marina, a field hand, went to camp meeting with Ervin, the coachman. Ervin came back without her. 'Mistus,' he reported, 'Marina done got religion. She stiff as a board.' 'Well, bring her home in the cart,' said Great-grandmother. Next morning Marina was no better, and Great-grandmother went down to quarters to see what was to be done. The overseer and all the hands were standing about.

" 'Give her the switch?' suggested the overseer. 'No,' said Great-grandmother. 'Sing over her,' suggested one of the hands. So they sang various songs such as 'The fifth wheel runs on the minute of the time,' 'Swing low, sweet chariot,' 'A billy le bumble ay; Oh my, de bell done rung!' ' 'Taint old age that makes me so; 'tis 'fliction, chile, 'tis 'fliction.'

"Still Marina never stirred and they tried pouring new milk down her throat. When this failed, Great-grandmother said sharply, 'Now, if you're not up in five minutes, girl, you're going to get the cowhide.'

"Marina recovered.

"Great-grandmother had three sons by her first husband. They didn't amount to much. At the same time there was a very bright [almost white] girl in the house called Milky. There was a strong suspicion that Milky was a half sister to the three boys. She always had a stool to sit on in the cart. Milky was very ambitious. Time after time, they would catch her kneeling at the door of the room where the boys were being tutored with her ear to the keyhole. No punishment could stop her. And every now and then she would break into poetry that she had picked up by listening:

> Down in a damp and mossy dell
> A modest violet grew.

"Ervin was Milky's half brother on the other side. There was a terrible excitement in the household when he came to Great-grandmother and reported that Milky had run away. Mother, then a little girl, dropped to her knees and prayed, 'Now I lay me down to sleep.' Milky never came back. Years later it was learned that she had gone to Philadelphia, married a white man and passed over. On his deathbed Ervin confessed that he had helped her escape.

"During the insurrection on the island of Santo Domingo, the white refugees brought their cooks and other house servants to Baltimore with them, and as they were very poor, they opened a school. This was in Grandmother's time. Grandmother sent Maria, her housekeeper, to the white ladies to be taught lacemaking, and her cook to their cooks to learn that art. Other Eastern Shore ladies did the same, and that is how Eastern Shore cooking became so famous.

"In the early days of the house, the gardens here were celebrated. They were laid out by the same man who designed the gardens at Wye House. We still have his original plan. There were thirty squares of box divided by gravel paths, each square containing flowers or vegetables. There was an arbor at each of the six principal intersections and eight archways at other points. At the water view, there was a kind of pergola with a floor for dancing on the second story. Around the outside of the entire garden grew what they called rose-water roses, hundreds of bushes. The rose water was distilled at home and sold to a druggist in Easton.

"The war, of course [she meant the Civil War], broke up everything here. The slaves were freed and went away. This was in my Mother's time and she was reduced to dreadful straits. Peter came home and begged to be taken back. 'I'se tired payin' doctor's bills and buyin' chillen shoes,' he said. So he was put to work in the stable. Ervin came to put flowers on his mother's grave. He had gone to Washington with $600 that he had saved from tips and trapping muskrats; and he had speculated and made money. When he saw how badly things were going with my mother, he offered in the most delicate way to lend money to her. She didn't take it, of course, but she never forgot the offer.

"Years later, Ervin paid her another visit. He had made more money. He left $30,000 when he died. 'Miss Mary,' he said to my mother, 'all my life I worked hard and now I want to see the world.' As it happened, my sister Claribel was living in Paris at that time, and my mother, never thinking anything would come of it, gave Ervin the address of her pension in Paris. And, lo and behold, one day he turned up there! The mistress of the pension wanted to ask him to dinner. Well, my sister couldn't do that, but she showed him all the sights of Paris, Ervin always insisting on walking respectfully one pace behind her!

"We have a great habit on the Eastern Shore of coining nicknames," said my friend in conclusion. "One of the funniest ones was for Robert Lloyd Tilghman. He used to sign his name Robert Ll. Tilghman, and so he got to be called 'Bobble Double Ell.' "

CHAPTER 18

The Lloyds of Wye

THE Wye is unique among the rivers of the Eastern Shore; its narrower, winding waters have little of the nobility of the Choptank or the Miles, but they reveal constantly changing prospects of a sweetness all their own. This part was settled at a very early date. Within a mile of its mouth it is divided by an extensive island, also called Wye. That part of the river which reaches to the west of the island is the Back Wye, while the southerly arm is the Front Wye; a channel connecting the two streams behind the island is called Wye Narrows. The Front Wye for the whole of its course forms the boundary between Talbot County and Queen Annes.

The Back Wye is divided from Eastern Bay by a long, narrow neck ending in Bennett's Point. Here stood the seat of Richard Bennett who, it will be remembered, was one of the leaders of the Puritan rebellion (1652) against Lord Baltimore. Like his friend, Edward Lloyd, he made peace with his lordship after the troubles, and, being one of the first on the ground, was able to leave his son, Richard II, the richest young man in the province. Richard II married Henrietta Maria Neal and, losing his life in a drowning accident not long afterward, left young Madam Bennett the greatest catch in Maryland. We shall go on with her story directly.

Opposite Bennett's Point lies Bruff's Island, a lovely spot covered with tall trees. Once there was a deep channel between it and the main, but it has filled up with sand, and Bruff's Island is no longer an island. On the shore of the main here stood the ancient town of Doncaster which, judging from its spelling in some of the old records, was called Donkster by its people. At other times it was called Wye Town. Probably never more than a tobacco warehouse, a chapel, and half a dozen houses, that was enough to earn it the name of town in the seventeenth century. Nothing remains of it now but a few foundation stones and, along the shore, a lonely gravestone bearing this inscription:

> Here lyeth immured ye bodye
> of Francis Butler, Gent. son of
> Rhoderick Butler, Gent. who was
> unfortunately drowned in St. Michael's
> River, the 3rd Mar. 1689, aged
> 42 years or thereabout.
> *Memento Mori*

All that is known of this unfortunate man is that he arrived in Maryland in 1688 bearing a powerful recommendation from the Countess of Tyrconnell, who was the famous "La Belle Jenyns" at the gay court of Charles II, and sister to Sarah, first Duchess of Marlborough. Lord Baltimore himself ordered that the countess's "commands" should be carried out; consequently, Butler was immediately appointed high sheriff of Talbot County—but in less than a year he was dead. No account survives of the accident that ended his life.

On the shore of Woodland Creek near-by is a tiny, ancient farmhouse with the familiar steep roof and gigantic chimney, which calls itself Wye Town. The present proprietor insists that this was the site of the old town, but it doesn't much matter now.

After passing Bruff's Island, we cross the mouth of Shaw Bay in the Front Wye, and presently enter Lloyd's Creek. On the shore, but scarcely visible from the water, rises Wye House, the most famous mansion of this country, though not necessarily the most beautiful. It is the seat of the Lloyds, premier family of the Eastern Shore. An imposing "five-part" wooden house, gleaming in its dress of white paint among the greenery, it is said to have been built or rebuilt in 1781 after a marauding party of the British had passed this way—the circumstances are obscure. A five-part house is one with a central block, having a corridor or colonnade at each side, and a wing at the end of each corridor.

The house looks down a broad swath of grass hemmed in with shrubbery on both sides, and known as the bowling green. This vista is closed by one of the most charming pieces of architecture on the Eastern Shore, the orangery, eighteenth century equivalent for a greenhouse. Constructed of ancient, moldering brick, the front is completely filled with a row of lofty arched windows to admit all of the sun. Unfortunately, no care has been taken to preserve the beautiful building.

On either side of the bowling green lie the astonishing box gardens. An elderly gardener on the place said he figured he had three miles of box hedges to keep in order. Naturally, they can be clipped only in a cursory manner, and many of the old alleys have closed up. Actually, the gardens are more beautiful and appealing in this state than if there were a brigade of gardeners keeping every leaf and blade of grass in place. Yet there is a note of sadness, too, in such a garden.

Beyond the garden, on the right as you face the orangery, stands the little steep-roofed brick house that was the original homestead of the Lloyds, built about 1661. Off to the left of the gardens lies the Lloyd burial rgound, the unique feature of Wye House. Here lie eight generations of Lloyds, the founder of the family having been buried in England. The Lloyds constituted a kind of family dynasty. The hearthstone at Wye was their altar. They are all buried here—even the sons-in-law and their offspring—except the first Lloyd. Surely there cannot be another such private graveyard anywhere in the Americas.

All these Lloyds one after another bear a strong family resemblance: stout men, hardheaded, prudent, eminently respectable, never given to excess, and singularly unimaginative. If there was a sport in this stock, it was Richard Bennett Lloyd. He was a disagreeable fellow—but, then, he was not the head of the family; in each generation the head of the family was a sound and steady man. Let the story tell itself; in a sense it is the story of the Eastern Shore:

Edward Lloyd, the founder, was the first of the Puritan immigrants from Virginia to rebel against Lord Baltimore. The Puritans were being persecuted in Virginia, it will be remembered, and Baltimore, the Catholic, invited them to Maryland, hoping thereby to secure immunity from the Puritan Parliament of England for his own party. The Puritans repaid Baltimore by seizing control of the government. They held it for six years, 1652-1658.

When Oliver Cromwell finally confirmed Lord Baltimore in his patent, the latter issued a general amnesty and, in Edward Lloyd's case, even went so far as to appoint him a member of Governor Josias Fendall's Council. Fendall turned traitor, too. It is uncertain what part Lloyd took in this brief rebellion; he appears to have kept his mouth shut. Fendall was fired, and when Philip Calvert, his lordship's brother, was appointed governor, Edward Lloyd became a member of his Council too. In early Maryland, the Governor's Council served as the upper house of the legislature.

In 1659 Edward Lloyd received his first Eastern Shore grant of three thousand acres lying between Choptank and Tred Avon, which he christened Hîr Dîr Lloyd (spelled in various ways), meaning Lloyd's long line, or road. In successfully promoting this tract, he laid the foundations of his fortune and quickly increased it by other land speculations, by planting tobacco, and in trade. He is supposed to have come over to Talbot in 1661, and built the first house at Wye.

In 1668, already a rich man, he abandoned Maryland for England. His idea was that his experience in America would enable him to trade with the colonies to advantage from the other side, and presumably he was right. He left with his son, Philemon, aged twenty-one, a power of attorney for the management of his estates in Maryland.

Philemon proved worthy of the trust. He promptly added Wye Island to his father's holdings and, young as he was, became the colonel of a militia regiment. From that day to this, each head of the Lloyd family has been called Colonel Lloyd in token of respect. Philemon quickly won the hand of Madam Henrietta Maria Neal Bennett, and so brought another great fortune into the family.

Madam Henrietta Maria Lloyd was very beautiful. She had spent her childhood in Spain, her father being a merchant there, and the romantic associations of that country clung about her; it was said that Henrietta Maria of Spain, who was Charles I's queen, had stood godmother for her. She was a Catholic, and she built the first little chapel of that faith at Doncaster, or Wye Town. As Madam Lloyd she soon became a very great lady on the Shore, second only to Madam Hampton of Mary's Lot. They were contemporaries; one would like to have seen a meeting between them. Even more widely than those of Madam Hampton, Madam Henrietta Maria's descendants are scattered today throughout the counties—and none of them ever forgets that she was his forebear. Madam Henrietta Maria Lloyd is the great ancestress of the Eastern Shore.

Philemon Lloyd, meanwhile, was rising in the world. In 1670 he was appointed one of the justices of the Quorum for Talbot, and was also elected to represent the county in the House of Burgesses at St. Marys. Only certain of the justices were "of the Quorum." Such a one had to be present at a trial, or it wasn't legal. In 1682 Colonels Philemon Lloyd and Henry Coursey negotiated a highly successful treaty with the Five Nations Indians, or Iroquois, at Albany in New York State. This greatly enhanced his reputation. He died in 1685, only thirty-eight years old, and is buried at Wye. Judging from the countless references to him in the early records, he was one of the ablest of the Lloyds. Since he predeceased his father, who still lived in England, he never actually came in for the Lloyd fortune.

His son and heir, Edward Lloyd II, was only fifteen at the time of his father's death, but he had his capable mother at his side. His grandfather died in England about 1695, and his mother, the beautiful Henrietta Maria, only fifty years old, in 1697. She had borne her husband three sons and seven daughters. Her tomb at Wye House bears an inscription supplying almost the only touch of sentiment in the burial ground—it was not composed by a Lloyd, but by her eldest son, Richard Bennett.

HENRIETTA
MARIA LLOYD
Shee who now takes her rest within this tomb,
Had Rachells face and Leas fruitful womb,
Abigails wisdom, Lydeas faithful heart,
With Martha's care and Mary's better part.
Who died the 21st day of May [Anno]
Dom. 1697 50 years [?]
months 23 days.
To whose memory Richard Bennett dedicates this tomb.

As soon as he grew up, Edward II began to succeed to his father's honors. All the rest of the Lloyds were Edwards, and in order to distinguish between them Edward II has been termed "the president." In 1697 he became one of the "Worshipful Commissioners and Justices of the Peace" for Talbot, and he was already called colonel. He was also a member of the Quorum. He had a brother, Philemon II, who likewise had an honorable career, though he lacked the advantage of heading the family.

In 1698 Edward II went to the House of Burgesses (or Delegates), and four years later to the Governor's Council. The chief business before the House while he was a member was the bill for establishing the Angelican Church of Maryland. It bore down hard on the Catholics and Quakers, and it is hoped that Edward II fought it for his mother's sake. After several stormy sessions, it finally received the royal assent.

With the name of this Edward and his brother Philemon

is associated the only romantic tale in the long annals of the Lloyds. Thus runs the story:

It was the custom of the Quakers to hold a great annual meeting at Third Haven. These meetings drew the Friends from all over the eastern and the western shores, besides a great crowd of those who had no interest in any sort of religion but merely came to see the fun. It was like a fair. The Quakers themselves were sore distressed by the booths for "tippling and trumpery," the side shows of every kind that sprang up around the grounds, and especially the horse racing, which was their detestation. They succeeded at last in having such unseemly amusements suppressed by law in the vicinity of the meetinghouse.

At the meeting in 1702, Edward Lloyd II and his brother Philemon rode over to Third Haven separately to see the fun. From different points of vantage, each young man witnessed the coming of a fair Quakeress seated on a pillion behind her father. The plainness of her dress accentuated her radiant beauty. A portrait of her which survives, in spite of the ravages of time, confirms the tale of her loveliness. Each young man fell in love on the spot, and upon making inquiries learned that the exquisite creature was Miss Sarah Covington of Somerset County.

Some days later Philemon, the younger, upon riding down to distant Somerset, found his brother Edward's horse, with the handsome accouterments saved for high days and holidays, tied outside the Covington door. No doubt Philemon's heart sank, for Edward was the chief of his clan. The brothers talked it over apart, and Philemon proposed that he who had seen her first should have the first chance to offer himself. Upon comparing notes, it was discovered that

Edward had caught sight of her on the road before she reached the meeting. And Edward won her.

Whatever truth there may be in the tale, it is a fact that Edward Lloyd II married Sarah Covington, Quakeress, in 1703. She, too, became a great lady and proved to have wonderful good sense in addition to her beauty.

Meanwhile, honors continued to be heaped on Edward II. In 1708 he became major general of militia, and from 1709 until 1714, now president of the Council, he served as de facto governor of Maryland. In 1715 the government was returned to the Lords Baltimore and Edward Lloyd continued to serve on the Governor's Council until his death in 1718. He left four minor children.

In 1721, Sarah Covington Lloyd, still beautiful and notable for her intelligence, married Colonel James Hollyday, a distinguished provincial figure in his own right, member of His Lordship's Council, Treasurer of the Eastern Shore, etc. During the minority of the Lloyd heir, he came to Wye House to live, and several of his own children were born there, including Henry, who was to marry Anna Maria Robins of Peachblossom and build Ratcliffe Manor for her, as heretofore described. Sarah Covington will come upon the scene once more.

Edward Lloyd III, termed the councilor, was the third son of Edward Lloyd and Sarah Covington. His elder brothers died before reaching their majority. Like his predecessors, Edward III went to the House of Delegates as soon as he reached years of discretion, and three years later was called to the "Honorable Council of Maryland" by Governor Ogle. In time he also became receiver-general of the province, a very lucrative employment. At this period, a few great families divided all the important provincial positions among themselves, forming a kind of oligarchy.

During the reign, as one might term it, of the third Edward, the French and Indian War was fought. After Braddock's defeat, all western Maryland even to Baltimore was in a panic, fearing a descent of the enemy, but this excitement hardly touched the Eastern Shore. During the conflict, a shipload of the unfortunate Acadian exiles was dumped off at Oxford. No provision had been made for them, and it was up to Colonel Lloyd, as the richest man in the county, to supply their wants. This he did throughout the winter of 1755-1756, but with much grumbling. It cost him £5 a week while the Acadians stayed at Oxford, and £12 weekly after they came to Wye.

The rich and childless great-uncle, Richard Bennett III, died about this time, making Colonel Lloyd his residuary legatee, and thus bringing another fortune into the family.

In 1760, Colonel Lloyd served on the commission that finally settled the Maryland-Pennsylvania boundary and arranged for the Mason and Dixon line to be drawn. The colonel may not have been a very astute man—perhaps he was too rich. At any rate, Marylanders have always claimed that the Penns put one over on their state.

As the troubles with the mother country began to thicken, Colonel Lloyd was faced by a painful decision. He was naturally conservative, he was a man of great wealth, and as a member of the Council was supposed to uphold Lord Baltimore in all his prerogatives. On the other hand, all Talbot was overwhemlmingly patriot. He never seems to have made a clear-cut decision. Some of his acts on the Council suggest that he sympathized with the people's cause, but for the most part he said nothing. His attitude toward the Stamp

Act is not known. Perhaps the mental and emotional struggle hastened his end. In 1769 he was forced to resign from the Council, and in the following year he died.

The almost identical tombs of this Edward Lloyd and his wife, who was Ann Rousby, side by side in the burial ground at Wye House are generally considered the most beautiful funerary monuments of colonial times. Each consists of a great stone urn mounted on a tall base, the whole exquisitely carved. The gray lichen that covers them now adds to their beauty and to their aspect of mourning.

There was never any doubt as to the sentiments of Edward Lloyd IV, who has been termed "the patriot." He was just of age when the Stamp Act was put into effect, and joined heartily in the demonstrations against it. He opposed the proprietary governor, Robert Eden, at every point. Eden was personally popular in the province; he had a hard row to hoe. After his father's death, Edward Lloyd IV was returned to the House of Delegates (the General Assembly, they were beginning to call it) in 1771, and in 1773 was re-elected. This was the last election under the proprietary government.

The actual administration of the province passed by degrees to the Revolutionary Convention, and in 1776 Governor Eden finally dissolved the Assembly, which was already functioning in a vacuum. Edward Lloyd IV was in the thick of everything; member of the Committee of Correspondence; a signer of the Association of the Freemen of Maryland; member of the Provincial Conventions of 1775 and 1776, and of the Constitutional Convention called late in 1776. In 1777, when Thomas Johnson was chosen first governor of the state of Maryland, Edward Lloyd became one of his

Council of five. He held that seat until 1779, and in that year became a candidate for governor, but did not get it.

In 1780 he went back to the House of Delegates, and in the following year was elected state senator. In 1783-1784 he was a delegate to the United States Congress, which was sitting in Annapolis at this time, where Colonel Lloyd witnessed the resignation of General Washington as commander in chief. In 1786 he was again elected to the State Senate. In 1787 he was a member of the United States Constitutional Convention. When it was put to the people, Lloyd was pro-Constitution, and his side carried Maryland, though opposed by two of the greatest men in the state, Samuel Chase and Luther Martin. In 1791 Colonel Lloyd was returned to the State Senate for the last time, and served there until his death.

Meanwhile, in 1781 Wye House had been looted and burned, or partly burned, by a marauding party of British sailors. No particulars of this attack have come down to us. There is a question as to whether the house was burned at all, but the marauders certainly carried off, among other articles of value, 336 ounces of plate, some jewelry and watches, 8 Negroes, £800 in cash, gold and silver, £181 in new state money, and much clothing. Colonel Lloyd claimed abatement of his taxes on this property.

In Colonel Lloyd the Patriot, the family reached its apogee. He was the greatest gentleman of them all; he established the tradition of opulence and luxury that has clung to the name ever since. In his day there was a saying in Talbot County that God Almighty never intended any white man should own a thousand niggers, but Colonel Lloyd had 999. A slight exaggeration; in a return filed in 1790, Colonel

Lloyd acknowledged ownership of only 305 slaves—but that was nearly four times as many as the next biggest holder.

He possessed 11,884 acres of land; he bought the magnificent unfinished house of Samuel Chase in Annapolis (still known as the Chase House) and completed it; the Lloyd yacht has been a byword for luxury on the Eastern Shore ever since. To be sure, it was just a trading vessel on ordinary occasions, but when used by the family on their frequent trips back and forth across the bay, it was fitted out with awnings, rugs and pillows like the barge of an Oriental potentate.

Colonel Lloyd the Patriot's luxuriousness may be illustrated by some extracts from his letters to his agent in London. This was for the yacht:

> Be pleased to send me a compleat Sett of American Colours for a Pleasure-Boat of about 60 Tons burthen. Ensign and Pennant with 15 stripes; my Arms painted thereon, the Field azure, the Lion Gold; let these Colours be full-sized. Six brass Guns with hammers, screws &c. compleat to fix on Swivels and to act in such a manner as to give the greatest report[!]; with the letters E. Ll. thereon, fitted to fire with Locks. Powder-horns, pricking-wires & charges, showing the quantity of Powder for each gun; and 200 ball, fitted to the size of the Bore. Have the guns fully proved before purchasing.
>
> A phaeton to be built by the best maker in London, fashionable, handsome carriage with two setts poles, wheels, harness for four horses, fitted to drive with or without postilions. It must not be too high, I being a gouty man.
>
> Sky-blue cloth sufficient for six Servants Coats and yellow ditto for Breeches and Waistcoats, besides best blue and yellow Livery Lace.
>
> Two pairs of Gentlemen's silver Shoe Buckles of the most elegant patterns . . . fashionable hats for the Family by Wagner of Pall Mall; morning caps for Mrs. Lloyd; four dozen Ladies'

white kid gloves for a small hand; two quarts of the finest milk of roses in small bottles; twenty pounds best perfumed hair powder.

For Wye House:

> An elegant Watch Clock proper to fix on a Chimney Piece; also a Sett of Fashionable Decorations to set off a dining or supper table that will accommodate 20 people—with a sketch showing how the Images are to be placed on the Table according to the Vogue. The cost of the ornament not to exceed 100 guineas.

When received, these ornaments proved to be a mirror in five sections, framed in silver and mounted on silver feet, together with a set of vases and mythological figures in bisque. The set is still at Wye House.

Colonel Lloyd the Patriot was no Philistine; he ordered many pictures and books. He collected a good library of a thousand volumes which is still intact at Wye House.

The Patriot had a brother called Richard Bennett Lloyd (after the rich great-granduncle), who must have been a thorn in his flesh. For Richard went to England and, joining the officers' mess of the Coldstream Guards, rose to the rank of captain. Richard, judging from his portrait, was an uncommonly handsome young man, and in England he married Joanna Leigh, one of the great beauties of her day, who has been immortalized by Sir Joshua Reynolds. The Lloyds knew how to pick them! After the war, the Richard Lloyds came to Maryland. Incidentally, it was Richard who brought over a coat of arms for the Patriot from Wales. In spite of the éclat that surrounded him as an officer in the Guards, Richard appears to have been something of a boor, as will shortly appear.

The Patriot was carried off by the gout in 1796 at the

early age of fifty-two. As is proper, his is the tallest monument in the burial ground at Wye. It bears no inscription save his name and the dates. He left one son and six daughters by his wife, who was Mary Tayloe of Mount Airey, Virginia.

Edward Lloyd V, termed "the governor," succeeded at the age of seventeen. Under his regime, the family wealth increased but he scarcely cut such a dash as his father. In Dr. Ennals Martin's "Grand Caucus," which has been mentioned, he was lampooned as "Lord Cock-de-doodle do"—which does not seem to have been just, because, while he was a very dignified man, he held the most democratic principles and was widely popular. He was one of the leading proponents of free suffrage. He supported Thomas Jefferson throughout, except in one particular: Colonel Lloyd took a much more militant stand in the troubles with England. Immediately following the *Chesapeake-Leopard* affair (1807), he was chosen captain of the Talbot Patriot Troop.

He went to the Assembly at the age of twenty-one, and served there four years. He was elected to Congress in 1806. In 1809, after a hot campaign in which his effective oratory and gracious manners served him well, he was elected governor of Maryland when only thirty years old, and was chosen again for the following year. At his second inauguration, he wore a beautiful suit of green merino spun and woven from the wool of his own sheep. In that year he had the satisfaction of seeing the last restrictions removed from popular suffrage and the ballot introduced.

He returned to Annapolis as a state senator and served there until 1815. When the War of 1812 broke out, he was a colonel in the militia, but naturally had no opportunity to see action. In 1812, one notes that he was defeated for presidential elector (an important office in those days) by a gentleman who bore the extraordinary name of Alemby Jump. In 1819 he was chosen United States senator, though his opponent was no less a person than Charles Carroll of Carrollton.

In 1824 he was appointed by Governor Stevens of Maryland as his representative to meet General Lafayette at Frenchtown and conduct him to Fort McHenry. In the following year, he was elected to a second term in the United States Senate, but soon had to resign for reasons of health, and in 1826, at forty-seven he was carried off by the family malady, the gout.

The governor, a handsome man, fair and ruddy with prematurely gray hair, was the country gentleman par excellence. He was the greatest and most successful wheat grower and cattle raiser in Maryland. He was a charter member of the Maryland Agricultural Society, the first of its kind, which subsequently, however, declined to a mere dinner club. He organized the Farmer's Bank, first on the Eastern Shore, which, as the Easton National, is still going strong. He loved hunting, fowling, cockfighting, horse racing. He owned some of the best horses in the state; he established a deer park at Wye Town farm.

So much for the official view of Edward Lloyd V, the Governor, a wealthy and a worthy gentleman of the Eastern Shore. As the greatest slaveholder of that country, he certainly bore no harder on his blacks than did others of his class. In fact, he had little to do with them directly, since he employed an overseer on each of his twenty or thirty farms, as well as a general overseer to direct all.

Today the old families of the Shore are likely to dwell on slave days with nostalgic regret. It is one of their pet articles of belief that slaves were never treated cruelly in that delectable country—or hardly ever. That, even if a slaveholder was inclined to be cruel, popular opinion would restrain him. "My grandfather never sold a slave," they will say. It is so easy to forget disagreeable things—for instance, the existence of slave traders and "slave breakers." To the latter sort of men, difficult slaves were hired out for a period, and in such cases the whippings, the chainings and the starvings were inflicted out of sight of the home plantation.

In 1817 or thereabouts (the exact date is unknown), a little slave baby was born at Tuckahoe over by Choptank. All the name he had was Freddy, since his father, a white man, was unknown and he had never been christened, anyhow. His mother was the property of Captain Aaron Anthony, general overseer for Colonel Lloyd. As soon as his mother was able to return to work, Freddy was boarded out with his grandmother at Tuckahoe in a little, dirt-floored cabin with a chimney made of clay and straw. In front of the fireplace there was a boarded-over pit where the sweet potatoes were kept in winter. There was a ladder in the corner, and as soon as the baby was able to climb it, he went to bed on a floor of fence rails above. He saw his mother only at long intervals, because it was twelve miles from Wye House to Tuckahoe and she had to walk it both ways on her Sunday off, but he loved her dearly.

In spite of hardships, this part of his life was happy because his grandmother was kind and he nearly always had enough to eat. His black grandmother was a famous woman in her way, because she had a "growing hand," as they say on the Shore. It was believed that her touch was required to make potato sprouts thrive, and she was in great demand on the plantations. The little boy was always wishing that he could stay little; an instinct told him that trouble was waiting for him as soon as he grew big.

Sure enough, when he was eight years old he was parted from his loving grandmother and carried to Wye House. His master, Captain Anthony, had a house on the Great House farm, and so Freddy became a part of the vast Lloyd establishment, though he was not the property of Colonel Lloyd. Here he did not see his mother much oftener than before, because she had no cabin of her own where she could keep him. All the little black children were put in the care of an old Negro called Uncle Isaac Copper, who administered castor oil and Epsom salts to cure their bodies and taught them the Lord's prayer with a hickory stick to improve their minds. Seemed like everybody wanted to whip somebody else, the little boy reflected.

There were many wonders at Wye House, chief among them the windmill at Long Point, with its white sails ceaselessly turning, and Colonel Lloyd's marvelous sloop, the *Sally Lloyd*. Master Daniel Lloyd, a younger son of the house, became Freddy's constant companion and playmate. His chief woe at this time was that Aunt Katy, his master's old Negro cook, had a spite against him and, when he asked for food, he was more likely to get a rap on the head. He was always hungry.

The last two days of each month were like a festival at the Great House. Each outlying farm then sent in its representatives to obtain the monthly allowances for the slaves. It was considered a great privilege to be chosen to go. All the bustle and noise provided a welcome relief from the monotony of field labor. The monthly allowance of food for a field hand was eight pounds of pickled pork or its equivalent in fish, one bushel of ground corn *unbolted,* and a pint of salt. Nothing more. A slave never knew how much meal he was getting until after he had sifted it.

Their yearly allowance of clothes consisted of two tow linen shirts, one pair trousers of the same for summer, one pair woolen trousers for winter, a woolen jacket, and a pair of coarse shoes. Children under ten got two linen shirts only, and if these wore out they went naked. Men and women got a blanket apiece, the children none. They stuffed themselves in all sorts of odd corners at night to keep warm. Places in front of the fire where you could bury your feet in the ashes were the best.

There were no beds for any of the field hands, young or old, but they hardly missed those. Time to sleep was what they craved. They were worked from daylight until dark, or say eighteen hours in midsummer, and they had to do their cooking, washing and mending on their own time.

On the Great House Farm, as elsewhere, the slaves used to sing at their work—they had to, if they knew what was good for them. The little boy noted that the overseers immediately became suspicious of a silent slave. "Make a noise there!" they would shout. "Bear a hand!" The songs were often impromptu.

> I am going away to the Great House Farm,
> Oh yea, Oh yea, Oh yea!
> My old master is a good old master.
> Oh yea, Oh yea, Oh yea!

The overseer was too stupid to hear the note of irony.

These were the field hands. How sickeningly they envied their brothers and sisters, the pampered house servants, selected for their grace and good looks, who were always beautifully dressed in their young masters' and mistresses' slightly

worn clothes, encouraged to keep themselves neat and trim and to dress their hair becomingly—and who always got as much as they could eat!

In the Great House, according to Freddy, there was one gorgeous, unending round of feasting. In his recollections he lists two whole pages of the delicious things he saw preparing in the kitchen, while the rich fumes of baking, boiling, roasting and broiling assaulted his famished little nostrils. For weeks at a time the Great House was like a hotel. Once in a while his friend, Master Daniel Lloyd, would give him a cake and tell him all about the guests and their doings.

In the carriage house there were three handsome coaches, besides gigs, phaetons, barouches, sulkies and sleighs. Thirty-five horses were kept for pleasure, and there was a slave on duty in the stable at all hours of the night and day. In a separate building there was kept a pack of twenty-five hounds.

The head coachman was old Barney, a man of wonderful skill, according to Freddy. Yet he never seemed to be able to please his master. Whenever the horses were brought around, Colonel Lloyd or the young masters or the young ladies were sure to complain that such or such was not right, while Barney stood, hat in hand, with lowered head, taking it in silence. Barney was a great man to little Freddy, and one day the boy had the horrible experience of seeing the coachman forced to kneel on the ground and take a whipping from Colonel Lloyd. Both old men, he thought, and the fathers of children.

Another coachman was William Wilks, a highly favored slave, who was believed to be the son of Colonel Lloyd. Wilks had a deadly enemy in Murray Lloyd, whom he strongly resembled. Murray gave his father no rest until he whipped Wilks. The whipping was robbed of its effect when Colonel Lloyd gave Wilks a handsome gold watch afterward. Finally, in order to solve an impossible domestic situation, the colonel sold Wilks to Austin Woldfolk, the prominent slave trader, and the young man was taken away to Baltimore in irons. However, when he was put up on the block, he outbid all bidders and bought himself in. It was generally supposed that Colonel Lloyd had slipped him the money for that purpose, but Freddy asserted that it was other friends who supplied the means. At any rate, William Wilks lived on, a free man in Baltimore.

In due course, Freddy's master hired him out to work for his brother-in-law in Baltimore. After serving other masters, both cruel and kind—including a slave breaker, Freddy escaped to Freedom and called himself Frederick Douglass. By that name he is known to the world, the first, or if not the first, the greatest of articulate slaves.

Edward Lloyd VI, next in line, termed "the farmer," was kept at home by illness during the period of education; consequently, he lacked some of the finish of his father and grandfather. In his time the lavish hospitality at Wye House was much restricted; however, Edward VI was a very good farmer indeed. Through long years of agricultural depression, he kept his farms together and even increased their value. He would not yield to the growing custom of renting his farms, but continued to employ an overseer for each one. He paid off his father's debts, and under adverse conditions became the richest of all the Lloyds. He was reputed to be a harsh master to his slaves, but this may be because Frederick Douglass's *Narrative* was published in 1845, and readers would not stop to figure out that the Colonel Lloyd whom

Douglass tells about was the Governor, not the Farmer. The latter would not sell his slaves, and they increased so fast he was forced to buy great plantations in Mississippi to provide work for them. He accompanied his slaves on the long trek to Mississippi by wagon.

This Colonel Lloyd had no political employment, except briefly as a member of the Maryland Constitutional Convention of 1851, and as state senator from Talbot, 1851-1852. As the clouds thickened before the Civil War, his sympathies naturally were with the South, but he took no part in public affairs. He was not much of a churchman—indeed, none of the Lloyds was—and his will began: "I desire that my funeral be plain and private without parade and preaching." He died in 1861, at the beginning of the great conflict.

Edward Lloyd VII, termed "Master of Wye," was the unfortunate member of the dynasty, the great slaveowner who had to stand up under the shattering impact of the Emancipation Proclamation. This Lloyd inherited seven hundred slaves in Maryland and Mississippi. He bore his losses with admirable fortitude. On the day when all his field hands dropped their work at the call of a recruiting officer and marched away in a body to the steamboat at Miles River bridge, he was the calmest man in Talbot, and was not heard either to bewail his loss or to blame anybody. After the war, many of his former slaves returned to his employ.

In his youth, at the outbreak of the Mexican War, Edward Lloyd VII raised a company in Talbot and was subsequently assigned to the staff of Brigadier General Tench Tilghman (the second of that name), but he was not sent to Mexico. Later he served two terms in the Maryland Assembly but, like a true Lloyd, kept his mouth shut on the burning question of secession. During the years of the conflict, when the Eastern Shore lay in thrall to the Union troops, no word or act of Colonel Lloyd's added to the strain. The property in Mississippi was rendered completely valueless, and many of the Maryland farms, too, of necessity went untilled or half tilled.

When the war was over, the Master of Wye spent the rest of his long life striving with courage, industry and skill to rebuild his shattered fortunes. In 1873 he went to the State Senate and was re-elected in 1877. In 1883 he went back to the Assembly. He lived to the age of eighty-two, dying in 1907. "A man of elevated character," was said of him, "with an amiable disposition, and refined, simple manners."

On a spring day in 1881, during the tenure of the Master, a trim revenue cutter nosed into Lloyd's Creek and anchored. A boat was sent ashore carrying a letter from the collector of the port of Baltimore to Colonel Lloyd, saying that he, the cellector, had as his guest Mr. Frederick Douglass, who, with Colonel Lloyd's permission, would like to re-visit the scenes of his childhood. As it happened, Colonel Lloyd was away from home, but his second son, Mr. Howard Lloyd, went out to the cutter as his father's representative to make Mr. Douglass welcome. Douglass was now a greater name in the nation than Lloyd. What a home-coming for the ragged, hungry little slave boy of fifty-six years before!

Upon being shown around the place, Frederick Douglass found fewer changes than he had expected. The house was still magnificent, the gardens lovely, though not so well cared for as in the days of Mr. McDermott, the Scots gardener, and his four hands. What Douglass chiefly missed were the squads of little black children once seen in all directions, and the crowds of slaves in the fields. There were seven thousand acres in the home farm; in 1825 sixty slaves were required to work it; in 1881 ten hired hands (with improved machinery) were sufficient.

Nearly all the buildings the little boy had known were still in place, including the house of Captain Anthony, his first master. Douglass paused in front of a certain window of this house, where he had been accustomed to stand and sing as a child when his hunger became too great to bear. His master's daughter, Miss Lucretia, would sometimes recognize the signal and hand him out a piece of bread. As an aging man he stood there and thought of all that had happened since.

After their tour of the place, Douglass sat on the great porch with the quality, and later they were all shown into the great dining room and "cordially invited to refresh ourselves with wine of most excellent quality."

"The abolition of slavery," Douglass reflected, "has not merely emancipated the Negro, but liberated the whites."

It is a regrettable conclusion to this long tale to have to say that Wye House, while still in the family, is passing out of the Lloyd name. Edward VII had a son, Edward VIII, who entered the United States Naval Academy as a youth, and at this writing (1943) is the last surviving commodore of the old navy. He has a son, Edward IX, who has a son, Edward X, but the commodore, interested only in his career, disposed of Wye House to his brother, the late Howard Lloyd, who had two daughters only.

CHAPTER 19

The Wye River

Many of the old mansions in the neighborhood of Wye House were built or purchased for sons and daughters of the Lloyds; Gross' Coate, Hope, Presq' Ile, Wye Heights, etc. Gross' Coate, on the other side of Lloyd's Creek, was patented to one Roger Gross in the seventeenth century who, in the fanciful nomenclature of that day wished to suggest that the land was his protection or covering, hence Gross' Coate. In 1687, with Lambeth, Courtroad, the Adventure and Knave-Standoff, it became Henrietta Maria's Purchase. In 1748 it was inherited by William Tilghman, the son of one of Henrietta Maria Lloyd's daughters. Since then it has been occupied by six generations of Tilghmans and is still in the possession of that family.

The age of the house is unknown. A comfortable and imposing mansion, very English in character, it has been extended and improved so many times that it bears the stamp of no era. It has never suffered from fire; consequently, it is full of old family treasures. Chief among them are three beautiful portraits by Charles Willson Peale painted in 1790. They represent (a) Richard Tilghman, a proud man, master of the house at that time, and irreverently termed Dick Yellowbreeches in the family; (b) his wife and children; and (c) his sister, Mary Tilghman.

It is related that Peale fell in love with Aunt Molly while staying at Gross' Coate and she with him. This is borne out by the exquisite delicacy and wistfulness depicted in Aunt Molly's young face. The proud brother would not hear of her marrying a middle-aged widower with children, and locked her up until Peale was out of the house. As she eventually married beneath her anyhow, she might as well have been given to the celebrated artist. The unhappy Aunt Molly lived to a great age, and the light tapping of her stick is still heard late at night in the corridors.

The old burial ground at Gross' Coate is crowded with graves, but has not many gravestones. This is due to a family superstition that he who puts up a stone for a departed member will be the next to go.

Hope, a five-part brick house of unusual architecture, restored not with entire success in 1906-1910, was purchased by Colonel Philemon Lloyd from two bachelors for "a case of spirits." The contracting parties proceeded to drink up the spirits under the magnificent beech tree which is still there. One of the bachelors died before he could sign the transfer, and Colonel Lloyd had a little difficulty in establishing his title.

Wye Heights, now called Cleghorne-on-Wye, was built by Edward Lloyd V, the Governor, for Edward VI, the Farmer. Later owners have extended and embellished the original house. Standing on a bold bluff above the spot where four streams come together, Wye Heights enjoys one of the finest sites on the Eastern Shore. The Front Wye stretches north and south, Skipton Creek comes in from the east, and Wye Narrows runs off to the west. Surely there cannot be

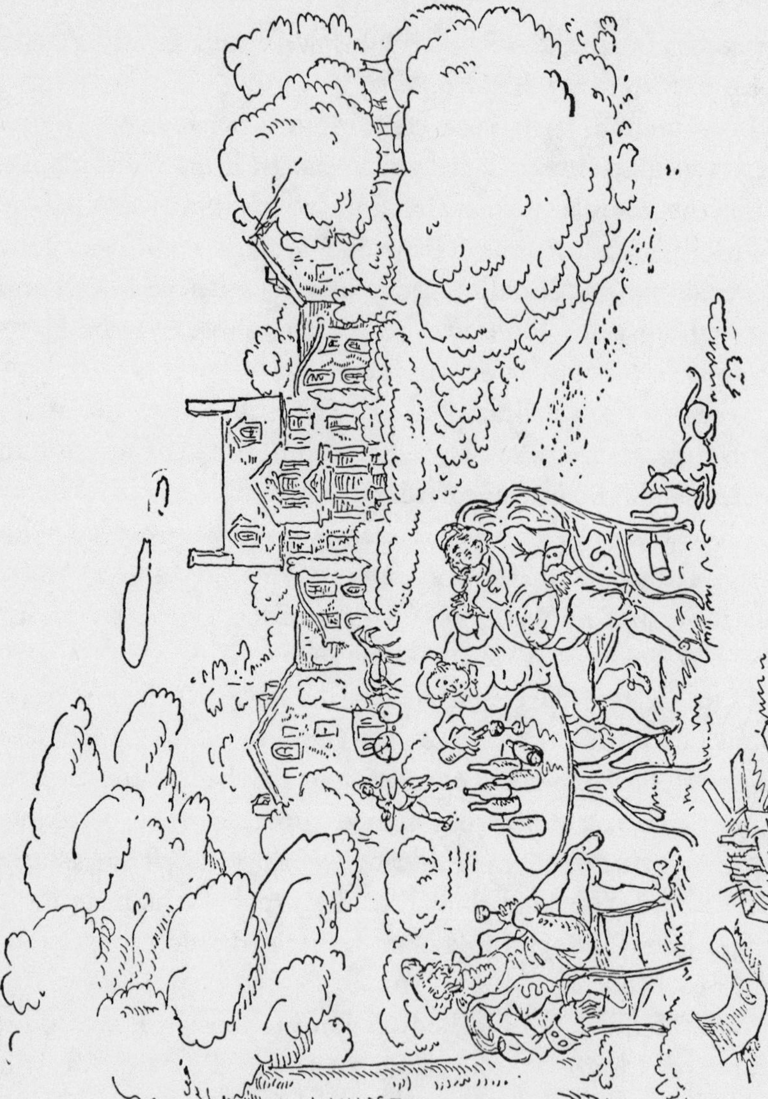

many such four corners on earth where two rivers appear to cross each other at right angles!

In Skipton Creek stood the first county seat of Talbot, which was called York. It has entirely disappeared except for some rubble and a hole in the ground. There was a courthouse and jail, with its accompanying stocks and whipping post, and a big stable for use on court days. When not in use, the courthouse was in the care of a tavernkeeper who must have abused his privilege, for in 1684 it was "Ordered by the Court that noe drink be sold in the Court House or dranke theire dureing the setting of the Court, in forefeiture of two shillings and sixpence for every Pott or Bottle or drink sold during the setting of the Court aforesaid." The Choptank Indian, Poh Poh Caquis, was tried in this courthouse.

Up at the head of Front Wye stands Cloverfields, homestead of the Hemsleys, with a stair tower and much beautiful interior woodwork. A little higher up the stream is Wye Mills, which ground flour for the Continental Army in 1776 and is still grinding, though it has a new millwheel. Near-by stands the famous Wye Oak, most glorious tree on all the Eastern Shore, which sprouted from an acorn a full century before the first white man came. Just beyond is the appealing little Wye Church, built in 1721 and in excellent preservation. It still has the original brick pavement with cushions to save the knees of the godly, candle sconces around the walls, and a slave gallery. In the chancel there is a marble tablet dedicated to the memory of the first rector "whose name has been lost."

Continuing west from the four corners through Wye Narrows, one presently comes to Wye Plantation, standing back on its low hill. This ancient house, stretching out its astonishing length to 160 feet, has a quaint Dutch aspect. Built by a Tilghman, its most famous owner was William Paca, the Signer, and third governor of the state of Maryland. There is a dispute as to whether Wye Plantation or Wye Hall across on the island was his favorite summer home. He is buried here at Wye Plantation. His city residence was the beautiful old house in Annapolis now known as Carvel Hall.

Wye Bridge, which crosses to the island, is a long, creaking, wooden structure, dry and silvery with age. In the middle it has a true drawbridge like the one at Crisfield, that is pulled back on rails with a winch. I saw the aged bridge tender, tall, lean and gnarled, a typical Eastern Shoreman, sitting on a bench in front of his tiny shack on the mainland bank. Since water-borne traffic has disappeared from these parts, I thought his job must be just about the least laborious in the world, and I asked him how it was.

"Oh, they still come through, they still come through," he said. "Since winter [this was May] I had to open the bridge, let me see, three, no, four times. That's right; four times, sir. . . . But at that I'll say it's a lonely spot," he went on. "I have to talk to myself or I'd lose the power of speech. Yes, sir, I asks myself questions and answers them myself."

Wye Island, which contains 1,800 acres, is associated with the names of two great Marylanders, John Beale Bordley and William Paca, and was at different times called by the names of each of them. Once a Lloyd property, as noted, it was devised by a granddaughter of Henrietta Maria's to her two daughters, who were respectively Mrs. Bordley and Mrs. Paca.

Bordley was a good patriot; it was through his passion for husbandry that he became famous. His aim was to prove to the colonies that they could support themselves independently of the mother country, and that Wye Island in particular might be made independent of all the rest of the world. In the course of time his place became a humming village of industry. It had a carpenter shop and smithy, always busy, and in other buildings many spinning wheels and looms supplied with the proprietor's own wool, hemp, flax and cotton. There was a ropewalk, a brickyard and kiln, a huge windmill of his own original design to supply power, a large brew house, a double milk house, a great warehouse or granary, icehouse, storehouse, hen house, pigeon house, stables, etc. The brewery was his particular joy, and he produced a wonderful beer.

Bordley used to dispatch boatloads of beef and flour, fruits and vegetables to the Continental military posts without waiting for requisitions. He conducted endless experiments to improve the methods of husbandry in vogue during his time. He wrote a book embodying all his innovations and recipes, which ran through several editions in his day, but it makes quaint reading now. Here is his recipe for making ice cream—something new in that day.

> Two pewter basins, one large, the other small, the small one to have a close cover; in this basin the cream is put and mixt with strawberries etc., to give flavor and color; sweeten it. Cover it close, and set the small basin in the large one. Fill this with ice and a handfull of salt, to stand for three-quarters of an hour; then uncover and stir the cream well together; cover it close to stand half an hour longer; and then it may be turned into a plate.

All this hive of industry has disappeared; Bordley's great house itself was destroyed by fire in 1879.

William Paca and his wife, Henrietta Maria's great-granddaughter, owned the other half of Wye Island. They were not happy in their oldest son, John P. Paca, a selfish, purse-proud, arrogant young man, and the father spoiled him still further by giving him carte blanche in building a new family mansion on the island. James Hoban, the architect of the White House, was engaged to design it, and the Signer poured his money into the building without stint. This was Wye Hall, celebrated alike for its magnificance and its horrors. In the final clearing of the stage through murder, suicide and madness, the story has the elements of a Greek tragedy. The house has been destroyed by fire three times. At present, the site is occupied by a modern mansion that is supposed to be a replica of the original, but it is hardly that.

Hoban's drawing of the front elevation, which survives, depicts a little palace in the Doric style surmounted by elegant balustrades embellished with statues. It is uncertain if this was carried out in all its elaborate details, but anyhow Wye Hall was the grandest house on the Eastern Shore, if not in the whole infant republic. There is a tradition that the six great drawing-room windows cost a thousand dollars each. The mirrors, plate, paintings, furniture and tapestries became legendary. One who visited the house before the last fire said, "Ruinous as is its present state, there is ample evidence of its past grandeur. Entering the house is like stepping back into the eighteenth century."

The worthy Signer died long before tragedy descended on his house, and in the course of years his son, John P. Paca, followed him, not much regretted. John P. left Wye Hall and its lands to his eldest son, William B., and Old Wye, or Wye Plantation, across the Narrows to a younger son, Edward. William B., like his father, was a handsome, narrow-minded, arrogant man, while Edward was generally popular. The brothers had never been able to get along with each other, and when their mother elected to live with Edward rather than with William, the latter began to nourish a deep and jealous hatred of the whole household at Old Wye.

William had married his cousin, Martha Phillips of Harford County, and of the eight children she bore him, five turned out to be mentally deficient in greater or less degree—"not hard good" is the Eastern Shore phrase. Every time William crossed the bridge upon leaving his grand house, he had to pass the gates of Old Wye, and the sight of his brother's healthy, spirited brood intensified his bitterness. There was little association between the two families. The grandmother died and was followed by her son Edward, still in his prime. The management of Old Wye devolved on Mariana Jones Paca, Edward's widow.

On the eve of the Civil War, a company of southern sympathizers was raised in the village of Queenstown near-by. William B. Paca exploded in terrible wrath when Ogle Tilghman was chosen over himself as captain. Moreover, the household at Old Wye was all for the South, and, for one reason and another, William became a Unionist. He raised a flying battery for the Union, and drilled it every Saturday on Queenstown green, but the folks all went to see Tilghman's men drill.

When the fighting began, Tilghman Paca, Edward's oldest son, went south with many other young men to join the Confederate Army. He subsequently rose to be a captain. This left his next brother, Jack, aged nineteen, as his mother's stand-by. Jack was as popular in the county as his uncle was hated. Folks called him "the honestest boy alive!"

He was a handsome fellow with black eyes, regular features, and the beginning of a promising mustache. When the slaves marched away, he put his own hands to the plow and the ax to win bread for his mother and the small fry.

William B. Paca, curdling with sullen wrath, informed the United States authorities that his nephew, Tilghman Paca, was serving in the Confederate Army and that his property, Old Wye, was therefore subject to confiscation. Old Wye was duly seized by a United States marshal. When it was put up at auction, William B. Paca bought it in at a fraction of its value. But Jack with his mother and the younger children continued to live there—it is likely they had no other place to go.

One afternoon William B. Paca and his daughter Sally (Sally was sane, and wonderfully attractive to boot) were driving toward home and, passing the Old Wye place, they came on young Jack Paca mending a fence with the assistance of his mother's brother, Alfred Jones. William B., in a passion, ordered them to stop because the place was no longer theirs, and young Jack told his uncle he could go to the devil. Uncle drove on fuming. Jack was sweet on his cousin Sally, and he told his mother when he got home that he didn't know what he would have done if Sally hadn't looked so pretty. To his younger brother, Henry, Jack said, "Old Bill will certainly give us trouble now." Jack loaded his gun and showed Henry where he put it.

At Old Wye next day they received a notice of eviction from the United States marshal. Jack, however, accompanied by Alfred Jones and brother Henry, went down to continue fixing the fence. This was March 8, 1865. Pretty soon the carriage from Wye Hall came trundling across the long bridge. In it were William B., his sane son, John P., and two of the imbeciles, James and Tilghman Chew. The imbeciles both had guns. A black servant on horseback followed. Henry, driving an oxcart, saw them coming and warned Jack. Jack sent him to the house for his gun.

Nobody knows exactly what happened. On the way back with the gun, Henry, accompanied by a little brother, Frederick, heard two shots. Springing forward, he found his brother Jack and his uncle, Alfred Jones, lying on the ground in their blood. Both were dying. The little boy, Frederick, dropped to the ground and took his brother's bloody head in his lap. The mother and her married daughter came flying from the house. She said to her brother-in-law:

"Have you added murder to your other crimes?"

"Their blood is upon your skirts," he retorted. "You encouraged them."

Henry was sent away to fetch a doctor and Judge Carmichael, a family friend. This was the same Judge Carmichael who had suffered so much at the hands of the Union forces. William B. Paca, boasting that the government would protect him, dispatched his sons in the carriage to Centerville to consult a lawyer. He took the horse from his servant and, coolly mounting it, rode away as if nothing in particular had happened.

To make a long story short, William B. and his three sons were arrested and lodged in the county jail at Centerville, where they enjoyed every luxury. The father obtained a change of venue to Talbot County, where the judge was said to be a Union man. At his trial he pleaded self-defense and, in defiance of public opinion, he was acquitted. John P., the sane son, was tried in Caroline County and he, too, was discharged. The two imbecile sons were not tried at all. The evidence indicated that one of them had fired the fatal shots.

Some said the courts were Union-controlled; others charged that the juries had been suborned by the wealthy William B. Paca. Be that as it may, a few months after the trials, the beautiful Sally Paca was married to Joseph Rasin, a man much beneath her in station, who had been a juror at her father's trial. In the course of a domestic quarrel, Sally was heard to cry out, "I was sold to you!"

A terrible retribution overtook the Pacas of Wye Hall. They shut themselves up as much as possible, but in the streets of Queenstown or Centerville, or on the steamboat, all old acquaintances pointedly turned their backs. William B. Paca, rich and prominent as he was, was refused accommodations at hotels. They stayed in Baltimore as much as they could, but it was the same there. They were outcasts.

Anna, the oldest daughter, who had a bright clear mind and was the apple of her father's eye, died in Baltimore of poison taken in mistake for medicine. When the family returned miserably to Wye Hall, the father himself died of what the doctors called a bilious dysentery. John P., the oldest son and administrator, who was supposed to be sane, soon afterward shot himself on his father's grave. James, the imbecile, who was said to have fired the fatal shots, while attempting to drown a dog from the bridge over the narrows (that same bridge where the old tender now waits to open the draw) drowned himself. Thus Mrs. William B. Paca was left alone with her other four feeble-minded children. She, who had always acted strangely, went completely mad and she and her children were confined in different institutions. To complete the tragedy, Wye Hall burned; only the old Signer's portrait was saved. The property was inherited by the two small children of John P. Paca, who had been carried away from the dreadful scene by their mother.

Continuing through Wye Narrows, the next landmark on the north shore is Cheston-on-Wye, the seat of the Courseys—or de Courcys, as they later called themselves. Their ancient house, destroyed by fire, has been replaced by a modern dwelling, but many of the superb trees have survived, including several of the finest specimens on the Eastern Shore. The sight of a herd of fawn-colored cattle grazing under these mighty trees with the horizontal rays of the setting sun striking upon them from across the water, is one not soon to be forgotten.

Three brothers, Henry, William and John Coursey, turned up in Maryland about 1653. Nothing is known about their former condition, except that they said they were related to Lord Kingsale of Ireland. Henry, who became famous in the province, seated himself on the Chester River; William and John settled here at Cheston-on-Wye. Henry afterward presented John with a part of the famous "thumb grant," and William became sole proprietor of Cheston.

William was evidently the oldest of the brothers, for in 1759, when the twenty-fourth Lord Kingsale died without male issue, William's grandson, William Coursey III, received an unexpected summons from the daughters of the old lord to come to Ireland and claim the title. This was more than a hundred years after the first William and his brothers had settled in Maryland. The old letters that passed reveal a curious story.

Lord Kingsale was of very distinguished ancestry, his peerage, the oldest in Ireland, having been conferred by King John upon John de Courcy in 1210. The unpopular King John was engaged in a dispute with King Philip Augustus of France over the duchy of Normandy and, being unable to find a knight to be his champion, he sent to the Tower of London for John de Courcy. King John had previously thrown de Courcy into the Tower for making disrespectful remarks about him. So formidable was de Courcy's appearance on the field that, at the mere sight of him, the French king's champion fled for his life and so King John kept Normandy. Ever since that day, the Lords Baron Kingsale have been privileged to wear their hats in the presence of the king of England.

The twenty-fourth lord had three daughters, from whom he had become estranged. For some years before his death he had been in a dithering, senile state, his daughters said, and had fallen completely under the influence of his agent, Lewis Leary, who kept the old lord confined in his, Leary's, house and had not allowed him to shave in five years. The daughters charged that this Leary had conspired with others to foist a bogus heir on the old man.

Sure enough, when Lord Kingsale died and his will was opened, it was found that, after cutting off his daughters with a shilling and some worthless lands (which belonged to them anyhow), he had left all he possessed to one John de Courcy, late of Rhode Island. He further designated this John as the rightful heir to his titles, and set forth his genealogy with great particularity. John therefore was accepted by the authorities and had taken his seat in the House of Lords.

The ladies raged against this John in their letters; "a despicable slave, bred a rope-maker and a waterman for hire. [This] the first peer of the Kingdom [of Ireland] and has exerted his right to wear his hat in the Royal presence." It was their contention that Leary was plotting to break the entail and secure the estates for himself. Meanwhile the ladies had heard that Mr. Coursey of Maryland was a gentleman. They promised him their full support if he would come over and present his claim. "The House of Lords would be glad to get rid of such a mongrel fellow," they wrote. Perhaps the ladies and their husbands had a hope of getting a slice of the lands out of it, too.

At any rate, William Coursey would not budge from Cheston-on-Wye. Perhaps he was well-advised. The Kingsale ladies, in showing forth his claim, offered some very questionable dates, and he may have known better. Or perhaps the Eastern Shore appealed to him more than the House of Lords. Edward Coursey, the son of William III, who distinguished himself in the Revolution, was sufficiently impressed by the incident to recommend in his will that his descendants should thereafter spell their name de Courcy, which they have done. Meanwhile, the descendants of that terrible fellow, the Rhode Island waterman, are still in enjoyment of the lands and dignities of Kingsale.

From Wye Narrows one enters the Back Wye, which comes straight down from the north, its shores broken by infinite little creeks and inlets. Only a few hundred feet separate its headwaters from a tributary of the Chester River. The British came up here in 1813 with a view of taking Queenstown from the rear, but they were checked at a place called Slippery Hill. I couldn't find any hill; all the country round about is as flat as the palm of your hand.

Slippery Hill also was the scene of a duel between Gustavus Wright and Benjamin Nicholson. They stood six feet apart and let fly. Wright shot Nicholson in the hand and in the side, and Nicholson missed altogether! This Gustavus was a fire-eater. All the Wrights had that reputation, and Gustavus was obliged to maintain it. At twelve years of age he acted as second for his father, Governor Robert Wright, when he met Governor Lloyd on the field of honor. It was the custom, when one of the parties chose to take the risk of reserving his first fire, to allow him to approach as near as he wished to his opponent. Governor Lloyd, a dead shot, took advantage of it and, coming close to Governor Wright, demanded, "What are you going to do, sir? Your life is in my hands!" Whereupon young Gustavus shrilled, "Tell him to shoot, pa, and be damned!" However, the matter was arranged without bloodshed.

Gustavus, when he grew up, killed a Captain Watson in a duel. His brother, Clinton Wright, when shot down by a Major Hook, proposed that they lie side by side on the ground and shoot again. The seconds protested that they must fight standing, whereupon Wright demanded that they lash him to a tree. However, both survived.

At the head of one of the upper arms of the Back Wye stands Bloomingdale, a grand old red-brick house of Georgian design, one of the best in Queen Annes. It is chiefly noted as having been the home of Sally Harris, a famous Baltimore belle of the early nineteenth century, a rival of the three peerless Caton sisters, each of whom married an English lord. Sally, in the end, never married anybody, and ended her life at Bloomingdale as one of a pair of old-maid sisters. One who admired her in later years said that the spirit, wit and vivacity of her conversation were united to the most direct and vigorous common sense. This is very characteristic of the Eastern Shore. She was a great versifier, and once, after a grand ball at Wye Hall, she turned out a long poem for circulation among her friends, lampooning everybody present. This is what she wrote about herself and her sister:

> There are other dames I'd quite forgot
> For they're grown staid and sober.
> One takes snuff but t'other don't
> Although she's two years older.

CHAPTER 20

The Chester River

KENT ISLAND, the largest island on the Eastern Shore, is barely an island, for the channel that separates it from the mainland is only a few yards wide. It is included within the bounds of Queen Annes County. This was the site of William Claiborne's trading post which occasioned so many alarums and excursions in the first days of the province, as described in an early chapter. Every trace of that settlement has disappeared, though there is one ancient house on the island, Kent Fort Manor, which may have been built soon after the destruction of the trading post in 1638, but it is questionable.

To enter the Chester River, one may pass through Kent Narrows on the inside of the island, or go outside and round Love Point at the top, a low headland of great beauty. On this course, one heads south into the river for a mile or two and then, sweeping all the way around after the manner of Eastern Shore rivers, travels due north, then northeast, and finally east. Near the mouth of the river Blackbeard's Bluff is another reminder of the pirate. Eastern Neck, with Eastern Neck Island which forces the river to go around it, ends in Hail Point, where the customs officers first hailed incoming ships in days gone by.

After the Choptank, the Chester is the noblest of Eastern Shore rivers, more than a mile wide until after passing Deep Point, then averaging half a mile almost all the way to the head of navigation. Toward the mouth, it is confused with a maze of deep inlets, like the other rivers, but the shores of the upper reaches generally roll up unbroken. The Chester for its whole length forms the boundary between Queen Annes and Kent counties.

Almost opposite Hail Point lies Lord's Gift, the seat of the eminent Colonel Henry Coursey whose name has been mentioned. Coming to Maryland in 1653, he is said to have been present at the Battle of Horn's Point (1655), when Lord Baltimore's men were so soundly whipped by the Puritan forces. Mr. Coursey (not yet a colonel) no doubt lay low for a while thereafter. In 1658 Lord Baltimore, having been restored in all his rights and privileges, granted Coursey (in gratitude, one assumes) as much land as he could cover on the map with the end of his thumb. Coursey applied his thumb to the southerly bank of the Chester, hence Lord's Gift. His thumb extended past the mouth of Queenstown harbor to the east, and this part was named Coursey's Neck. Henry transferred it to his brother John, who sold it to the Blake family, and it has borne the name of Blakeford ever since. Henry's quaint little house at Lord's Gift still stands, but so altered and extended he would never know it now.

Colonel Henry Coursey was one of the three great Indian negotiators in the early days of Maryland, the others being Colonels Philemon Lloyd and William Stevens. It was undoubtedly due to the efforts of these three (backed by the wisdom of the second Lord Baltimore) that the province was spared such disasters as overcame some of the sister colonies.

Baltimore wrote of these three that he had "special trust in their fidelity, prudence and circumspection."

Of the three, Coursey seems to have been the ablest; at least he was the most often employed on such missions. When the provincial authorities were looking for a man to treat with the dreaded Five Nations of northern New York, Major Peter Sayer, a fellow officer, recommended Coursey, then "Commander in Chief of all his Lordship's foot militia in Cecil and Kent Counties," as "the fittest man to be imployed in any negotiations with the Indians, [he] being known to the Chiefs of all their Nations."

So Henry Coursey was sent on that long journey (1677) as sole commissioner. This was his greatest single service to the province. Raiding parties of the Five Nations, or Iroquois, offered a perpetual threat to the outlying settlers on the western shore. They didn't often kill white men, but they were fond of butchering the "friend Indians" who were Maryland's wards—and buffers! Colonel Coursey's mission was highly successful, despite the veiled opposition of the governor of New York (Sir Edmund Andros) and despite the fact that the Maryland authorities appear to have been rather niggardly in providing gifts for the Indians.

Attawachrett, sachem of the Oneidas, after having dryly called attention to the fact that the belt of wampum presented to him was of the smallest size, said, "We doe thank you and our heart is good, and we doe give a Small Beaver (!)."

The treaty then made was fairly well kept by the Indians for five years. In 1682 Colonel Coursey, now a member of His Lordship's Council, was sent back to Albany to confirm and renew it. In his second mission he was joined with Colonel Philemon Lloyd, speaker of the lower house at the time. Once again the Marylanders were met by the New York authorities with fair words and something less than full co-operation. Nevertheless, this mission was a success also, and the relations of the province with the Five Nations were much improved thereafter.

The proceedings of these missions as spread upon the Maryland Archives make quaint reading. The highly figurative language employed by the sachems of the Five Nations afforded much amusement to the Englishmen of that day. The Duke of Newcastle, in bidding farewell to a friend who was sailing for the colonies, thus parodied it:

"For God's sake have a care of your health and eat stewed prunes in the passage. And pray my dear Excellency, take care of our good friends the Five Nations. The Toryories, the Maccolmacks, the Out-o'-the-Ways, the Crickets and the Kickshaws. Let 'em have plenty of blankets and stinkubus and wampum; and your Excellency wont fail to scour the kettle and boil the chain and bury the tree and plant the hatchet."

Although he was a Protestant, Colonel Henry Coursey loyally supported Lord Baltimore during the Protestant rebellion of 1689. Upon being deprived of his administrative powers, Baltimore suggested that, of all the men in Maryland, Colonel Henry Coursey was best fitted to be governor for the crown—but of course, at that juncture, his recommendation was ignored. Colonel Coursey died in 1695.

Almost next door to Lord's Gift is the village of Queenstown, on a pretty, natural harbor. Today it is a sprawling, featureless little place, but in 1813 the British thought it worth taking. They sent ashore a force of 1,400 men in two parties. The first party was checked at Slippery Hill, as already mentioned, by the ingenious Colonel Massey, who deployed his eighteen men like an army. The second party, aiming to take the village in the rear, landed at Blakeford and, finding a large, deep creek between them and Queenstown, went back to their boats in disgust.

The principal object of interest in the village is Bowlingly, an ancient house that has had a checkered career. The huge porches which now surround it were added by the Queen Anne's Railway, when it operated the house as a summer hotel. Bowlingly was once the property of James Neale, who came to Maryland in 1635. He had been a merchant in Spain, and was employed on many commissions by King Charles I. It was his eldest daughter, Henrietta Maria, who married first Richard Bennett II, and secondly Colonel Philemon Lloyd, and so became the great ancestress of the Eastern Shore. Under the trees at Bowlingly, Ogle Tilghman drilled his Confederate company, while William B. Paca's flying battery for the Union side exercised in Cherry Lane.

Over on Eastern Neck Island, across the river from Queenstown, is Wickliffe, the home of the Wickes family for nearly three hundred years. Part of the original house is embodied in a later structure. Augustine Herman stopped here on his first journey into Maryland. When Major Joseph Wickes died here in 1693, an inventory of the contents of his house was taken, which today provides an interesting item for the antiquary. There was only one picture on the walls, "a Mapp of Man's Mortality," but from them hung in various rooms no less than eleven guns and powder horns, "all in good order."

Wickliffe was the home of Lambert Wickes, the gallant and appealing young officer who commanded the *Reprisal* in the Revolution. He carried Benjamin Franklin on his mission to France, and afterward (1777) was lost with his ship in a gale off Newfoundland.

Eastern Neck was the site of the first lasting settlement on the Eastern Shore. Little Church Creek over here is a reminder of St. Peter's, the first church on the Shore. The church disappeared so long ago that its very existence had been forgotten until lately, when a farmer, breaking several plow points in his field, investigated and uncovered some old gravestones sunk in the earth. Near-by, on the larger Gray's Inn Creek, there was actually a town in the seventeenth century called New Yarmouth. Kent County's first courthouse and jail stood here, besides two shipbuilding establishments. The place rapidly declined when the county seat was moved upriver in 1696, and today nothing remains but a few imported stones that mark the site of the old landing place. Eastern Neck has its full quota of fine old houses.

Near the head of Gray's Inn Creek, the village of Rock Hall spreads over to Chesapeake Bay. This is the terminus of the oldest turnpike in the country. The packets from Annapolis landed their passengers here, whence they took horse to Philadelphia and points north. George Washington used this route eight times, and it was at Rock Hall that Lieutenant Colonel Tench Tilghman started his famous ride to carry the news of Yorktown to Congress.

Back across the wide Chester, there is a little creek called Tilghman's, and above it rises the Hermitage, the cradle of the most widely spread family on the Eastern Shore. The Tilghmans were prolific, and in addition to sons, they had many daughters to marry into other first families; consequently, almost the whole quality of the Shore shares in the Tilghman blood. Their progenitor was Dr. Richard Tilghman, who pitched his tent on this spot about 1659, and practiced up and down the river in a batteau with a leg-o'-mutton sail, or, when the wind was adverse, rowed by his slaves. There is a tradition that Dr. Tilghman was no other than the "R.T." who signed the petition that brought King Charles I to trial. Hence the need for a flight to America ten years later, when the tide was running the other

way. Matthew Tilghman, the patriarch of Maryland, was Dr. Richard's grandson, and Tench Tilghman a great-grandson through another line.

There have been two fires at the Hermitage, and the present house, dating from 1859, has no architectural pretensions, but the ancient avenue of approach is magnificent and the terraced garden, with its sunken parterres, still lovely. Within a crumbling brick wall, close beside the house in affectionate intimacy, is the family burial ground containing rows and rows of departed Tilghmans. The in-laws have not intruded here to the same extent as at Wye House. Chief among the graves is a huge slab covering the remains of Dr. Richard Tilghman with this inscription:

Always remember
The 5th of November
But do not forgett
Death will have no lett
Consider thy end
And thy time well spend
& so shall thou have
A crown in thy grave
Vale
Ita Dixit
Richardus Tilghmannes B.M.
In Artiqui Chirurgi Magister qui
sub hoc tumulo sepultus est
Obiit Janu 7 mo Anno 1675

The next opening on this side of the river is Reed Creek, with Grove Creek flowing into it. The point of land between is Wright's Neck, and this was the principal stamping ground of a family famous hereabouts, of whom one member, Gustavus the duelist, has already been mentioned. Reed's Creek House, their home, is an eighteenth century mansion in the grand style. It looks forlorn now, for the trees are gone. In a house of many interesting details, the most notable thing is a painting on wood above the fireplace in the paneled dining room. The whitish stains on the wood suggest that some prudish housewife has vigorously scrubbed the panel with lye.

But still shadowed forth in spite of the lye is a lovely nude Venus attended by cupids.

A member of the Wright connection has described how they hunted the fox from Reed's Creek House, *circa* 1850. The fox was turned out of a bag on the front lawn at sunup, the dogs being shut up to give him a fair start. While the hunters waited there was always great argument as to the respective merits of the dogs, Mr. Ellick Wright's Fanny Gray, being generally held the best. At the right moment, Uncle Peregrine Tilghman stood up in his stirrups and blew his bugle horn, and the hunt was on. The dogs were not allowed to kill the fox. He was saved for another day. Cousin Henry Wright wrote a song for the fox-hunting set. One stanza:

Hark boys, to the shout o'er the waves of the Grove!
[Grove Creek]
The Squire's [Uncle Peregrine] old signal you know 'tis to move.
Already impatient he's chiding our stay
And Fanny Gray's piping her musical lay
Tally-ho! Ho! Ho! Tally-ho! Tally-ho!

In those days Miss Serena Spencer, another cousin, was a frequent visitor to Reed's Creek House. Here is a pen portrait, pure Eastern Shore:

She was widely known as an intelligent, companionable lady. . . . Her conversation was a volley of Italian and French phrases. She was proficient in music and never forgot the sweet strains she had learned in her young days, among them Auld Ang Syne [*sic!*] with variations, which she executed with great expression and correctness when over fifty years of age. Her fingers glistened with diamonds, rubies and emeralds as they glided gracefully over the snowy keys . . . Her tastes were "gay." She doted on operas, lively dance tunes, novels Francaise. . . . When she landed at

Queenstown wharf she was always greeted with a smile of welcome by multitudes of friends, Mr. Alexander Wright often meeting her. . . . Their mutual salutations were heartfelt and demonstrative.

'Cousin Ellick, how are you?'

'Oh, I feel like a three-year-old! How is my fairy queen?'

Cousin Serena's weight was at least two hundred!

Other Wright homes in the neighborhood are little Walnut Grove across the fields, once called Warplesdon, and Peace and Plenty over on the Centerville road, a house of the same character as Reed's Creek House. According to family tradition, it was so christened by the bride of the Wright who built it. Her home was called Hungry Hill! Walnut Grove was built by Solomon, the first Wright, a great man in his day. Probably the oldest house in Queen Annes, it is a little gem, so beautifully fashioned that the paneling of one of the tiny rooms is said to have sold for sixteen thousand dollars, and this did not include the superb carved chimneypiece with its odd little cupboards, still in place. Unfortunately, one has to close one's eyes to a gambrel-roofed addition that is hopelessly out of character. Magnificent Blakeford also was a Wright home for several generations.

The next inlet on this side is the Corsica River, though it is no more a river than Langford Bay opposite is a bay. If all the other inlets are creeks, these are creeks too. In a country where all the waterways are beautiful, the Corsica is pre-eminent. The steep, heavily wooded banks rise to an elevation of fifty feet, something we have not seen lower down on the Shore. Here and there the bold scene is relieved by green fields rising gently from the water. The Corsica, only five miles long, ends abruptly at the foot of a bluff on which stands the town of Centerville, county seat of Queen Annes.

Centerville is a bowery village, unpretentious, wholly American in character, and therefore dear to its sons and daughters. The population is slowly shrinking; mechanical industry has not touched it; it has changed very little since, say, 1875. When the world is too much with us, such a village takes a strong grip on the affections. It is the sort of place where the boys and girls sing in the choir and Pa practices on the flute after supper.

Once upon a time the young fellows of Centerville had a band of music and on moonlight nights they would drive around in a wagon behind a pair of "spanking bays" and serenade the belles of town and county, Dr. Robert Goldsborough's pretty daughters at Church Farm or Colonel Thomas Wright's interesting family at Peace and Plenty.

"Bully" Hemsley played the French horn with great effect. That is to say, it was wonderful to see him puff out his cheeks and blow, but the horn did not seem to lend any volume to the music and the other players became suspicious. One night, in the middle of "Oh, don't you remember sweet Alice, Ben Bolt," they all stopped by prearrangement. Bully continued to demonstrate a tremendous puffing, but not a sound issued from the horn! On Sundays it was a treat to see Bully handing the pretty girls out of their carriages in front of the Episcopal church and escorting them to the door. He sang in the choir, but the only air he knew was the bass to "Villanella," and that had taken him months to learn.

On the other side of the Chester, Langford Bay extends a couple of crooked fingers deep into the land. With its countless points and coves and creeks, it reminds one of the famed Thousand Islands, though there is but one island here,

Cacaway, a striking wooded headland dividing the two arms of the bay. Such commanding, tree-clad points alternate with wheatfields of so gentle a slope that they seem to slip imperceptibly under water. Here and there stands an old house; they are not all beautiful; even so, they grace the scene because of their beautiful trees. The little coves are lined down to the water's edge, with a green so dense as to appear black in the hollows; the lower branches dip into the water. One of these inlets, called Lovely Cove, is justly named. Langford Bay is especially beautiful in a light rain, when the vivid green shores fade away into nothingness behind successively thickening gray curtains. Its glassy waters are broken by an occasional pair of wild duck (even in summer), by leaping fish, and perhaps—rare sight!—a snowy heron.

Up near the head of the westerly arm stands St. Paul's, the most satisfying of all the ancient churches on the Eastern Shore because it has been restored with care and taste, and because of the beauty of the churchyard. These aged oaks started growing long before there was a church. That was built in 1713; the little vestry house near-by, a little later. One of the pleasing things about St. Paul's is that it is still very much a going concern, and well-filled on Sundays. The thirty-four original pews were offered in perpetuity for a thousand pounds of tobacco. One of these is occupied today by the tenth in line from the original purchaser.

Quaker Neck, lying between the east arm of Langford Bay and the Chester, has always been a desirable neighborhood; in the beginning because the land was rich, and latterly because the society was good. Of the many ancient houses in Quaker Neck, the most interesting is the smallest, a little place on the bay that has been known variously as

Ruth's Farm, Reward, and Walnut Point Farm. The present owners have revived the name of Reward.

The land on which it stands was patented as long ago as 1650, and the house must have been built soon afterward. The front part may have been raised half a story at some later date; nevertheless, Reward still retains more original seventeenth century work than any other house on the Eastern Shore I have seen, including much of the first type of paneling employed by Maryland builders. This consists of no more than random-width matched oaken planks stood on end to divide the rooms. There are also several handsomely carved chimneypieces, corner cupboards, a rear stairway of the earliest type, original doors with diagonal battens, wooden latches complete with latch strings, a secret drawer in the wainscot, and so on, all in an excellent state of preservation. Reward is a dream house for lovers of the antique.

Quaker Neck Landing, on the river side, is a scrap of a village arranged around three sides of a tiny green as decoratively as a stage setting. The fourth side is open to the water as to an audience. The old wharf has been filled in with earth and a house built upon it; there is a promising weeping willow springing from the spot where the hand trucks used to thunder. Down on the beach I ran into an old steamboater. We sat on a turned-over skiff while he talked about former days.

He had served aboard most of the vessels of the Chester River Line, in one capacity or another: the *Emma Ford,* the *B. S. Ford,* the *Corsica,* the *Gratitude.* To help in moving the peach crop, the line would charter extra vessels such as the *Hamilton* and the *Transit.* The latter vessel could carry eighteen thousand baskets.

"We used to carry the whole of the wheat crop in bags,"

said Captain Will. "The railroads couldn't take that business from us because they was in no position to return the bags to the farmer like we did. The *Corsica* could stow ten thousand bushels in the hold and on deck. But little by little the wheat and corn left the river; then the trucks took all, and the boats had to stop. The passengers had taken to riding to town in cars, too. Oh, my life and time! what funny people passengers were! I mind one man started to sue the company because he got left on the wharf! And once when I was second mate on the *B. S. Ford*, leaving Baltimore in a heavy nor'easter, lady said to the captain: 'Cap'n, don't you think it's too risky?' And the captain said: 'Lady, I think just as much of my life as you do.'

"Once on the *B. S. Ford*, when we was leavin' Bal'more Sunday afternoon at the same time as the *Eastern Shore* [of another line], she almost cut us in two. We was a-backin' out of Pier 7 with three licensed men in the pilothouse, and the *Eastern Shore* she only had the captain and a boy on deck. Cap'n was astern, leaving the boy alone in the pilothouse. She struck us just aft our pilothouse. Cap'n of the *Eastern Shore* got his license suspended for one month, and they passed a law to keep three licensed men in the pilothouse.

"When I was mate on the *Corsica*, making three trips weekly to Crumpton, we broke down in the middle of the bay off Seven-foot Knoll, and anchored and blew four whistles for assistance. *Tred Avon* was in sight, but her mate didn't hear us and she passed on. By and by a tug with mud scows come along, anchored the scows and asks us $175. Cap'n told him to go you know where. Under the law, the tug was forbidden to leave us. So there we stayed looking at each other until he come down to $75 and towed us in.

"The old side-wheelers was better sea boats than the propellers. The *Corsica* was a propeller. One Christmas Eve when I was mate aboard her, we lay here at Quaker Neck loading all night with cases canned goods, oil drums and so forth. At daybreak we started downriver and made Love Point Light on the ebb, and there we run into a heavy nor'easter, which was soon jumping the *Corsica's* propeller clean out of the water. At Buoy Rock, though we had two passengers and I and George at the wheel, she wouldn't answer her port wheel and I say to George, 'Hadn't we better head up to Seven-foot Knoll?' but he wouldn't.

"At Five-fathom-lump buoy I seen a puff coming. Struck us on the starboard bow and knocked her side to, and she rolled until the water come up to the pilothouse door. She rolled the flagpole right out of her. Down below the passengers was lying on the cabin floor. 'How much more of this have we got to stand?' they was saying. George agreed to turn back to Love Point then. We went back before the wind ten miles in half an hour. After shifting two hundred cases canned goods astern to keep her screw down, we started out again and made Baltimore by 8:00 P.M. Which proves that two heads is better than one, even if one is a cabbage head. I missed my Christmas dinner.

"Ain't nothin' stopped the Chester River steamboats ceppin ice. I mind one winter, when I was on the *B. S. Ford* as a young fellow, they was four Negroes in the Chestertown jail accused of murder, and the mob was determined to lynch them. So Governor Frank Brown, he ordered them brought to Baltimore, but the *B. S. Ford* was froze hard and fast to Chestertown wharf. Now the governor felt bad, because these was young boys and they hadn't any close connection with the murder, so he ordered out the icebreaker

Latrobe and he come over across the bay on her and fetched the boys away without the mob knowing anything. They got to Chestertown at 2:00 A.M. and went right back, and gemmen! by nine o'clock in the morning the whole river was froze from shore to shore and men was skatin' across.

[Captain Will was right as to his main facts. This was the celebrated Hill murder about 1893. But according to my information, Governor Brown did not cross the bay on the *Latrobe,* but remained pacing the floor of the Executive Mansion all night until she returned.]

"Another time the *B. S. Ford* was froze to the wharf in Chestertown," Captain Will continued, "some tough fellows come aboard and engaged in a game of poker with the crew down below. There was a fight over the winnings, and during it the *Ford* caught fire and burned. She was rebuilt, but afterwards she was never allowed to lie at Chestertown overnight.

"The *B. S. Ford* was my favorite. The man she was named after rose from clerk to captain in the early days of the line. And *Emma Ford* was called after his wife. Afterwards, B. S. was president of the line, and then he was pretty much the whole thing on Chester River; but that was before my time. B. S. was drowned at Ocean City in 1879. They fed us right good on that boat, passengers and mates. For breakfast they would give us bacon and eggs, fried fish, sausage, fried apples, biscuits and coffee. Evenings it was like a social party in the cabin, with the captain doing the honors.

"The old *B. S. Ford* come back home a few years ago. They had moved the pilothouse back on top the ladies' cabin, and taken off the house on the bow. Jes' a barge bein' towed by a goddam tug! Dog my breeches, if it ain't make me feel bad to see that!"

Across the river from Quaker Neck Landing, at the top of a long, green slope, stands Readbourne, one of the most elegant Georgian houses on the Shore. It was built in 1733 by Colonel James Hollyday after his marriage to the widow, Sarah Covington Lloyd. Sarah Covington, it will be remembered, was the beautiful Quakeress for whose hand the brothers Edward and Philemon Lloyd had contended. According to tradition, it was Sarah herself who designed this lovely house while her husband went to England to order the materials and furnishings. In drawing her plans, she had the assistance of Lord Baltimore. This would be Charles, the fifth lord, who by this time had recovered the government of his province from the crown.

Sarah lies in the little burial ground near the house. One of her sons, Henry, built Ratcliffe Manor in Talbot County, a house of the same type as Readbourne, for his bride, Anna Maria Robins. Seven generations of Hollydays lived at Readbourne. The house was then purchased by a New Yorker, who required a hall with a twelve-foot ceiling in which to hang a priceless set of mural paintings by Vernet that he possessed. The murals are at Readbourne now, and look as if they had been painted for the hall they adorn.

Above Readbourne on the Queen Annes side opens Southeast Creek, the last inlet of any size from the Chester. It heads at the village of Church Hill, which takes its name from the venerable St. Luke's, dating from 1731. This ancient brick edifice is of unusual design, having a heavy gambrel roof, arched windows, and a semicircular apse that also has a gambrel roof. The church possesses handsome antique silver and (the gift of Queen Anne) a pair of very beautiful black-enameled brass tablets, one bearing the Ten Commandments, the other the Lord's Prayer. The church records are said to be intact from the beginning.

CHAPTER 21

Chestertown

In Maryland, Chestertown is second only to Annapolis in the number of beautiful eighteenth century dwellings that have survived; the Kent County town has something that even Annapolis cannot boast of—a whole street, albeit a short one, of such houses. A rich tradition of leisure, breeding, sport and good living still governs Chestertown. Up to twenty years ago, nobody in Kent County had any money. Since then an influx of wealth from the North and West has given town and county a fresh start.

Chestertown started in 1698, when the county seat was finally brought here, just a few years after Annapolis became the provincial capital. Chestertown always had its eye on Annapolis, but it was something more than a mere copy, being a busy port in its own right. Chestertown's ships kept her directly in touch with the great world. The town has always had a strong Anglican flavor; even today, the people still refer to the "Courthouse Green" and the "Customhouse Green," and guests are invited to "tea." Yet Chestertown is not Anglophile; in 1774 they had another kind of tea party when the tea, brought by the brigantine *Geddes,* was thrown overboard. Neither did the fashionable town neglect the graces of learning. Washington College was founded in 1782;

its roots are to be found in schools that go all the way back to 1707.

Chestertown always had a spendthrift reputation, and this naturally reached its height during the lavish generation preceding the Revolution. Gaming, dancing and horse racing had long been features, and theatrical performances when they could be had. Smuggling was rife; Bordeaux wines were cheap and plentiful; Antigua rums, Martinique cordials and Schiedam schnapps were on most sideboards. John Beale Bordley of Wye Island, writing in 1771 to a friend in London, says disgustedly:

"Foppery, idleness and dissipation are striding briskly on to bring about a general change of proprietors for our land; the incoming cargoes of trash this year imported is astonishing!"

For the men, such "trash" included: curled and powdered perukes, small swords, tall canes with tassels, knee breeches of black satin or red plush (one Maryland gentleman ordered eight pairs of silk breeches at a time), paste buckles, lace cravats and ruffles, long embroidered waistcoats, cocked hats, snuffboxes, signet and mourning rings. A London tailor, sending a velvet suit to a Maryland customer, thus describes it:

"Of a fine Garnett colour lined with pea green sattin and embroidered with a very genteel silver embroidery, not very rich, but handsome and quite a new pattern which I dare say you will approve of. I have also sent an embroidered sword knot to match it."

Rising men, such as overseers, redemptioners and so forth, were always pressing close on the heels of these extravagant cockerouses. "Cockerouse" was Maryland slang for an important man.

The ladies, of course, were not forgotten. Coaches and sedan chairs were imported for them, and all sorts of delicious dress materials: China silks, brocades, taffetas, lutestring, sarcenet; also red-heeled slippers for the minuet. The dancing master peregrinated from one great house to another with his fiddle under his arm. The ladies titivated in their coaches during the long drives to a ball. This custom persisted right down to the introduction of the motorcar. The "family carriage" would halt near the scene of a ball. Curtains were let down and candles lighted so that the young ladies could add the finishing touches and arrive with every hair in place.

The young men were stalwart dandies. They chased the fox through brake and brier, or stood up to their waists in water during November bringing down canvasbacks with their long ducking guns. Royal suppers of wild duck and hominy followed, with rum punch and old Madeira from the wood; then long pipes and cards before a blazing fire, and bed—bed would be a shakedown if the house was full.

In Chestertown's gaudiest days there was always that mixture of style and homeliness so characteristic of the Eastern Shore. A shrewd English visitor observes: "An idea of equality seems to prevail and the inferior order of people pay but little external respect to those who occupy superior stations." One notes a court order that "the public houses in the county shall be hindered from keeping their ninepins on the street during the sitting of the court."

In 1786 the Reverend Francis Asbury, the famous traveling preacher, entered this in his *Journal:* "Sunday 9th . . . I preached at night in Chestertown. I always have an enlargement in preaching in this very wicked place."

In Chestertown, during the Revolution and after, lived Mr. James Tilghman, a grandson of Dr. Richard of the Hermitage. Mr. James was in retirement because he was a loyalist, otherwise a Tory. His large family was divided in sympathy; his eldest son, the celebrated Lieutenant Colonel Tench Tilghman, being a member of General Washington's "family," two younger sons ardent patriots, while sons Richard and Philemon held commissions from the British. He had several daughters too, one of whom, Molly Tilghman, a lively, warmhearted girl, has left some letters that throw a revealing light on life in Chestertown and indicate that the girls of the Revolution were not very different from our girls. The letters are addressed to her bosom friend, Polly Pearse, who lived at Poplar Neck on the Sassafras River. The series starts with a warning from Molly to Polly to destroy her letters—but Polly didn't!

Molly Tilghman to Polly Pearse, undated, possibly 1782. Sister Nancy Tilghman has called upon Mrs. Wright in Chestertown. Years later, this lady's husband became governor of Maryland.

> She [Nancy] had the pleasure of being dressed very fine and passing a stupid, silent Afternoon in a bitter cold Room which smoak'd so monstrously that they came home half blind and almost frozen. Tho' the Lady of the House is a Wit, she did not choose to exhibit her talents, but when she did speak, her discourse was directed to Miss Caroline and Master Bob [her children] who were fighting on the carpet during the whole visit. . . .
>
> [In Philadelphia] Mrs. Lloyd is more followed and admired than ever she was. [This was Mrs. Richard Bennett Lloyd, the lovely Joanna Leigh, whose portrait had been painted by Sir Joshua Reynolds. Her husband, though born at Wye House, was a captain in the Coldstream Guards.] Old ladies who have not ventured into public these 30 years, have drawn forth their broad-backed robes and crowded to the Assembly to gaze at the Divinity. See what it is to be a beauty! . . . The first night that she

appeared in public her dress was a White Sattin habit and coat covered with crape. A Gauze Apron spangled with Gold and black Velvet Stars, and looped up with wreaths of flowers. A small cap ornamented with white feathers. . . .

Molly Tilghman to Polly Pearse (1785?):

Yesterday found me doing the Honours of the Table to a dozen Gentlemen. Just after dinner Captain Richard Bennett Lloyd and his train made their appearance at Worrells and my father most unmercifully ordered me to go and ask the Ladies to lodge here. As there was no help for it, I obey'd with the best grace in my power, but Mrs. Lloyd was so much indispos'd that she cou'd not leave her chamber, and I was oblig'd to give up the pleasure of entertaining her. Never did I see a Woman more alter'd. I protest to you she is not even pretty, but it is no wonder, such an Abominable Husband is enough to break any Woman. The Creature was quite drunk yesterday. He overwhelm'd poor Cousin Polly [Ringgold] with his compliments and absolutely kissed Sister Betsey twice by way of showing his joy for her recovery.

Molly Tilghman to Polly Pearse, spring 1785: Molly was "put almost out of her wits with joy yesterday by receiving a packet from England." It brought news of her brothers Dick, who had been ordered to India, and Phil, an officer in the British Navy. She goes on:

After much debate and irresolution the Collegians [Washington College had been established three years before] have fixed on the tragedy of [the] Atoners to act next at the Commencement and Billy Hemsley is to act the Princess Ormisinda. I dare say you will make a point of being here on the occasion when I tell you that Mike Earle is to represent Maria the heroine of the farce [that is to follow]. Figure to yourself, my dear Polly, that antique face of his for a blooming young Girl just from Boarding School. It will really be too farcical.

Molly Tilghman to Polly Pearse, August 5th (1785?). Molly is writing from Bayside and talking about "Going to Church." She was visiting her sister Henrietta who had married cousin Lloyd Tilghman, son of the old Patriarch.

In the first place I broil'd 6 miles by water to the Bay Side church [at St. Michael's] in such a sun it was enough to coddle common flesh. I was then so stupefied with old Gordon's [The Reverend John Gordon who maintained a race-track behind the church] slow croaking that I began to dream a dozen times before the Sermon was over, and finally I got into the chariot of Aunt Tilghman [Mrs. Matthew Tilghman] who met me by appointment and encountered a perpetual Cloud of Dust which prevented our seeing the Horse's Heads, or speaking a word lest we be choak'd. I came off alive, it's true, but suffered so much in the Battle that I have made a Vow to say my prayers at home until it rains, which I begin to think it never will again. . . .

Oh, this Henny of ours [Henrietta was in an interesting condition] is the saddest Creature you can conceive. If she drags her bloated self to the Wind Mill, she thinks so prodigious an exertion entitles her to groan and complain the whole evening until nine o'Clock when she departs and is seen no more until the next morning.

Molly Tilghman to Polly Pearse, April 13, 1786. She is describing, ironically, a certain Major Forman:

I am more than commonly anxious to meet him since his late modest and generous declaration "that he is to be bought" and that the price of so generous a heart is only twenty thousand pounds. There's humility and moderation for you! . . . The moment that I draw the high prize in the Lottery I shall fly to Swan Harbour to get my good friend Mr. Earle to negociate with the sprightly youth for me. . . .

When my father left Baltimore my brother [Lieutenant Colonel Tench Tilghman] was better, though still too far from being well.

Tuesday morning.

Johnny Relpe has promised to send this Letter tomorrow by a safe hand. Alas! my dear Polly, I am too unhappy about poor Tench to write you more than we had Letters on Saturday which informed us that he was no better, but had rather lost strength. My God! what his situation this moment may be! Indeed I fear he is in great danger.

Lieutenant Colonel Tench Tilghman died on April 18, 1786.

Molly Tilghman to Polly Pearse, January 2, 1787:

There was a Ball the night after Christmas which was much indebted to the Majors of Queen Anne's, the formidable Clealand, the woeful looking Emory and the handsome Smyth. Mrs. Galloway flashed upon them in her Muslin attended by her admiring spouse in his Rock of Gibraltar Coat. They had 16 couple and spent a very agreeable Evening. The play came next night which afforded a few unexpected incidents. Some Bucks of true spirit which was increas'd by good Liquor, broke open one of the Windows to the great dismay of the Ladies. As to the Play, it exceeded no ones expectations. However, the Eyes of the Audience were oblig'd by a vast display of fine Cloaths and Jewels, which more than made up for any faults in the acting. Our Duke [?] really looked very handsome, he wore Mat Tilghman's white sattin waistcoat &c, a black star brilliant with paste and fourteen black and white feathers. Last night it was again repeated with the addition of the Irish Widow. The Ball gave such a spring to the Spirit of our Beaux they have made up a Subscription for Assemblies and the first is to be to-morrow night . . .

Molly Tilghman to Polly Pearse, October 6, 1787, from Chestertown:

On my way from Talbot I had the ill luck of meeting that abominable old winking Tommy Goldsborough at Miles River. The moment I saw him I had a presentiment that it would be the worse for me. My dear Polly, he is worse than ever. Not content with worrying the company in general, with his *interregnum* observation (which he did several times) he singled me out for the victim of his vulgarism, for which if I forget him, may I be condemned for life to his counterpart if such a one exists. As my evil genius wou'd have it, Billy Goldsborough asked us to ride and look at his house. From that one circumstance the Wretch took it into his Head (or rather pretended to think so) that a Match was in agitation, and said such things, such shocking things, as hardly left me the power of leaving the room, which was all I had for it.

We learn from the postscript to a later letter that, the "abominable" Captain Richard Bennett Lloyd having died, his widow, the lovely Joanna, had married a Captain Beckford of the Guards, a handsome man of twenty-two with —— guineas a year. The all-important word is undecipherable.

The years are passing, and poor Molly tends more and more to become the spinster sister, sick nurse and guardian for her whole family. She never married. On January 29, 1789, after having described the "lying-in" of brother Phil's wife, Harriet, she proceeds directly to another blessed event:

The 15th of this month Henny produced a Daughter (yes, another Daughter) with as little trouble as might be. What shall we do with such a tribe of Girls? She is called after my Ladyship, not Molly nor Polly but Mary, and I have the additional honour of being her God Mother. . . .

Late as it is, I must tell you that last night we were at a Ball at Petty Jackson's [Perpetual Jackson!] where we staid till one o'clock. It was really a very genteel entertainment. We had twelve Couples. I went determined not to dance, but who can resist the temptation of a super-excellent partner? It was not in nature to refuse Jack Chew with whom I danced three dances.

We had some of the most capital figures I have seen for a long time. Oh, that you had been there, my dear Polly! . . .

Fain would I dissect Miss [Anna] Garnett for your edification. Did you ever of a rainy day empty all your Drawers on the Bed in order to set them to rights? If you can recollect the confused mixture of Ribbon, Gauze, Flowers, Beads, Persian feathers and Lace, black and white, you will have the best idea I can give you of Miss Garnett's Hatt. Such a Hoop and Handkerchief, too, was never seen on mortal Woman before. Mrs. Bordley's Head without a Hatt was quite equal to the other. The tremendous majesty of her Tete will never leave my memory, which with the fabric erected on it made her almost as tall as myself.

The last letter is dated Chestertown, May 8th (1789?).

Since my return from Talbot I have had little leisure and not much more inclination for my pen. The very evening I got home I took up the employment of Mistress, Nurse and Housekeeper.

She goes on to tell of the illnesses of her stepmother, sister-in-law and various servants. Of the visiting of other members of the family, and visits to come, and ends sadly:

So what chance has poor Mary of getting to Cecil [where Polly lived].

In Kent County a few miles to the northwest of Chestertown lies Caulk's Field, where the only land battle ever fought on the Eastern Shore took place. It was a very small battle and the result indecisive, but the Americans may be said to have won because they inflicted a greater loss on the British than they sustained. The Negroes of the vicinity used to call it Marse Peter Peter Parker's war.

In August, 1814, when the main British fleet sailed up

the Patuxent River on the western shore with a view to attacking Washington, Captain Sir Peter Parker was detached in the frigate *Menelaus*, accompanied by some smaller vessels, to create a diversion on the Eastern Shore. On August 20th, he was in the neighborhood of Rock Hall. Proceeding northward, he landed a detachment which burned an unfortunate farmer's house, barn and crops, and returned to the ship. On the 30th he landed another party in Fairlee Creek, burned some more buildings and carried off four Negroes. By this time the British had taken Washington and set it afire, but Sir Peter could not have known that. When his men were ashore at Fairlee, they heard news of a regiment of Maryland militia encamped in the neighborhood. Upon being told of it, Sir Peter immediately ordered a strong landing force to be prepared, and he brought them ashore himself that night "to have a frolic with the Yankees." Before leaving his ship he wrote a little note to his wife:

H.M.S. Menelaus
August 30th 1814

My Darling Marianne:

I am just going on desperate service and entirely depend upon valor and example for its successful issue. If anything befalls me I have made a sort of will. My country will be good to you and our adored children. God Almighty bless and protect you all. Adieu, most beloved Marianne, adieu!

Peter Parker

P.S. I am in high health and spirits.

One hopes that his country *was* good to Marianne and the children.

He had 260 men. Under the guidance of one of the slaves he had captured, he set off in the dark to find the Americans, who were reported to number 170. There may have been more than that; the exact number is in dispute. The best account of what followed is to be found in the report of Lieutenant Colonel Philip Reed who commanded the Americans.

Reed was on his way to try to protect the isolated farms along the bay. According to a local tradition, his troops had bivouacked in old St. Paul's the previous night, where they had a terrible scare when a flock of sheep strayed into the church. Upon hearing that the British were coming after *him*, Reed ordered a retreat to a gentle eminence he had in mind, where he could lie concealed and take the British in flank as they came marching along the road. This was Caulk's Field. Caulk's ancient house still stands beyond it; the rolling wheatfield looks just the same; the road by which the British came from the bay is not yet improved; the only new thing is a modest monument of fieldstone at the edge of the field.

Reed posted an advance party to cover the road while his line was forming across the field. After greeting the oncoming British with a sharp fire, this party retired to take their places on the right of the line. The enemy deployed and fire became general, sustained by our troops, says Reed, with determined valor. Very few of them had ever heard the whistle of a ball. Foiled in front, the enemy re-formed and attacked the left flank. It was unavailing.

The British fire was slackening when Reed learned, to his dismay, that the American ammunition was almost exhausted. Every man had brought twenty cartridges to the field. The artillery was entirely out of ammunition. He was forced to order his line to fall back to another position that was partly fortified. Here they waited for the British in a kind of desperation—but the British never came. They were on the way back to their barges, carrying their wounded commander. He died on the way.

The Americans lost only one man killed and three wounded. The British admitted to the loss of fourteen killed and twenty-seven wounded. A few days later the British made a full-dress sea and shore attack on Baltimore and were definitely repulsed. That ended their activities in Chesapeake Bay.

For about ten miles above Chestertown the broad Chester follows a placid course between low banks, with moderately high ground behind, and an occasional little hill. It is a pastoral scene of rich bottom lands, patches of intensely green woods, an occasional old house on a point of vantage. At the end one comes to the first village, Crumpton, a very small village. Here the steamboats turned around and went back. Years before there were any steamboats, this is where the gay young Henry Callister settled down to die after age and bankruptcy had soured him. In those days there was no bridge, and Crumpton was known as Callister's ferry. Comegys' Farm, which looks down on the present bridge, is the quaintest of all the old houses hereabouts.

The actual head of Chester is at Millington, five miles farther upstream. Here the river splits into several little branches, which have their sources in the swamps of Kent County to the south or across the state line in Delaware.

CHAPTER 22

The Sassafras and Bohemia Rivers

As one travels northward, the land is always rising by imperceptible degrees, and for this reason the Sassafras is the most beautiful of Eastern Shore rivers and quite different in character from the streams farther south. The steep, wooded banks rise to a bench eighty feet above water level; it is only occasionally that one glimpses a sloping wheatfield behind a screen of trees. Each of the many inlets winds away to disappear mysteriously in the shadows of its lofty banks. The variety is endless. Each point, as you round it, reveals a green surprise. The course is like a succession of little land-locked lakes; you can never see far. The Sassafras is something special in rivers, yet few know it, even in Maryland.

Like the other rivers, it has an immense estuary, but within a couple of miles it narrows down. At the mouth there is a sprawling summer resort called Betterton, but this is for visitors and has little to do with the Eastern Shore. Once past Ornery Point, you are in the real river and that is a solitary stream, rarely disturbed nowadays. Up on the bench there are rich farms, and many a fine old house, but these are mostly too high and too well-screened to be seen from the water. The man in a boat is alone. Every mile or two there will be a wharf, now rotting away. Each wharf is built at the mouth of a gully, in order to secure an easy grade for a road up to the farms.

Lloyd's Creek on the Kent County side is different from all the others. The opening is almost a mile wide and across it runs a low spit of land decorated with a charming, serrated file of trees, leaving only a narrow opening at the east end. Inside, there is a lagoon branching off in various directions, and in the middle of the lagoon rises a tiny, high and wooded island as if painted there by an artist to complete his composition.

Upstream, Ornery Point is another low spit running out from the high Cecil County shore for nearly half a mile and forcing the river to go around it. One might suppose it was called "Ornery" because sailors had so much trouble weathering it in a head wind, but as a matter of fact there used to be a tavern or ordinary on this point run in connection with a ferry. It is a spot of singular charm.

Opposite Ornery Point lies the narrow opening of Turner's Creek, which spreads out within in an intriguing confusion of high points and still coves. The wharf here was once an important one, serving a prosperous invisible community above. At the head of one of the arms of Turner's, Shrewsbury church has stood since the eighteenth century. The present church, built in 1832 out of the materials of its predecessor, is insignificant, but the churchyard with its ancient ruined trees has a lingering, mournful beauty.

The grave of General John Cadwalader is here, Washington's stanch friend in his darkest years. Cadwalader challenged General Thomas Conway, Washington's principal detractor, to a duel and shot his teeth out, saying, "I have stopped the damned rascal's lying tongue at any rate." Conway survived and abjectly apologized to General Washington. The long epitaph on Cadwalader's gravestone was composed by no less a person than Tom Paine, but he who goes to the trouble of deciphering the lichened lettering will be disappointed in its literary quality, considering who wrote it.

Near-by a brown headstone, sinking into the earth, commemorates an humble tragedy. Under a rudely etched fat cherub, blowing what appears to be a penny whistle, appears this legend:

> Here lieth the bodies of Iervis and Hannah,
> son and daughter of Henery Spencer
> who departed this life Feb'y the 10th
> 1742/3, Iervis aged 13, Hannah 16.
>
> —o—
>
> Farewell our Friends and Parents dear
> We are not dead but sleepeth here.
> Our debts is paid, our graves you see,
> Prepare yourselves to follow we.

Captain John Smith, it will be remembered, called the Sassafras River the Tockwogh, which was as close as he could render the guttural name of the tribe who occupied its shores. On his map Captain John places their village, where he was so well-entertained, on the Kent shore just above Turner's Creek. According to tradition, this was later to have been the site of Shrewsbury, one of the towns that Lord Baltimore commanded to be built in 1683, but it never took. Higher upstream, however, Georgetown, founded in 1707, became an important place in a small way.

On the Cecil side the entrance to Back Creek cannot be seen until you are immediately opposite it; inside, it spreads out wide with many branches. On the Kent side, by way of variety, Freeman's Creek strikes in straight and narrow, while just beyond, the shore flattens down for a space to provide in the twin creeks, Island and Mill, an inlet of quite another style.

Upon rounding a double bend in the river, one is surprised by civilization in the shape of two villages connected by a modern bridge, Georgetown in Kent County and Fredericton in Cecil, named for two sons of George II. The slope of the banks is more gradual here, and odd little streets run this way and that, conditioned by the lie of the land. The white houses are half hidden among the trees. This is a popular rendezvous for small yachts and in summer there is always a fleet of them anchored in the pool below the bridge. On the Fredericton side there is a famous boatbuilding yard, and adjoining it the house and wharf of the Tockwogh Yacht Club.

Above the bridge one may continue to follow the beautiful, crooked course of the river for half a dozen miles more to the Head of Sassafras. At Budd's Landing on the Cecil side, there is a fine reach with high wooded shores and deep gullies, black in the shadows. The floors of the gullies are filled with an almost tropical tangle of greenbrier, honeysuckle and wild grape. Where there is an overgrown road coming down to a rotting wharf, it will be lined with wineberry canes. On the other hand, at the mouth of Duffy Creek there is a spread of salt marsh for a change.

At the head of tidewater, there is an old village called Sassafras, sleeping under immense trees. Here the river divides into two runs, one of which comes pouring through a breach in a ruined milldam. The wide floor of the millpond inside is now covered with goose grass, greenest of all the greens.

Only once in the course of our history has the quiet of the Sassafras River been rudely broken. On May 5, 1813, a flotilla of small boats from the British fleet came rowing up the river. Besides the sailors, they had 150 marines aboard and five cannon. They were under the command of Lieutenant Westphal of H.M.S. *Marlborough,* and Rear Admiral Cockburn was with them. It was the same party that had burned Havre de Grace on the western shore two days before.

The British (especially Admiral Cockburn) were greatly feared and hated because of the stories of outrages committed down at Hampton, when the fleet first arrived in the Chesapeake. These acts, the British claimed, had been committed by a regiment of renegade French prisoners rescued from Spanish prisons and organized as Chasseurs Brittanique. One of the British officers (Sir Charles James Napier) confessed that they ought to have been hanged at once. Such outrages had not been repeated up the bay, but Admiral Cockburn could not live them down.

The twin villages had sent a couple of men down in a boat to watch the river. Two miles below, they were captured by the approaching British and sent back with the admiral's terms. Nobody in the villages should be molested, he promised, unless they resisted the British.

Nevertheless, when the flotilla appeared, it received the fire of a field gun and three or four hundred militia muskets. When the British returned the fire, the militia fled. The British thereupon started firing all the houses in both villages except those where the occupants (according to the admiral's terms) were found staying quietly at home. This is the British account. They told of one man wearing gaiters (i.e., military trappings) who begged so hard that "though he had no doubt assisted in firing on the British, his home was spared."

The British were confused by the lack of uniforms in the militia. Accused of firing on noncombatants, they said: "The fact is, every man in the United States under 45 years of age is a militia man and during the war attended in his turn to be drilled or trained. He had always in his possession either a musket or a rifle-barrel piece; knew its use from his infancy and with it therefore could do as much execution in a smock frock or plain coat as if he wore the most splendid uniform."

It is not reported that anybody was hurt by the shooting at Georgetown. On his way downriver, the admiral visited a village situated on a branch. (This might have been Stillpond at the head of Lloyd's Creek.) Here the people, warned by what had happened above, adopted a peaceable demeanor and shook hands with the admiral. Their houses were spared, and everything the British took from them they paid for. Like other marauders we have heard of, the British wanted to be loved!

The affair at Georgetown has given rise to one of the most cherished bits of lore on the Eastern Shore: how Kitty Knight kept the British from burning her house. Kitty lived to a great age, and the story has been taken down in her own words. The truth is much more interesting than the popular versions of the story. As a matter of fact, her house *was* burned by the British. It was another woman's house that she saved.

Catherine, or Kitty, Knight was born about 1775 of a prominent Kent County family. In her youth she was a beauty and a great belle, and in afteryears she liked to tell of how she was noticed by President George Washington at a theatrical performance followed by a ball in Philadelphia. She was escorted by Mr. Benjamin Harrison of Virginia, father of William H. Harrison and great-grandfather of Benjamin. Here is Kitty's story:

I must explain the manner in which the theatre was built. The stage proper could be removed in sections, disclosing a circus in which horses and animals could be used. This was protected by heavy iron bars so that the horses would not jump into the space allotted to the audience. General Washington in moving around, speaking pleasantly to his personal friends, crossed the hall and possibly noticing that I was with Mr. Harrison, said to me, passing his hand down these iron bars: "You are well guarded, Miss." Then I said to him: "I am surely, Sir, in your presence," and curtsied.

In respect to the attack on Georgetown, Kitty said—one can picture the old lady in her rocking chair, telling the story in well-chosen words:

The British, after landing, commenced to burn all the lower part of the town, which was largely of frame. There were, however, two brick buildings on top of the hill [they are there still] which had not as yet been fired. In one of them was an old lady sick and almost destitute, and to this building the Admiral and his sailors and marines proceeded at a rapid gait. I followed them but before I got to the top of the hill, they had set fire to the house in which the old lady lay. I immediately called the attention of the Admiral to the fact that they were about to burn up a human being and that a woman, and I pleaded with him to make his men put the fire out. This I finally succeeded in doing, when they immediately went next door, not forty feet distant and fired the second of the brick houses. I told the commanding officer that as the wind was blowing toward the other house the old lady would be burned up anyhow, when, apparently affected by my appeal, he called his men off but left the fire burning, saying 'Come on, boys!' As they went out of the door, one of them struck his boarding-axe through a panel of the door.

Kitty stayed behind and put out the fire herself with her broom. The door with the mark of the ax is still there.

She died in 1855, and I quote from her obituary in the local newspaper: "She had read all the old poets and the British classics and but a short time before her death could quote page after page of her favorite authors . . . she was gifted with rare conversational powers."

In 1899 the citizens of Georgetown decided to change the name of the steamboat *Trumpeter,* which had served them for many years, to *Kitty Knight.*

We are now approaching the head of Chesapeake Bay. Five miles above the mouth of the Sassafras, the Elk River comes down from the northeast. At its mouth, the country for the first time assumes an aspect of grandeur. Down Elk Neck, on the westerly side of the river, marches a chain of mountains rising steeply from the water and ending in the bold promontory of Turkey Point. They are only hills, really, the highest summits running up to little more than three hundred feet, but in the flat country to which we have become accustomed the effect is tremendous. The view of the hills from across the river, either from the water's edge or from the high bench behind, is glorious. Seagoing ships are continually passing, bound to and from the entrance to the Chesapeake and Delaware Canal above. The sight of ships steaming through a narrow strait, with steep, green-clad hills behind, is anywhere in the world a sight to gladden the eyes.

Five miles up the Elk, the Bohemia River comes in from the east. As a river, it is a small affair, but its name is forever associated with one of the great figures of the Eastern Shore, Augustine Herman. Born in what is now Czechoslovakia, it was he who named the river after his fatherland, and also called his home Bohemia Manor.

In the first half of the seventeenth century, Herman was a leading citizen of the Dutch colony of New Amsterdam. A vital man with a curious mind, who had been trained as surveyor and mapmaker, he was a valuable accession in a new land. He was sometimes a supporter, but more often in opposition to the autocratic and peppery governor, one-legged Peter Stuyvesant. Herman's "bouwerie" was on the site of the present Lafayette Street in New York, adjoining the Stuyvesant farm, and his town house was at the corner of Pine and Pearl Streets. He was a great experimenter, and grew indigo and tobacco on Manhattan Island, but the latter crop was a failure. After serving as agent for a house in Amsterdam, Holland, he went into business for himself in 1645, dealing in slaves, tobacco, etc., with Jamestown, Virginia, London and Amsterdam. By contriving to evade the English navigation laws, he did very well for himself. In the Chesapeake Bay country his agent was Dr. George Hack of the eastern shore of Virginia.

For six years Herman was one of the famous "Nine Men of New Amsterdam," who served as a kind of council to the governor, and stoutly opposed Peter Stuyvesant's more oppressive acts. In 1649 Herman and Adrian van der Donck, in the name of the Nine Men, wrote a remonstrance to the home government, and three of the nine carried it to Holland. It is a great document; as a result, the States-General sternly rebuked Governor Peter Stuyvesant, who thereupon very naturally swore enmity against Herman.

In 1651 Herman, through assuming the debts of a friend, was almost ruined. At the same time the tobacco market failed. He turned to his neighbor, Peter Stuyvesant, for aid, and Peter not only refused it but exerted all his power to hasten Herman's ruin. Herman wrote to his friend Anna, wife of Dr. Hack in Virginia: "In fine, matters are so situated that only God's help will avail; there is no trust to be placed in man."

It is pleasant to relate that Anna Hack immediately started on the long and difficult journey to New Amsterdam to assist her friend. Peter Stuyvesant set to work to bring her down too, but Anna was an experienced businesswoman and she foiled him. During the winter of 1651-1652, which she spent in New Amsterdam, Augustine Herman's enemies brought one suit after another against her and she won them all. In the spring, Herman, "having settled with his creditors," was granted "liberty and freedom," and the capricious Peter Stuyvesant thereupon became his friend again. Governor Stuyvesant had lost face through having made a disastrous treaty with New England, and he needed friends.

He sent Augustine Herman and Adrian Keyser to Rhode Island with a letter to governor Coddington which, upon being opened, was regarded as so insulting that the New Amsterdam emissaries were thrown into prison at Newport. It was only with the greatest difficulty that they got Peter Stuyvesant to clear them. A year later, Herman was sent to Boston to appease the New Englanders, and acquitted himself with credit. About this time he married Annetje Verlett in New Amsterdam. She is supposed to have been Anna Hack's sister, but the record is not clear.

In 1659 Governor Peter Stuyvesant was assailed by trouble from the other direction. The Dutch settlements on the Delaware River which were under his jurisdiction, besides being unprofitable, were distracted by the quarrels of the local director and vice-directors. The debt-ridden settlers were slipping away to Maryland, leaving their debts behind them. To Josias Fendall, governor of Maryland, this seemed like a good opportunity to assert Lord Baltimore's claim to all the land on the west side of the Delaware up to the 40th parallel. This would take in all the Dutch settlements on that river.

Colonel Nathaniel Utie of Maryland, who was sent up to New Amstel (Newcastle, Delaware) for this purpose, carried himself in a very highhanded manner. He not only ordered the Dutch to get out instantly or take an oath of allegiance to Lord Baltimore, but he went from house to house in the little town trying to persuade the settlers to revolt against their Dutch administrators. There was keen competition to secure settlers in those days. Utie told the authorities he had an armed force ready to march on them. Finally, he allowed them three weeks in which to communicate with their overlord, Governor Peter Stuyvesant.

The rage of that choleric gentleman upon receiving this news can be pictured. "He raged and fumed in his usual manner," one of his men said. Why hadn't they arrested Utie and sent him under guard to New Amsterdam? he wanted to know. However, he acted quickly. In three days he had outfitted and dispatched a force of seventy-five men for the defense of the Delaware settlements. Also, he sent Augustine Herman (Heermans, the Dutch called him) and Resolved Waldron direct to the governor of Maryland, with a letter embodying a vigorous protest.

Herman kept a diary of that journey. He and Waldron set out from New Amstel with a few soldiers and Indians for guides. It is only a few miles from the Delaware to the streams that empty into the Chesapeake. Coming to the Elk River, they found a skiff on the shore and sent back their guides. Herman goes on:

Shortly after we pushed off, the boat became almost half full of water, whereupon we were obliged to land and turn the boat upside down; we caulked the seams somewhat with old linen, our people having left behind the tow which had been given them for that purpose, and thus made it a little tighter, but one was obliged to sit continually and bail out the water. In that way, we came with the same tide a good league and a half down the Elk River and found ourselves at its east branch [the Bohemia River?], where we built a fire in the woods, and proceeded with the night ebb on our journey with great labor, as the boat was very leaky, and we had neither rudder nor oar but merely paddles.

Herman did not yet know the country, and his route is a little hard to follow. Apparently they entered the Sassafras River after descending the Elk, and stopped at the plantation of John Turner (on Turner's Creek?). Here they met a runaway soldier from New Amstel, who refused to return but made them a pair of oars. Upon re-embarking, they met two men in the river who claimed to own the boat they were in, but after great difficulty they succeeded in getting away from them.

Upon leaving the Sassafras, it was apparently their intention to cross over to Colonel Utie's place on Spesutie Island (*Spes Utiae*, Hope of the Uties). But as they approached the island they heard music and much firing of guns, and supposing this to be the armed force Utie had promised to send against New Amstel, they kept on down the middle of the bay, passing to the east of what Herman calls Pooloo Island. Its right name is Poole's. This was a pretty hazardous voyage in their leaky little skiff.

On the evening of the fourth day, they were off the Eastern Shore at Love Point, where the Chester River empties, and here Captain, later Major, Joseph Wickes took them in at Wickliffe. There was a warm discussion that night between the gentlemen as to a charge that the Dutch were trying to incite the Indians to rise against the English—a charge that was always trotted out when colonists quarreled in the seventeenth century. Captain Wickes let the Dutch ambassadors have a better boat, but charged them a stiff hire for it: twenty pounds of tobacco a day for the boat, and twenty pounds more for a man to help row it.

On the following day they arrived at "Seaforn" across the bay. This no doubt refers to the Severn River, where Annapolis now stands. Here there was another row about the boat, and to pay for it Herman was forced to give a draft for fifteen hundred pounds of tobacco in Maryland, or the equivalent in brandy at Manhattan.

Next day (October 6th) they were at Colonel "Coortsey's" (our old friend, Henry Coursey) in Patuxent River, who was "very courteous and conversed pleasantly."

Nine days, however, elapsed before a meeting was arranged with the governor and his Council. During the interim, Herman lost no opportunity of promoting the Dutch claims in discussion with the other gentlemen of Maryland whom he met. Finally they got together at the house of William Bateman at Patuxent, and after a courteous reception and many compliments proceeded to dinner.

The long-winded discussions that followed stretched over four days. Amidst a mass of verbiage, it may clearly be seen how astutely Herman presented the Dutch case and kept his temper. He immediately succeeded in putting Colonel Utie (who was present) in the wrong, and provoked that gentleman to such a burst of temper as to call down a rebuke from the governor. Herman discovered a phrase in Lord Baltimore's patent that proved a stumblingblock to the Marylanders for years and finally cost his lordship the land under dispute. It was this: Baltimore was granted land that was not already settled by Christians. The Dutch were able to show that the Delaware was settled by white men before the Baltimore patent was issued.

The conference ended inconclusively, but the honors

were Herman's. The Marylanders, shaken by the flaw in Lord Baltimore's patent, required time to communicate with his lordship in England. Resolved Waldron carried Herman's report back to New Amstel and Manhattan, while Herman proceeded to Virginia to see Governor Richard Bennett and, as he says, "create a diversion between them." It is supposed that Herman's wife joined him at Jamestown, having come by sea, and that they spent the winter of 1659-1660 at the home of their friends, the Hacks, on the Eastern Shore.

The boundary dispute went on for years. In 1664 the Dutch settlements at Manhattan and on the Delaware fell to the English fleets without a struggle. In 1670 the Dutch recaptured them, but four years later they passed to the English for good. Lord Baltimore's claim was then taken up with the proprietor of Pennsylvania, and to this day it makes a good Marylander hot under the collar to remember how his state was done out of her due by the "oily" William Penn. Otherwise, the city of Wilmington and a part of Philadelphia would be in Maryland today.

Meanwhile, though the Dutch kept their settlements on the Delaware for the moment, they lost their vigorous and able envoy. Augustine Herman loved the amenities, and the large style of living at the Hacks' that winter must have made a strong appeal to him. He could no longer have had any respect for Peter Stuyvesant; perhaps he foresaw the approaching end of Dutch rule in North America. He was not a Dutchman. Perhaps that night when he built a fire on the shore of the Bohemia, he saw the noble bank where he subsequently built his house, and fell in love with it.

He went back to Manhattan, but not to stay. That same year (1660) he received from the Maryland authorities "letters of Denization," permitting him to own land in the province. Charles Calvert, later the third Lord Baltimore, came over as governor and was much taken with the sturdy Herman. Herman agreed with Calvert to make a map of the province, for which he was to be paid in grants of land. In 1662 he received his first grant of four thousand acres on the site he had chosen, christened it Bohemia Manor, and started to build his "great house." When it was finished he brought his family to Maryland and began to live as the great country gentleman he wished to be. In 1666 the family became the first foreign-born persons to be naturalized in Maryland. Meanwhile, the Hacks had taken up land on the south shore of the Bohemia.

Augustine Herman gave ten years of labor to the famous map. In 1673 the original drawing was sent to London, where it was engraved by William Fairthorne. The result is considered a fine piece of cartography, but Herman was dissatisfied with the engraver's work. He "slobbered over it," Herman said, "defiling the prints by many errors." Nevertheless, it was so good a map that no other was required for many years. Only two copies of the original are known, but it has often been reproduced.

The able and vigorous Herman was greatly esteemed by the governor, and Calvert showered him with whatever honors were in his gift. Herman was his lordship's deputy at the head of the bay, with full powers for dealing with malefactors and with Indians, a commissioner of one thing and another, and a justice of the Quorum. He received many grants of land, Mill Fall, Small Hope, Misfortune, Bohemia Sisters, etc., about fifteen thousand acres in all. On the Eastern Shore he was the greatest personage of his day.

Herman's wife, Annetje, having borne him two sons, Ephraim George and Casparus, and three daughters, died about 1664. Two years later he married Catherine, the daughter of Henry Ward of Baltimore County. Nothing has survived of her except a portrait depicting a lady with a long nose and a morose expression. There is also an abusive reference to her in the diary of two travelers: "a miserable, doubly miserable wife, but so miserable that I will not relate it here. All his children have been compelled on her account to leave their father's house." So wrote Sluyters and Dankaerts, emissaries of the Labadists—not, however, a very credible pair of reporters.

The Labadists were followers of Jean de Labadie, a former French Jesuit who had established a small Protestant sect in Holland whose beliefs and practices resembled those of the Quakers. Sluyters and Dankaerts were seeking land for a colony in America. They fell in first with Ephraim George Herman (who seems to have been rather a feeble character, "a fly-up-the-creek," they say on the Shore), and he brought them to his father. This was in 1679. Augustine Herman, always seeking colonists for his wide acres, received them well and promised them three thousand acres of land.

However, the Labadists had converted Ephraim George, and under the influence of their teaching the young man felt obliged to live apart from his wife. This annoyed his father, and he withdrew his promise of land to the missionaries. Moreover, he added a codicil to his will, appointing trustees for Ephraim George for fear his son would give away everything he had. Ephraim George subsequently recanted and went back to his wife.

In 1683, to Augustine Herman's great annoyance, Sluyters and Dankaerts returned with a hundred colonists to claim the three thousand acres. They brought suit against the old man and won their case. As a religious colony the Labadists lasted but forty years; however, they brought some good blood to the province, and founded several honorable families in Maryland and Delaware.

Toward the end of his life, Augustine, having become reconciled with Ephraim George, transferred most of his property to his son with this odd proviso: Ephraim George was to pay his father annually five thousand pounds of tobacco, six barrels "of good beer and strong beer," an anker (ten gallons) of rum, two ankers of good wine, one hogshead of the best cider out of the orchard, a hundred pounds of Muscovado sugar, all "for my private spending." Moreover, if Augustine left home, Ephraim George was to pay him two thousand pounds of tobacco additional "towards my board and £25 in money should I happen to go to New York."

Augustine Herman died in 1686, and Ephraim George three years later. Augustine's wife married again and her second husband managed to get most of the great property into his hands. Litigation followed which lasted through more than two generations. The Herman line died out in the third generation, but several prominent Eastern Shore families claim descent from the mapmaker through the female line.

No description of the great house that Augustine Herman built has survived, but there is a touch in the Labadists' diary that brings the seventeenth century scene winging back: "We were directed to a place to sleep but the screeching of the wild geese and other wild fowl in the creek before the door prevented us from having a good sleep." The palatial modern dwelling of a remote descendant now stands on or near the spot where Herman built his house. His grave was found, but when the stone was lifted his bones were gone. The grave has been re-erected in the modern flower garden.

Many traditional stories cling to the Herman name; stories of his lavish hospitality and the blazing fires that were lighted to warm travelers; of his formal gardens, his deer park (though the surrounding country swarmed with deer!), his coach and four, his collection of paintings. He was the first to visualize a canal to connect the waters of the Chesapeake and the Delaware. Failing that, he built a portage road which for generations was known as "the old man's path."

Only less famous than the old man is his beloved white horse. After he had brought his family to Maryland, one version of the story runs, he returned to New Amsterdam to settle his affairs there. Accused of being a traitor to the Dutch, he was arrested and cast into prison, some say threatened with execution. Feigning insanity, he asked to be allowed to say farewell to his horse. A good-humored jailer brought the animal up the steps and into the "Round House" where Herman was confined. Herman sprang on his back and put him to one of the tall windows. The horse crashed through and, landing unharmed fifteen feet below, carried his master to the bank of the North River and swam it in safety. According to the story, the horse was maintained by his grateful master for the rest of his life without working, and provided with a handsome tombstone when he died.

There is always some foundation for such a story, however fanciful the details. Herman afterward had himself painted with the white horse. The original was destroyed in the fire that consumed his gallery of paintings, but a copy had been made and that survives in the modern Bohemia Manor. The painter was not a very good one—though he has rendered the head of the horse beautifully; Herman is depicted as a little man with a flat-topped head and a highly suspicious expression—but that may be because he didn't like the painter.

The Elk River and the Northeast River a few miles north of it are both geographically on the Eastern Shore of Chesapeake Bay, as a glance at the map will show. The Northeast, though it has a great estuary like the other rivers, is unimportant either way, but the Elk, and particularly the Head of Elk (the present town of Elkton) occupies an important page in the history of our country. While there was no battle here during the Revolution, the armies were continually passing back and forth or landing or taking to the water. There are other interesting circumstances, too; the first steamboat on the Chesapeake ran up here (1813), and there was a quaint railway in operation as early as 1831.

Nevertheless, I have determined to omit the Elk because the people of that neighborhood have little connection with the Eastern Shore. Head of Elk, since the beginning of our country, has been astride the main route of travel between North and South, and on that account a different culture has resulted; whereas the Eastern Shore is on a branch line and its culture is *sui generis.* If I took up Head of Elk, I should be beginning a new story, so I choose for my dividing line no river, but a man-made ditch, the Chesapeake and Delaware Canal; upon crossing it a traveler recognizes that he is leaving the real Eastern Shore.

In concluding this Eastern Shore excursion let me quote a description left by John Bernard, a popular Anglo-Irish actor of the eighteenth century. Bernard, while playing a season at Annapolis in 1798, hired a sloop and took part of his company over to Chestertown for a few performances. They were stranded on the way back, so Bernard can hardly be accused of favoritism toward the Eastern Shore.

It always seemed to me a collection of country houses where people had been born with wealth or had retired to spend it; a spot which, from a happy union of influences in its soil and sky, had so molded its denizens' characters as to become one wide temple of mirth and sociability. Here the grand product was good-humor;

the great exchange hospitality; the one avocation enjoyment. Here the most inveterate wanderer was tempted to stay his step. The doors seemed to me a useless device; they were made to stand open. And almost equally unnecessary were the roofs, for the sky was always smiling approbation on what was doing below. People of every nation and prejudice met here to subside into brotherhood, and the genius of their hosts expended itself but in the invention of new spells to support such influence. To sum up in a word—this was the Ireland of America. Surely there was never such a permissable corruption of a name as that by which people pronounced this region Merryland.

A bit of the blarney, of course, but founded on what Bernard himself experienced. This is still the ideal of the Eastern Shore, though in the complicated life of today it may be difficult of attainment.

ACKNOWLEDGMENTS

THE appended list of sources does not give the measure of the debt I owe to the late Dr. Samuel A. Harrison; and a particular acknowledgment is called for. Dr. Harrison confined his essays to his own county, Talbot, but though his field was small he exhibits the qualifications of a notable historian. Some of his articles appeared in the newspaper press of his day; others have been printed as pamphlets; but the greatest part of his work has been gathered together by his son-in-law, the late Oswald Tilghman, and incorporated in Tilghman's *History of Talbot County*. Would that all county histories were as easy to read as this one! I have also had the advantage of consulting Dr. Harrison's collected papers in the Maryland Historical Society. Another book that is not so well known as it ought to be is Henry Chandlee Forman's *Early Manor and Plantation Houses of Maryland*, with its wealth of unique photographs.

It will be noted that there are a number of privately printed books listed among the sources, and many more books that have been published by a local printer. It is somewhat the fashion to disregard books that do not bear the cachet of an established house; but in a work like this, purporting to be a social history, the smallest of local events may be characteristic, and such little books therefore have been invaluable to this author. I owe especial thanks to the staffs of the Pratt Library's Maryland Room, the Library of the Maryland Historical Society, and the Easton (Maryland) Public Library for their assistance in running down such out-of-the-way items. Talbot County Free Library has a Maryland Room also.

On my various tours around the Eastern Shore by land or water, nearly everybody I talked to has contributed something to this book. Among those who have helped me appreciably are: Eben Hearne, Arthur H. Shettle, and Dr. E. J. Clarke of Pocomoke; Lorrie C. Quinn of Crisfield; Rives Matthews of Princess Anne; Colonel C. L. Vincent of Snow Hill; Clarke Gardner of Salisbury; Dr. Guy Steele and Willis White of Cambridge; John Dickinson of Crosiadore; J. Ramsay Spear of the Wilderness; Walter F. Austin, Mr. and Mrs. Robert G. Henry, and Miss Alice Cox of Easton; Judge J. Owen Knotts and Mrs. Mary Melvin of Denton; Leon Andrus of Centerville; William Fahnestock of Readbourne; Dr. Gilbert W. Mead, President of Washington College, and Miss Dorothy Paca of Chestertown; Mr. and Mrs. Clifton Miller of Hinchingham; Dr. R. V. Truitt, Director of the Marine Biological Laboratory at Solomon's Island; and George T. Ross of Philadelphia, who masquerades as *Minnie Wheeler's* Boy-Friend. The late Swepson Earle, formerly Commissioner of Conservation for Maryland and author of *The Chesapeake Bay Country*, has done me the kindness of reading the script for obvious errors and omissions.

SOURCES

Books

ABBE, CLEVELAND JR., *Report on the Physiography of Maryland.* Baltimore, 1898.

ANDREWS, MATTHEW PAGE, *History of Maryland.* Garden City, N. Y., 1929.

ARBER, EDWARD, F.S.A. (ed.), *Travels and Works of Captain John Smith,* new edition, with introduction by A. G. Bradley (2 vols.), Edinburgh, 1910.

ARCHIVES OF MARYLAND, with special reference to Vols. 45, 47 and 48.

ASBURY, REV. FRANCIS, *Journal.* New York, 1852.

BANNING, JEREMIAH, *Log and Will.* New York, privately printed, no date.

BARRIE, ROBERT & GEORGE JR., *Cruises.* Philadelphia, 1909.

BERNARD, JOHN, *Retrospections of America.* New York, 1887.

BOOGHER, WILLIAM F., *Miscellaneous Americana,* Vol. 1. Philadelphia, 1883.

BOWEN, REV. L. P., D.D., *The Days of Makemie.* Philadelphia, no date.

BREWINGTON, M. V., *Chesapeake Bay Log Canoes.* Newport News, 1937.

——— *Chesapeake Bay Bugeyes.* Newport News, 1941.

BROOKE, HENRY K. (compiler), *Book of Pirates.* New York, 1841.

CANNON, LUCRETIA P., *Narrative*. Georgetown (Del.), 1841.

CAPEK, THOMAS, *Augustine Herman of Bohemia Manor* (pamphlet). Praha, 1930.

CAROLINE COUNTY, MARYLAND, *History* (A compilation by the Teachers and Children of the County). Federalsburg (Md.), 1920.

CLAIBORNE, JOHN HERBERT, M.D., F.A.C.S., *William Claiborne of Virginia*. New York, 1917.

CLARK, WILLIAM BULLOCK & EDWARD B. MATTHEWS, *Physical Features of Maryland*. Baltimore, 1906.

COTTON, JANE BALDWIN (ed.), *Maryland Calendar of Wills*, Vols. 2 and 3. Baltimore, 1906-1907.

DOLE, ESTHER MOHR, PH.D., *Maryland During the American Revolution*. Privately printed, 1941.

DOUGLASS, FREDERICK, *The Life and Times of Frederick Douglass, Written by Himself*. Boston, 1892.

EARLE, SWEPSON, *The Chesapeake Bay Country*. Baltimore, 1938.

——— (ed.), *Maryland Colonial Eastern Shore*. Baltimore, 1916.

EMORY, MRS. MARY EDWARDINE BOURKE, *Colonial Families*. Baltimore, 1900.

FOOTNER, HULBERT, *Maryland Main and the Eastern Shore*. New York, 1942.

FORMAN, HENRY CHANDLEE, *Early Manor and Plantation Houses of Maryland* (with 320 photographs). Easton (Md.), privately printed, 1934.

FOX, GEORGE, *Journal*.

GOLDSBOROUGH, EDMUND K. H., M.D., *Ole' Mars' and Ole Miss*. Washington, D.C., 1900.

GREENBIE, MARJORIE BARSTOW, *My Dear Lady* (The story of Anna Ella Carroll). New York, no date.

HALL, CLAYTON COLMAN, LL.B., A.M. (ed.), *Narratives of Early Maryland.* New York, 1910.

HANSON, GEORGE A., M.A., *Old Kent.* Baltimore, 1876.

HARRISON, SAMUEL A., M.D. (see TILGHMAN, OSWALD).

——— *Wenlock Christison* (pamphlet). Baltimore, 1878.

——— *A Memoir of Hon. William Hindman* (pamphlet). Baltimore, 1879.

HAZARD, SAMUEL, *Annals of Pennsylvania,* 1600-1682. Philadelphia, 1850.

HECK, EARL L. W., *Augustine Herrmann.* Englewood, N.J., privately printed, 1941.

INGRAHAM, PRENTISS, *Land of Legendary Lore.* Easton (Md.), 1898.

JOHNSTON, GEORGE, *History of Cecil County Maryland.* Elkton (Md.), 1881.

JONES, ELIAS, *Revised History of Dorchester County, Maryland.* Baltimore, 1925.

KENT, FRANK R., *Alexander Brown & Sons.* Baltimore, 1925.

LANTZ, EMILY E., *Spirit of Maryland.* Baltimore, 1929.

MARINE, WILLIAM M., *British Invasion of Maryland, 1812-15.* Baltimore, 1913.

MARSHALL, JOHN A., *American Bastile.* Philadelphia, 1883.

MARYLAND, *American Guide Series* (WPA). New York, 1940.

MARYLAND ARCHIVES, With particular reference to Vols. 45, 47 and 48.

MARYLAND HISTORICAL MAGAZINE, all bound volumes, 1 to 36, have been searched for pertinent matter.

MATHEWS, EDWARD B., *Counties of Maryland.* Baltimore, 1907.

MORRIS, JOHN D., D.D., *The Lords Baltimore* (pamphlet). Baltimore, 1874.

MURRAY, REV. JAMES, *History of Pocomoke City*. Baltimore, 1883.

SCHARF, J. THOMAS, *History of Maryland* (3 vols.). Baltimore, 1879.

SETH, JOSEPH B. and MARY W., *Recollections of a Long Life on the Eastern Shore*. Privately printed, no date.

SEMMES, RAPHAEL, *Captains and Mariners of Early Maryland*. Baltimore, 1937.

——— *Crime and Punishment in Early Maryland*. Baltimore, 1938.

SHANNAHAN, JOHN H. K., *Steamboat'n Days*. Baltimore, 1930.

——— *Tales of Old Maryland*. Baltimore, 1907.

SPENCER, RICHARD HENRY, *The Thomas Family of Talbot County*. Baltimore, 1914.

STEINER, BERNARD C., PH.D., *Maryland During the English Civil Wars* (pamphlet). Baltimore, 1906.

——— *Maryland Under the Commonwealth* (pamphlet). Baltimore, 1911.

STREETER, SEBASTIAN F., *The First Commander of Kent Island* (pamphlet). Baltimore, 1868.

STUMP, H. ARTHUR JR., *Augustine Herman* (pamphlet). Baltimore, 1929.

TILGHMAN, OSWALD, *History of Talbot County, Maryland* (largely compiled from the papers of Samuel A. Harrison, M.D. (2 vols.). Baltimore, 1915.

TORRENCE, CLAYTON, *Old Somerset on the Eastern Shore of Maryland*. Richmond, Va., 1935.

USILTON, FRED G., *History of Kent County* (*Md.*). Chestertown, Md., privately printed.

VALLANDIGHAM, EDWARD NOBLE, *Delaware and the Eastern Shore*. Philadelphia, 1922.

WALLACE, ADAM, *The Parson of the Islands*. Philadelphia, 1861.

WILSTACH, PAUL, *Tidewater Maryland*. Indianapolis, 1931.

WISE, JENNINGS CROPPER, *Ye Kingdom of Accawmacke*. Richmond, Va., 1911.

Magazine Articles

PALMER, JOHN WILLIAMSON, "By the Waters of the Chesapeake," *Century Magazine*, Vol. 47.

ROWLAND, KATE MASON, "Old Portraits," *Dixie Magazine*, 1899.

WILSON, REV. ROBERT, "Wye Island," *Lippincott's Magazine*, Vol. 19 (1877).

SOLLERS, BASIL, "Transported Convict Laborers in Maryland" (from the Society's Collections), *Maryland Historical Magazine*, Vol. 2. "Action between American and British Barges" (from the Society's Collections), *Maryland Historical Magazine*, Vol. 4.

PLEASANTS, DR. J. HALL (ed.), "Letters of Molly and Hetty Tilghman," *Maryland Historical Magazine*, Vol. 21.

VINCENT, JOHN MARTIN, "European Background of the War of 1812," *Patriotic Marylander*, Vol. 1 (June, 1915).

Newspapers

Baltimore *Sun,* Old files for morning, evening and Sunday editions; also clipping file, with particular reference to *History of the Steamboat on Chesapeake Bay,* by Emily Emerson Lantz in *Sunday Sun,* running from January to June, 1908.

Centerville (Md.) *Observer, Queen Anne's County,* a series of articles by Frederic Emory, running from January 5, 1886, to May 3, 1887.

Democratic Messenger (Snow Hill, Md.), Contributions of Eben Hearne.

Easton (Md.) *Star-Democrat, Talbot County Necks,* a series of articles by Wilson M. Tyler, 1927-28.

Maryland Journal and Baltimore Advertiser, 1781-1782, for items relating to the Refugee Boats.

Maryland Gazette, 1781-1782, for Refugee Boats.

Philadelphia *Times,* April 27, 1879, *Wye Hall* (anon.).

Preston (Md.) *News,* Contributions of "Minnie Wheeler's Boy-friend" (George T. Ross).

Saturday Morning Visitor, (Baltimore) Dec. 15, 1832, for Frenchtown and Newcastle Railway.

Worcester *Times-Democrat,* (Pocomoke, Md.) Contributions of Eben Hearne.

Manuscripts

EASTON (MD.) PUBLIC LIBRARY, The Caile Letters, The Letter of Henry Callister, and general mss. files.

HISTORIC DORSET, A series of articles (anon.) loaned by Walter F. Austin.

LIBRARY OF CONGRESS, Papers relating to the Coursey claim to the Barony of Kingsale.

MARYLAND HISTORICAL SOCIETY, The Calvert Papers, The Harrison Papers, The Scharf Papers; miscellaneous ms. files for Commodore Grason's Journal, and other references to the Refugee Boats.

WASHINGTON COLLEGE LIBRARY, A ms., anon. and without title, relating the story of the Paca murders.

Index

Acadians, 278
Accomac, 15, 24-26, 40
Active, schooner, 50
Africa, 26
Algonquin tribe, 137
Allen, Hervey, 177
Almodington, 111-112
Anglicans, 35, 235
Annapolis, 38, 51, 52, 84, 206, 326, 351
Anne, Queen, 168-169
Annemessex River, 40, 44, 46
Annemessex River, Big, 98-100
Annemessex tribe, 112
Arcadia, 12
Argoll, Sir Samuel, 24
Ark, the, 27
Asbury, Francis, 171, 193-194, 329
Assateague tribe, 13, 41-44, 74, 112, 187
Attawachrett, 311

Backgarden Creek, 152
Baltimore, Lords, 8, 26, 35-37, 68, 74, 111, 113, 115, 177, 200, 206, 234-235, 240, 351-353
(*See also* Calvert)
Baltimore, 97, 98
attacked by British, 253
Banning, Captain Jeremiah, 207, 209, 217, 220-221, 223, 231
Barney, Joshua, 194, 240
Barrel House, 83
Barren Creek, 144
Beckford, 117
Bennett, Richard, 36, 37, 269, 275, 352
Bennett, James Gordon, 200
Berkeley, Sir William, 35, 41, 42, 46
Bernard, John, 357-358
Beverly of Somerset, 113-114
Beverly of Worcester (Thrumcapped), 69
Big Blackwater River, 153, 160
Blackbeard, 156-158, 223
Blackbird, schooner, 124
Black duck, 155-156
Blackwater Migratory Bird Refuge, 160
Bladensburg, Battle of, 97
Boatbuilding, 240, 253
Bohemia River, 346-354
Bonaparte, Jerome, 114
Bonfield, 177
Bordley, John Beale, 298-299, 327
Bosman, William, 112
Breckenridge, Senator, 102
British fleet (1812), 244, 248-253
Brooklyn Museum of Art, 190
B. S. Ford, steamboat, 321-324
Buchanan, Admiral, 256, 262
Bugeye, 89
Bullock's Channel, 14
Butler, John, 33, 34

Cabin Creek, 190
Cadwalader, General John, 340-341
Callister, Henry, 209-210, 214, 216-217, 338
Calvert, Cecil, 27, 39, 40, 231, 310
Calvert, Charles, 40, 44, 46, 48, 190, 353-354
Calvert, Governor Leonard, 27, 30, 33
Calvert, Philip, 273
Cambridge, 182-185, 229, 230
Carmichael, Judge Richard Bennett, 233-234

Cannon, Patty, 83, 145-151, 186
Carroll, Anna Ella, 102-103, 169
Carroll, Colonel Henry James, 101
Carroll, Thomas King, 101-102, 169, 176
Castle Haven, 175-177
Catholics, 36, 275
Caulk's Field, battle, 335-337
Cedar Straits, 68
Centerville, 319
Chamberlaine family, 177, 178
Chancellor's Point, 204
Charles I, King, 26, 32, 36, 274, 313, 314
Charles II, 39, 41
Charles, Cape, 6, 15, 58
Chesapeake Bay, 5, 13-14, 19, 314, 338, 346, 356-357
Chesapeake Bay, canoe, 89, 105
Chesapeake and Delaware Canal, 357
Chester River, 22, 26, 309-325
Chestertown, 326-338
Chicamacomico River, 153, 160
Chicone Creek, 144-145
Chincoteague Bay, 11-12, 58
Chlora's Point, 178
Choptank, steamboat, 128-129
Choptank River, 8, 62, 170-204
(*See also* Little Choptank River)
Choptank tribe, 186-189
Christ Church, Cambridge, 183
Christison, Wenlock, 258, 262
Chrysler, Walter P., 176
Church Creek, 166-169
Church of England, established, 235
City of Salisbury, barge, 122
Civil War, 124-126, 174, 180, 184, 232-233, 267
Claiborne, William, 26-39, 186, 309
Clifton, 111
Clippers, Baltimore, 90, 240
Cockatrice, shallop, 31, 32, 68
Cockburn, Admiral, 252, 343
Compton, 179
Conway, General Thomas, 340
Cooke, Ebenezer, 172-173
Cooke's Point, 172
Cooper's Strait, 18
Cornwallis, Lord, 54, 258, 259
Cornwallis, Captain Thomas, 31, 32, 34
Corsica, steamboat, 321-323
Coursey, Henry, 201, 305, 310-312, 351
Coursey family, 305-307, 310
Covington, Sarah, 215, 276, 277, 325
Crisfield, 86-92
Critchett, Aunt Polly, 166
Crockett, 59
Cromwell, Oliver, 38, 272
Cropper, Colonel, 62-63
Crosiadore, 181, 182
Cryer, Jesse, 203
Curtis, Captain Edmund, 36
Cypresses, 69-70, 76, 83

Dashiell, Captain George, 60-63
Dashiell, Colonel George, 50, 51, 54, 62, 64
Dashiell, Colonel Joseph, 51, 52, 64
Dauntless, H.M.S., 164
Dauphine, 11
Deal's Island (Devil's Island), 104-108
Debedeavon, 15, 24
Declaration of Independence, 98, 182
Decoy, armed boat, 52
Defense, barge, 58-61, 64
Delaware tribe, 188
Denis, Captain Robert, 36
Dennis, Donoch, 69
Dennis, John Upshur, 70
Denton, 197-199
Dickinson, Charles, 200
Dickinson, John, 181-182
Dickinson family, 181
Dividing Creek, 83
Dixon, Ambrose, 46, 170
Dolphin, state boat, 50
Doncaster, 270
Doolittle, Mamie, 193
Dorchester County ("Dorset"), 182-183
Dorchester Marshes, 135, 152-162
Douglass, Frederick, 253-254, 285-293
Dove, pinnace, 27
Dover Bridge, ferry-house, 202
Dow, Lorenzo, 78-79, 171
Dresser, Paul, 195
Dutch, 45

Eastern Shore, 8-11
explorers, 11-23
history and geology, 1

Eastern Shore (*continued*)
rivers of, 5-23
settlers, 8-11
soil, 7
Eastern Shore, steamboat, 86
Easton, 229-233, 236, 253
Elizabeth, bark, 13
Elk River, 20, 21, 346, 349, 350, 356-357
Elzey, Arnold, 112
Elzey, John, 40, 45, 46, 111
Emancipation Proclamation, 291
Emma Giles, steamboat, 255
English settlers, 9
Ervin, 266-268
Evans, William, 92
Evelin, George, 32-34
Experiment, barge, 55

Farragut, Admiral, 257
Fearnought, barge, 64
Fendall, Josias, 39, 273, 349
Fenwick's Island, 43
Ferry, rope, 129, 158
Fiddlers, 77-78, 104
Fishing Bay, 152, 153
Fishing Creek, 163
Fleet, Captain Henry, 29
Flying Fish, supply boat, 60-62
Foster, Cunliffe and Company, 206, 207, 216, 217
Fox, George, 74, 186-187, 234
Fox hunting, 174, 329
Fox Island, 59, 60
France, Richard, 257
Francks, Peter, 58
Franklin, Benjamin, 313
Frazier, Captain Solomon, 58-65
Frazier, Captain William, 193
French and Indian War, 278
Fuller, William, 38
Fur trade, 19, 28

Gabriel, 78-79
Gale, Captain Levin, 126
George III, 64
Georgetown, 342, 344, 345
Gibson, Jacob, 221-222, 240-245, 248-249, 252, 253
Gilbert, Bartholomew, 13
Girod, Mayor, 114
Glasgow, 184
Golden Fortune, 206
Golden Lion, 38
Goldsboro Creek, 221-222
Goldsborough, Judge Robert, 262, 319
Goldsborough, William L., 176-177
Goose Creek Farm, 189
Gordon, John, 255-256, 262
Grason, Commodore Thomas, 54-56, 67, 238, 255
Great Eastern, steamship, 173
Green Hill Church, 130
Greenwood, 99-100
Greyhound, schooner, 57
Guinea, frigate, 36
Gwynn's Island, 58

Habnab, 112
Hack, Anna, 348
Hambrook, 184
Hampton, Mary (*see* Jenckins, Mary)
Hampton, Virginia, 15
Handy, Lieutenant Joseph, 62, 63
Handy, Lieutenant Samuel, 60
Haney, Uncle, 91-92
Hanna, Mark, 176
Harford, Henry, 48
Harrington (Emerson C.) bridge, 182
Harris, Sally, 308
Harris Creek, 173
Harvey, Sir John, 27
Hatton, Thomas, 37
Helen, steamboat, 79
Henry, John, 71, 136
Henry, Robert, 72
Herman, Augustine, 346-357
Hermitage, 314-316
Hicktopeake, 15
Highland Light, steamboat, 79
Hindman, James, 232
Hindman, William, 232, 263
Hole-in-the-Wall, 180
Hollyday, Henry, 214-215, 224, 325
Hollyday, James, 277, 325
Hooper, Colonel Henry, 49, 51, 53
Hooper's Island, 133, 160-162
Hooper's Strait, 132
Hoover, Herbert, 176
Hopkins, 65-66
Horn's Point, 38, 176
Battle of, 310
Horsey, Stephen, 45, 98-99, 170
Humber, Captain, 29

Hunting Creek, 191, 193
Hurst Creek, 186
Hutchins, Colonel Charles, 141

Ice cream, 299
Indentured servants, 210-211
Indians, of Eastern Shore, 7-23
  attacked by settlers, 41, 42, 44
  trade with, 24-39, 141
  (*See also* individual tribes)
Iroquois tribe (Six Nations), 19-22, 143, 188, 274, 311, 312
Island Creek House, 177-178

Jackson, Andrew, 200
Jamaica Point, 203-204
James II, 41
James Island, S. C., 49, 163
James River, 20
Jamestown, 15, 23-25, 42
J. B. Meredith, schooner, 159
Jefferson, Thomas, 143, 283
Jenckins, Francis, 70, 71
Jenckins-Henry-Hampton, Mary, 70-73, 100, 136, 262
Johnson, George, 46, 170
Jones, Sam, store, 168
Jones' Creek, 112
Joppa, steamboat, 122, 225, 226
Juba, 78
Julia Harlow, schooner, 157

Kecoughtan (Hampton, Virginia), 15, 20, 26
Kedge's Straits, battle, 49-65
Kent Island, 26, 29-31, 33, 34, 39, 309
Kent Point, 64
Kidnapper, barge, 63
Kidd, Captain, 223
King, Nehemiah II, 113, 114
King, Sir Robert, 71, 112
King, Thomas, 100, 101
King's Creek, 112
Kingston Hall, 100-103, 113
Kirk, Colonel John, 184
Kline, Ada, 195, 196
Knight, Kitty, 344-346

Lafayette, Marquis de, 179, 284
Lake, Lavinia (Lovey), 161
Languedoc, 59-62
Latrobe, icebreaker, 324
Lawson, 65
LeCompte, Anthony, 175-176
Lee, Euel, 85
Lee, John, 145
Lee, Thomas, 145
Lee, Thomas Sim, 54
Levi, Uncle, 95
Lincoln, Abraham, 102, 103
Little Annemessex River, 86-98
Little Blackwater River, 153, 158, 160
Little Choptank River, 163-169
Lloyd, Edward (Hîr Dîr), 177, 269, 272-273
Lloyd, Edward II, 274-277
Lloyd, Edward III, 277-279
Lloyd, Edward IV, "the Patriot," 279-283
Lloyd, Edward V, "the Governor," 283-291, 295
Lloyd, Edward VI, "the Farmer," 290-291, 295
Lloyd, Edward VII, "Master of Wye," 291-292
Lloyd, Philemon, 201, 273-274, 295, 310
Lloyd family, 269-293
Lloyd's Creek, 271, 340
Long Point (Nanticoke River), 136
Long Tayle, pinnace, 28-31
Lord's Gift, 310
Lynn, Captain John, 64, 65

Maggie, steamboat, 79
Makemie, Francis, 71, 72, 74, 171
Manokin River, 40, 44, 46, 104-119
Manokin tribe, 112
Marina, 265-266
Marlborough, H.M.S., 343
Martin, Daniel, 178
Marshyhope Creek, 145
Maryland, 5-8, 12, 13, 15, 26-28, 44
  saved to Union, 102
  Toleration Act, 36, 39
Maryland Assembly, 35, 36, 55, 67
Maryland Convention, 238
Maryland, steamboat, 225
Maryland Herald, 241, 242
Maryland Journal and Baltimore Advertiser, 55-57
"Mary's Lot," 71, 72, 74, 100, 274
Massawomeke tribe (*see* Iroquois)
Mattapony, 29

Matthews, Captain Samuel, 215
May, Henry, 257
Maynadier, Mrs. David, 180-181
Merrimac, ironclad, 256
Methodism, 78, 171
Methodist, canoe, 104-105
Metropolitan Museum, New York, 112
Miles River, 236, 255-268
Miles River Neck, 239
Minnie Wheeler, steamboat, 191, 193, 196, 199, 226, 227, 229
"Minnie Wheeler's Boy-Friend," 191, 193, 196, 229
Morris, Robert, 180, 206-209, 215-217
Murray, William Vans, 143, 183
Muskrat pelts, 153-155
Myrtle Grove, 262

Nanticoke River, 7, 8, 16, 50, 135-151
Nanticoke tribe, 44-46, 74, 111, 112, 137, 138, 187
Napoleon, 114
Nassawango Creek, 83, 84
Neale, James, 313
Neal, Henrietta Maria, 273-275, 294, 298-300, 313
Negroes, 100-102, 105, 113, 122, 126, 142, 145-151, 174-177, 210, 229, 280-281, 285-293
New Nithsdale, 126
Newton, 77-78
North East River, 20, 256-257
Northampton Protest, 98
Norwood, Colonel, 43-44

Old Coventry, Episcopal church, 73-74
Onancock, 58, 59
Oneida tribe, 311
Ornery Point, 339-340
Otwell, 222
Oxford, 205-217
Oystermen, 90-91, 107, 236, 253

Paca, Governor William, 62-64, 298, 300
Paca, William B., 300-304, 313
Paine, Tom, 341
Palmer's Island, 26, 28, 35
Panquas, 142, 143
Parker, Mrs. James, epitaph, 130
Parker, Captain Sir Peter, 335-338
Parsons, Captain Allison, 125-126
Patapsco River, 18
Patterson, Betsy, 114
Patuxent River, 23, 28, 29
Patuxent, 38
Peachblossom, 215, 222, 223
Peale, Charles Willson, 294-295
Penn, William, 235, 353
Perry, Captain, 191, 200
Perry, Uncle, 174
Perry Farm, 182
Peyton, Valentine, 51
Piankatank, 57
Picaroons, 48-67, 238
Pinke, Henry, 26
Pirates, 223
Piscattaway, 74
Plaindealing Creek, 218
Plater, state boat, 52
Pocomoke City, 76-77
Pocomoke River, 7, 12, 40, 46, 68-85
Pocomoke Sound, 31, 32, 48, 49, 52, 68
Pocomoke tribe, 42, 47, 74
Poh Poh Caquis, 201-202, 297
Point, the, 184
Pole Cat, brig, 64
Porpuss, sloop, 50
Potato Neck, 100, 105
Potomac River, 19, 23, 57
Potter, William, 197
Potter, Captain Zabdiel, 197
Powhatan, 15, 19, 21, 24
Preston, Richard, 37, 38
Preston, *News*, 191, 193
Princess Anne, 115-119, 121
Protector, barge, 51, 62, 63, 239
Providence, 38
Pyle, Howard, 259
Pungy, 89
Puritans, 35-39, 269

Quakers, 40, 45, 47, 74, 98, 170, 234-236, 275-276
Quaker Neck, 320
Quaker Neck Landing, 321, 325

Raleigh, Sir Walter, colony, 13
Ranger, brig, 56
Rappahannock River, 23, 57
Ratcliffe Manor, 215, 223-224, 277, 325
Readbourne, 325
Reed, Colonel Philip, 337

Reed's Creek House, 316-318
Rehobeth, 72, 74
Republican Star, 241
Revell, Randall, 40, 44, 45, 109-111
Revelly, Captain, 50
Revenge, 55
Revolution, American, 48, 49, 117, 118, 161, 171, 184, 204, 206, 210, 231, 238, 313, 327, 357
Reward, 321
Rich Neck Manor, 237
Richardson, Colonel William, 194
Robins, Anna Maria, 214-215, 224, 277, 325
Robins, Susanna, 218-219
Rock Hall, 314
Rockawalkin Creek, 126-127
Rousby, Ann, 279
Russell, Walter, 14, 15
Russell, Dr., 20

St. George's Island, 56
St. Helen, pinnace, 31, 68
St. Luke's Church, 325
St. Marguaret, pinnace, 31, 68
St. Marys, 28-30, 32-34, 138, 188
St. Michaels, 236-254
St. Paul's Church, 320
Salisbury, 120-125
Sally Lloyd, sloop, 286
Samuels, Dan'l, 82
Sassafras River, 7, 20-22, 339-346
Saulsbury House, 203
Savage, Thomas, 24, 25
Saxis Island, 69
Scarburgh, Captain Edmund, 25, 26
Scarburgh, Colonel Edmund, 25, 40-47, 68, 74, 99, 111
Scharf, *History of Maryland,* 65, 67
Secretary Creek, 189-190
Seneca tribe, 188, 190, 201
Seney, Joshua, 241
Sewall, Henry, 190
Sewall, Jane, 190
Sharp's Island, 172
Severn River, 38
Shawnee tribe, 143
Shelltown, 69
Ship's Point (Turner's Point), 223
Shoal Creek, 186
Simmons, Captain Thomas, 56
Sinepuxent Bay, 43
Skillington, Thomas, shipyard, 223
Slaves, 210, 280-293
Slippery Hill, 312, 313
Smallwood's Flying Camp, 232
Smith, Captain John, 14-23, 24, 31, 45, 138, 341
  map, 68
Smith, Captain Thomas, 28, 30, 32-35
Smith's Island, 14, 16, 24, 68, 86, 91
Snow Hill, 77, 84-85
Speddon, Captain, 57, 60-63
Spocot, 165-166
Stagge, Thomas, 36
Stamp Act, 231, 278-279
Steamboats, 79, 82-83, 122-134, 224-229, 321-325, 357
Sterling, Aaron, 52-53
Stevens, John, 179
Stevens, Samuel, 179
Stevens, Colonel William, 74-76, 117, 139-140, 170, 310
Stevens, William, of Compton, 234-235
Stewart, Major John, 50
Stone, William, 36-38
Stuyvesant, Peter, 347-349, 353
Sue, steamboat, 79
Surprise, steamboat, 255
Susquehanna River, 5, 20, 22, 26
Susquehannock tribe, 22, 33, 74
Sylvester, John, 69

Talbot County, 231
Tangier Island, 55, 58, 94
Tangier Sound, 49, 68, 86, 132, 135
Taylor, Philip, 32
Teach, Captain (*see* Blackbeard)
Teackle, Littleton Dennis, 118
Teackle Mansion, 117-118
Tedious Creek, 152
Tennessee Valley, 102
Terrapin, 84, 88
Third Haven, 235
Thomas, Coloney Zarvona, 124-125
Thomas, Reverend Joshua, 92-98, 104-108, 171
Thompson, Absolom Americus Vespucius, 173
Thompson, Dr. Absolom, 237
Thorne, William, 45
Tilghman, Anna Maria, 238
Tilghman, Matthew, 53, 232, 237-238

Tilghman, Mary, 295
Tilghman, Molly, 330-335
Tilghman, Dr. Richard, 314-316
Tilghman, Captain Samuel, 206
Tilghman, Lieutenant Colonel Tench, 238, 258-259, 262, 314, 333
Tilghman's Island, 236, 237
Timmons, Michael, 54, 57
Tobacco, 208, 216
Tockwogh tribe, 21, 22
Tockwogh, 341
Todkill, Amos, 14
Toleration, Act of, 36, 39
Tories, 48, 49, 161, 171, 231, 232, 330
Townsend, George Alfred, *The Entailed Hat*, 118
Transquaking River, 153, 158, 160
Trappe Creek, 180, 181
Treaty Oak, 168
Tred Avon River, 205, 218-235
Tred Avon, steamboat, 226, 227
Trippe's Creek, 222
Troth's Fortune, 201
Trueman, Captain Alexander, 52
Tuckahoe Creek, 194, 199
Tweed, "Boss," 258, 262
Two Johns, 195-197
Tyng, Hannah, 24

Ungle, Squire, 219
Utie, Colonel Nathaniel, 349-351

Venus, schooner, 64
Verrazano, Giovanni da, 11-13, 42
Vicksburg, 103
Vienna, 53, 136, 144, 158
Villa, the, 257-258
Villebrune, Chevalier de, 57
Virginia, 5, 15, 24, 25, 36, 55
Virginia Assembly, 27, 98
Virginia, House of Burgesses, 25
Virginia Merchant, 43
Vue de Leau, 189

Walley, Commodore Zedekiah, 12-14, 51-54, 57-63, 67, 79, 239
Walnut Grove, 318
War of 1812, 97, 184, 232, 283
Warren, Lieutenant, 30-32
Washington, George, 54, 64, 259, 262, 280, 314, 330, 340, 344, 345
Washington, D. C., burning of, 253, 336
Washington College, 326, 331
Washington Hotel, Princess Anne, 118
Watkins Point, 68
Watts' Island, 59, 68
Weston, 136-137
Whaland, Joseph, 49-51, 54, 56-57, 63, 64, 66, 67, 239
Wheeler, Captain Caleb, 191, 193
White House Farm, 158-159
White Marsh Church, 180
Wickes, Lambert, 313-314
Wicomico Creek (Little Wicomico), 130
Wicomico River, 7, 50, 120-134
Wighcocomoco, 15 , 16, 31, 45 (*see also* Pocomoke River)
Wilderness, the, 178
Will, Captain, 321-324
William, King, 41
Williams' Conquest, 99
Willmott, Captain, 49
Windmere, 166
Worcester County, Maryland, 12
Wreck Island Inlet, 58
Wright, Captain Charles W., 128-129
Wye Church, 297
Wye Hall, 300-304
Wye Heights, 295
Wye House, 271, 272, 279, 280, 293
Wye Island, 273, 299, 300
Wye River, 239, 294-308, 269
Wye Town, 270, 271, 274

York, 297
Yorktown, 55